Cognitive Coaching^{SM}:
Weaving Threads of
Learning and Change Into the
Culture of an Organization

Cognitive Coaching^SM:
Weaving Threads of Learning and Change Into the Culture of an Organization

Edited by

Jane Ellison
and
Carolee Hayes

With Foreword by Arthur L. Costa and Robert J. Garmston

Christopher-Gordon Publishers, Inc.
Norwood, Massachusetts

Dedication

This book is dedicated to
Bob Garmston and Art Costa,
mentors, friends, and colleagues to each of us.
Their work sustains and inspires us, enriching our lives
and providing the platform for our ongoing
development as self-directed persons.

Copyright Acknowledgments

Every effort has been made to contact copyright holders for permission to reproduce borrowed material where necessary. We apologize for any oversights and would be happy to rectify them in future printings.

Information from the International School of Tanganyika used with permission.

Christopher-Gordon Publishers, Inc.
1502 Providence Highway, Suite #12
Norwood, Massachusetts 02062
800-934-8322
781-762-5577

Printed in the United State of America
10 9 8 7 6 5 4 3 2 1   07 06 05 04 03

ISBN: 1-929024-57-6
Library of Congress Catalogue Number: 2003101604

Table of Contents

Foreword

Over the past 15 years, thousands of teachers, staff developers, administrators, teacher educators, and corporate leaders have been trained in and have begun to practice Cognitive Coaching[SM]. Many readers of this book are already acquainted with the principles, purposes, and practices of Cognitive Coaching[SM]. They have found that Cognitive Coaching[SM] becomes not only an interactive strategy intended to enhance the self-directedness of others, it becomes internalized into a way of being and an important part of an individual's identity. It is this unique attribute of Cognitive Coaching[SM] that makes the work so powerful and as many people have reported, so life changing.

This book now directs attention to how these same principles can inform the identity of an organization. Its intent is to transform a system's identity by applying practices congruent with Cognitive Coaching[SM]. We believe that the search for consistency transforms the life of the organization as well.

Just as people's behavior is informed by meanings, values, beliefs, perceptions, and thinking processes which lie at the level of deep structure within human beings, so too, is an organization's behavior influenced by the values, beliefs, perceptions, and thinking processes that lie at a deeper level. It is only by interacting with these generative meanings and thinking processes that permanent and self-directing change is accomplished.

Fractal qualities can be found in all organizations. What is core to an organization's deepest identity, values, and missions are woven in repetitive patterns forming the system's tapestry. Principled design can be disclosed by watching anyone, whether it be a classroom dialogue between a teacher with her students, an administrator conducting a faculty meeting, a school secretary interacting on the telephone with a concerned parent, or the district personnel officer interviewing perspective employees. In any organization there is congruence woven into patterns of behavior. No matter where one looks, parallel threads create the organization's fabric regardless of the roles and levels of the people.

Organizations striving for excellence do so by maintaining integrity. They constantly reflect on themselves by asking, "Who are we as an organization?"

and "To what degree do our actions reflect that identity?" Identity is a framework for understanding oneself. It is the self of the system that compels it to different agendas and actions. An organizational identity may be summarized in three major dimensions:

- What is taken by the organization to be the central to its work

- What insiders believe makes the organization distinct from other organizations

- What is perceived by members to be an enduring quality of the organization

Central to the work of Cognitive Coaching[SM] are its

- Values— including self-directedness and holonomy

- Beliefs—the distinct ideas that humans construct their own meaning and have the capacity to draw forth the Five States of Mind to learn, solve problems, and resolve conflicts

- Mental maps—which guide Cognitive Coaching interactions

- Coaching skills—among them, many verbal and non-verbal tools

Much of school improvement is an add on. Schools today are being described as places where people are feeling overwhelmed and fragmented. Witness the inconsistency of content standards, tests, textbooks, and accountability practices. Schools that lack clarity lurch back and forth from one panacea to another. If an organization's real beliefs are tattered, this is displayed in patchwork practices, often at odds with one another. This book demonstrates how Cognitive Coaching[SM] can be used as an integrative force that penetrates rather than fragments practices. This important book offers descriptions in different settings that help system leaders determine who we are as an organization, what is our central work, what makes us distinct, and what qualities are perceived as enduring.

There is a greater likelihood that teachers will teach and students will learn the ideals of Cognitive Coaching[SM] if those ideals are apparent in the school's curriculum and its culture. Teachers will adopt visions of self-directed learning for their own students and will value exacting standards, flexibility, cooperation, and creativity in thoughtful, interdependent environments. Students will become more self-directed, more capable of constructing their own meanings, and better able to interact with others in powerful, non-judgmental, and empathic ways. Integrating Cognitive Coaching[SM] throughout the school culture and curriculum requires valuing, understanding, and making a commitment to constructivist principles of learning that place the natural human quest for understanding at the center of the educational enterprise.

We are pleased to report that within the field of Cognitive Coaching[SM], in which we have labored for nearly two decades, we continue to learn.

        Arthur L. Costa   Robert J. Garmston

Acknowledgments

This book is the product of many colleagues' experimentation, exploration, and application of Cognitive Coaching[SM] over the last 18 years. We are indebted to Art Costa, Bob Garmston, and the Center for Cognitive Coaching[SM] Training Associates for their ongoing support and collegiality in pioneering the frontiers of Cognitive Coaching[SM]. We are particularly grateful to Bruce Wellman, our Foundation Seminar® Trainer, who introduced us to Cognitive Coaching[SM] and developed us as coaches and trainers. We appreciate the many school districts and other systems that have allowed us to work with many special individuals who have embraced the mission of Cognitive Coaching[SM]. They have provided us with new insights, meaningful contexts, and an opportunity to learn from educators and practitioners around the world.

We celebrate and thank the contributors to this book, who have shared their experiences and wisdom. Each of them has offered a unique perspective—collectively they represent the creativity and diversity of the Cognitive Coaching[SM] Community. Their patience, persistence, and commitment have honored us as we developed this book.

Sue Canavan and Hiram Howard were invaluable to us as they encouraged and supported us in the development process. Their faith in us and in the contribution of this work provided us with the motivation we needed to complete the project.

And finally, to our families, we say thank you for valuing the importance of our work and supporting us as we focused our energies on our professional growth.

Introduction

A culture is a socially constructed understanding of how humans choose to live and work together. It is organic, dynamic, and constantly changing based on the interactions of the human players. Schools often focus on innovations, that is, programs and practices rather than student learning. Our contention is that to impact student learning, the culture should be the focus of leadership. A culture is, metaphorically, much like a woven fabric. Each and every human interaction adds a thread to the fabric of the culture. Cognitive Coaching^{SM} is a process that provides threads for weaving a culture of reflective practice and enhanced learning for all members of an organization.

This book is written with the intention to support leaders and group members in becoming even more skillful in weaving cultures that support improved processes for student learning. The authors presume knowledge of Cognitive Coaching^{SM} on the part of the reader. The book represents the thinking of many individuals and groups who have learned Cognitive Coaching^{SM}, valued its premises, practices, and outcomes, and found ways to lace it into the fabric of the cultures in which they work. The title *Cognitive Coaching^{SM}: Weaving Threads of Learning and Change into the Culture of an Organization* was chosen from other possible metaphors because of the concept of constructing a product from interwoven threads. The product is the culture. A fabric is made up of threads woven together to create a design that represents an image that the artist has in mind as he or she conceives of and constructs the fabric. That is precisely the process that one might use in an organization as he or she creates a vision of what the organization would look like, sound like, and be like, if the appropriate threads ran throughout all aspects of the organization. We feel this metaphor is particularly applicable to Cognitive Coaching^{SM} as we believe that Cognitive Coaching^{SM} can truly impact the entire culture of an organization if it is visible in all the policies, procedures, and practices that guide and support the actions of each individual and team.

At a basic level, a weaver begins with a loom, threads, and a shuttle. One set of threads is the warp, made up of yarn stretched lengthwise on the loom.

The other set of threads is the weft, the yarn that crosses the width of the warp. The weaver uses a shuttle to carry the weft thread or yarn through the warp. Using this metaphor, we have conceived of the loom as the structure of a school district; the warp as the system, school, and classroom; the weft as the maps, tools, capabilities, and States of Mind of Cognitive Coaching[SM]; and the shuttle as the leadership guiding the implementation of Cognitive Coaching[SM]. Each chapter is a unique application made by a practitioner exploring the threads of culture-building. It is the task of leadership to examine each thread and find the best ones to weave a strong fabric that serves students first and foremost, while also expanding the development of professional staff. With time and patience, the leadership creates a picture of self-directedness in an organization in which both teams and individuals are self-managing, self-monitoring, and self-modifying.

The history of weaving also supports the use of this metaphor for implementing Cognitive Coaching[SM] in an organization. Twenty to thirty thousand years ago, mankind developed the first string by twisting together handfuls of plant fibers. Preparing thin bundles of plant material and stretching them out while twisting them together produced a fine string or thread. The ability to produce string and thread was the starting place for the development of weaving, spinning, and sewing. In a similar way, a classroom teacher, a building principal, or a district leader might begin using the maps and tools of Cognitive Coaching[SM], twisting them into a thread that might connect the practices in a classroom, school, or district.

In some cases, weft twining occurs in weaving. Weft twining is a method of weaving that creates a strong, decorative fabric. It is sometimes called twined tapestry because of the similarity in appearance to tapestry weaving. Whereas tapestry weaving is made by passing one weft across at a time within a limited area, in weft twining two ends are passed across, one over and one under the warps. Weft twining is often confused with embroidery, because of the type of surface it creates and the wide range of designs that are possible with the technique. In our metaphor, weft twining might occur when the maps, tools, capabilities, and States of Mind of Cognitive Coaching[SM] are not individual weft threads, but intertwined in such a way as to create weft threads that are stronger and more colorful than single threads. Such a process in a school district might result in an even richer picture of self-directedness.

Structure of the Book

In this book the chapters represent the warp threads of the system, the school, and the classroom. Each chapter describes a unique application of the maps, tools, capabilities, and States of Mind of Cognitive Coaching[SM]—the weft threads that create the woven fabric. The uniqueness is an application that goes beyond the original conception of Cognitive Coaching[SM] as a way for principals to support the thinking of teachers. The result of these applications is a fabric that covers much more of the organization than the dyad of teacher and principal.

Part 1 begins by looking at the organization as a system. The chapters included in this section consider applications of Cognitive Coaching[SM] that impact practices and outcomes at an organizational level. Weaving these threads requires an orientation towards systems thinking and organizational development.

Part 2 focuses on the school as the unit of change. These chapters describe specific processes that enhance the varied functions of leadership at the school level. Weaving these threads invites schools as subsystems to rethink traditional ways of working and thinking.

Part 3 illuminates classroom practices that bring coaching into the lives of students. These chapters create a vision of classroom cultures where thinking and collaborating are norms for everyday interactions. Weaving these threads involves professionals as well as students and parents in the culture of the organization.

There are many creative ways in which the weft threads have been passed over and under the warp threads to create the fabric that becomes a representation of self-directedness. While this book includes numerous examples of applications of Cognitive Coaching[SM] in a variety of settings, we invite educators to also remain vigilant for new learning and additional opportunities to invest Cognitive Coaching[SM] in their own and their organization's practices—to create new fabrics.

Jane Ellison   Carolee Hayes

Part 1

System Applications

The chapters in this section take a macro-view of the organizational culture. When the threads of learning and change are generated by the leaders of a system, there are strong, consistent, and well-defined patterns throughout the fabric. These applications have the greatest potential for impact on the culture of a system.

This section ranges from applications that focus directly on enculturation to those that include specific strategies. These chapters also represent multiple perspectives in a system: board of education, superintendent, principal, and teacher. One chapter contrasts coaching in the business world with coaching in an education setting, illuminating the importance of cultural values.

Chapter 1

Enculturating Cognitive Coaching[SM] in a Complex System

By: Joe Saban

Introduction

Educational institutions have historically adopted innovations with good intentions that are short-term efforts with minimal results. The initial practices are implemented by some practitioners, but often never become institutionalized practice. High investments are made with little return for staff and students.

Joe Saban, retired superintendent of District 155 in Crystal Lake, Illinois, describes one district's effort to be systemic in moving Cognitive Coaching[SM] from peripheral innovation to embedded practice. The threads of Cognitive Coaching[SM] are primary, prominent, and strong fibers in the fabric of this district. Using a metaphor of how animal cultures evolve to new norms and ways of thinking, a model for institutionalizing Cognitive Coaching[SM] as a way of working and thinking emerges. Key processes for addressing individual and institutional needs are described. This chapter considers means for developing ownership, broadening impact, and sustaining coaching work over time as prominent threads in the cultural fabric.

"The Tale of the Hundredth Monkey"

The Japanese tell a story about Macaca fuscata, a monkey that lived in the wilds of their islands. It seems that scientists studying these monkeys on one of the islands had been dropping sweet potatoes to attract them to a scientific observation point. This particular island, similar to the other nearby Japanese Isles, had an especially sandy soil that clung to the potatoes. However, this generally did not deter the monkeys from eating the potatoes.

After a while the scientists observed that a year-old, female monkey named Imo began washing the sand off her potatoes before eating them. The interested scientists documented that she was the only monkey engaged in the washing routine. But even more interestingly, Imo began to teach this practice to her mom and then to her playmates. The mom and the playmates found the washed potatoes to be preferable to those unwashed. The playmates subsequently taught their moms to wash the potatoes as well. The scientists noted this cultural innovation and how it was spreading among the monkeys.

Then something startling took place. In the autumn of 1958, a number of monkeys were observed washing sweet potatoes—99 of them to be precise. During the day, the hundredth monkey learned how to wash his sweet potato. Then it happened! It is said that by that evening every monkey on the island was washing the potatoes. Several hundred of them! Intriguingly, the change did not stop on that island. The scientists observed that colonies of the same type of monkey on other islands who did not previously wash their potatoes had adopted the practice too!

The "Tale of the Hundredth Monkey" leads us to contemplate what happens at the point where if only one more individual tunes in to a new awareness, the awareness becomes adopted by almost everyone. It also speaks to field theory, communication, and learning that occur in unforeseen and seemingly magical ways.

The implementation story and subsequent enculturation of Cognitive Coaching[SM] in Community High School District 155 in Crystal Lake, Illinois, is revealed through the metaphor of the hundredth monkey. The reader of this chapter should not misunderstand the comparisons of those humans involved in District 155 to the Japanese study except as a metaphorical viewpoint through which to better understand the enculturation of innovation in a complex system.

1991: The Beginning—Washing the First Sweet Potato

Much of the life of a professional educator is spent in search of sweet pota-toes, that is, innovation that nourishes the learning process and educational community. Workshops, seminars, and other staff development opportuni-ties in cooperative learning, thinking skills, learning styles, and the like are well attended by educators in the hope of finding yet another tool or strat-egy to extend the abilities of students. Early in the 1990s one such innova-tion landed in District 155 in Crystal Lake, Illinois. Administrators participated in a 7-day Cognitive Coaching^SM seminar hosted by Art Costa and Bob Garmston. This initiation to the Cognitive Coaching^SM process was, in the opinion of the attendees, significant to the degree that the future of their school district might be forever changed. The teachings of Costa and Garmston were tightly aligned with the values of the District 155 leadership and of the organization.

A vision of a school district whose entire staff . . . no, whose entire com-munity . . . engaged daily in coaching one another was articulated. This Dis-trict would be a place where supervisory energies centered on personal and professional growth—a renaissance community for the future. Plans were made to spread the word to other important decision-makers in the system. A small number of formal and informal district leaders were approached with the vision. Interested in what they heard, they traveled to Lake Tahoe for advanced training to learn more. The sand had been washed from the first potato.

1992/1993: Spreading the Word—Teaching Playmates

Meanwhile, back on the island (also know as the District), those who had experienced the 7-day training were busy creating venues for others to learn of the Cognitive Coaching^SM vision. The entire administration was intro-duced to the important tenets of the vision through the regular weekly ad-ministrator meetings, a summer retreat, and department chair gatherings. Those who had gone to Lake Tahoe, along with Senior Associate Laura Lipton, presented seminars that were intended to build interest in this innovation. The administration, from the superintendent on, quickly embraced the val-ues and vision of the innovation and agreed to plan further.

Leadership, while deliberating the next steps, decided to put the future of Cognitive Coaching^SM in the hands of the teaching staff. Teacher union lead-ers, decision-makers on the staff, and other informal leaders were invited to participate in a 7-day Cognitive Coaching^SM training during the regular school day. They were told that at the conclusion of the 7-day training they would be asked to vote on whether or not to build Cognitive Coaching^SM into the district's culture. They were promised that if this group felt that Cognitive Coaching^{SM} did not have a place in the system, they would never hear of the program again. The 7-day long sessions were broken up into two 2-day sessions and one 3-day session to lessen the impact on the educational processes in classrooms across the district. Also invited to attend were all administrators from all district and building levels not previously benefiting from coaching training. One hundred percent of those invited agreed to attend. Upon completion of the 7-day training a vote among the teacher group was taken. Promisingly, a unanimous decision to proceed with establishing Cognitive Coaching^{SM} as an important paradigm in our preferred culture was cast. The word began to spread. A cadre of teaching staff and administrators were dispatched to the advanced training with the intention to develop in-district trainers. Playmates were beginning to wash potatoes.

1994: Securing the Needed Resources and Support—Teaching the "Moms"

Marshaling the resources critical for a cultural change in a school district can be daunting. There are so many "moms" to answer to. Most notable of the "moms" are the school board and the state agencies, that is, those who finance and provide the wherewithal to support meaningful change and innovation. Our leadership decided to outline the scope of the cultural change we envisioned for our school district. We did so by addressing the school board in public session and the State in the State Capitol. Surely if the "moms" bought in (as in any family we knew), the path would be further cleared for progress.

The District had been using grant money to support trainings for Cognitive Coaching^{SM} up to this point. Now it was time to influence the school board to contribute to the innovation in an ongoing manner. To do this, the innovators staged a Board of Education meeting to be a mini Cognitive Coaching^{SM} training. Board members were trained to use the coaching maps and then engaged in real time coaching first led by experienced Cognitive Coaching^{SM} trainers and then with each other. This was a risky endeavor, but with skillful advocacy and coaching the Board granted permission to enter into meetings to negotiate contract language with the district teacher union that would seat Cognitive Coaching^{SM} in the teacher contract. This was accomplished by making Cognitive Coaching^{SM} an alternative to the traditional evaluation plan found in most school systems. Those who administered the teacher contract knew full well that the contract had to be funded. The Board of Education, a significant "mom" was washing potatoes.

While the negotiation with the teacher union was proceeding, another important "mom" in the form of the State of Illinois was approached with the innovation. As with most states, in Illinois teacher evaluation is outlined and regulated by statutory school code. The Cognitive Coaching^{SM} model clearly did not fit with the state plan. The state model required strong judgments by the administrator and little teacher self-direction. The task at hand was to persuade the State that a coaching model could coexist with more traditional clinical models. The rationale shared with state officials was that one must "graduate" from a traditional clinical supervision model into a professional growth-oriented coaching model. To satisfy the State's perceived need for high administrator judgment, the coaching plan required teachers entering the Cognitive Coaching^{SM} model to have earned the rating of excellent under the traditionally oriented state evaluation model. The evaluation rating under the state model was awarded biannually by the school principal. By now the District 155 principals were Cognitive Coaching^{SM} advocates.

The District was able to place most teaching staff into the coaching alternative by assigning teachers an excellent rating. Using the district plan, the principals serve as the gatekeepers for those who are permitted to go into and out of the coaching alternative. The State liked the concepts presented in the district plan. Yet another "mom" washed potatoes.

The Union and Board approved the contract language. The State granted the first exemption of this sort ever in the State of Illinois. The table was set. Sweet potatoes were on the menu!

1995/2002: Reaching a Critical Mass—The 100th Monkey and Beyond

The foundational pieces for innovation were in place. The vision was alive and the values at work. The "moms" had approved it all. Now it was time to spread the knowledge in the school community in every conceivable way. Seven-day Cognitive Coaching^{SM} trainings open to all staff were established two or three times a year (summer, fall, and winter semesters) every school year. In-district trainers who had learned at the feet of the masters, Art Costa and Bob Garmston and their Senior Associates, taught these trainings. Soon over 200 of the 250 teaching staff were trained, as were many of the support staff.

Those tenured individuals who trained became eligible for the coaching alternative to traditional evaluation. They were assigned a trained coaching colleague who had similar free time during the school day. To satisfy the terms of their newly revised employment contract, these coaching pairs engaged in a mutual coaching relationship in which goals were set, coaching maps and techniques were used, and follow up assessments discussed. Logs of the coaching episodes were kept and shared with appropriate staff supervisors at the end of the coaching cycle. As a result of this initiative, the quality of the lessons the teachers were producing began to improve, more innovation was finding its way into the classroom, and teachers were engaged in highly productive conversations about their professional practice.

In a separate but related innovation, a cost-free, in-district Masters Degree was developed in partnership with a local university targeting the young, non-tenured District 155 staff. Cognitive Coaching^{SM}, taught by District staff, was a required course for graduation under this new program of study. The innovators felt those who were at entry level with no previous experience (or scars) would adopt coaching mannerisms most easily. This was a perfect opportunity to inculcate coaching into the district culture. New staff members were paired in a coaching relationship to practice coaching skills while enrolled in the master's degree classes. Because of a new staff requirement to take Cognitive Coaching^{SM}, today roughly 90% of the current 350 teaching staff are trained as coaches.

Additionally, an existing District 155 new employee-mentoring program was modified in support of the coaching innovation. Each incoming employee was assigned a mentor. With the wide acceptance of the coaching model, every mentor assigned to a new employee was trained in Cognitive Coaching^{SM}. Never before had all new staff been engaged in reflective and productive conversation of this nature. More and more potatoes were being washed.

1995/2002: Coaching Breaks Ranks— Innovation Spreads to Other Islands

While the Cognitive Coaching^{SM} model proliferated in its conceptual design, new forms and expressions of the model morphed "to other islands." Each of these forms and expressions was a unique way for innovators to wash sand off differing island potatoes. The following are examples that are interesting in their application to a developing culture.

One such expression can be found in the chapter titled "Designing and Constructing the Holonomous School" in which coaching concepts were used to influence school building design and construction. The subtle architectural features support promoting States of Mind development. To this author's knowledge, it was the first brick and mortar manifestation of Cognitive Coaching^{SM}.

Another innovation that has traversed the islands of the district is level two training for those who wish to move beyond the basic 7-day training. This program was developed in concert with the Institute for Intelligent

Behavior (now the Center for Cognitive Coaching) and offers students a deeper understanding of coaching through advanced paraphrasing, pace and lead, and other techniques. This course is offered once a year and is taught by in-district staff.

Still another Cognitive Coaching^{SM} innovation that has found a way into the culture is the "Coaching Luncheon." These are scheduled luncheons (lunch provided by the district) where staff can go to extend or refresh their knowledge base relative to coaching and to have guided practice for their skills. These generally take place once or twice a semester and are open to all trained coaches and mentors.

Group coaching (see chapter titled "Cognitive Coaching^{SM} with Small Groups" for more information on this process) is now a common technique utilized in the district. Administrative cabinet meetings are group coaching episodes, as are building department chair meetings. Group techniques are also used when working with parent groups such as Booster Clubs or Blue Ribbon Committees. Group coaching has been found to be especially effective when controversial or important group decisions need to be examined.

Special Education staff members are utilizing coaching tenets when doing placement staffings with parents and in IEP determinations. States of mind development among students has even become a goal for all special education students.

Trained deans of students implement Cognitive Coaching^{SM} techniques when dealing with unruly students or parents. Disciplinary meetings are now viewed more positively as deans believe they possess adequate coaching finesse to deal with tense situations. Furthermore, the deans report they feel they are in more of a guidance and learning mode with problem students when using coaching than that of the traditional dean metaphor as a "hatchet man."

Teachers regularly make their supervisors aware of the use of coaching techniques in communicating with parents regarding disciplinary, curricular, or athletic issues. Many innovative teachers are now training students in the use of coaching techniques when students are actively engaged in group work, interpersonal conflict resolution, and self-advocacy.

On another island, Cognitive Coaching^{SM} is used to interview candidates for employment or services to the district. Interview questions have been crafted by staff to probe candidates' states of mind. Revealing answers to these questions lead decision makers to those they believe possess a values match with the school district. One notable example of this was the selection of an architect to build a new school. The firm awarded the job was the one who, through the interview questioning process, was determined to be the most holonomous firm and thereby the most favored! This particular decision turned out to be extraordinarily positive and has led to an ongoing relationship.

All this said, the most notable influence and evidence of the positive effects of coaching on this culture are detected when one stops to listen to the conversations that take place within the school district itself. Whether during formal meetings, at the lunch hour, in the lounge, at interviews, or by the copy machine, coaching skills are widely employed by the school community. "Will you coach me on this?" is a question now commonplace in the system. As a result, the quality of interaction between staff members has improved markedly. Evidences of this are witnessed by more collegial labor negotiations, virtually no grievances filed from the staff, and a culture of dedicated professionals who are more prone to listen and to share with colleagues.

Sweet potatoes were being washed on "islands" one would not have initially predicted!

2002/2020: The Future of Cognitive Coaching^SM—What of This "Magic"?

One might ask, "Where will this all go as the years progress?" Happily no one knows, and that is the beauty of it! The possibilities for Cognitive Coaching^SM seem endless. There are so many islands. Coaching advocates pose many visionary questions such as: "Can we envision a time when all staff, parents, and students are using Cognitive Coaching^SM in their everyday lives?" "Might those who have learned and internalized Cognitive Coaching^SM carry the techniques to contextual venues unimaginable at this time?" "Could the culture of one school district have a profound effect on larger systems in our community or in our world?"

Of course those in District 155 believe the answers to these questions to be, "Yes, yes, and yes." They expect this because they have, over a decade's worth of time, experienced the "magic" of Cognitive Coaching^SM while striving toward establishing a renaissance school community. They have personally experienced the cognitive shifts so critical to being a thoughtful and reflective professional. They have become grounded through positive interpersonal relationships and hold dearly the belief that one can be a high functioning individual contributing to a high functioning organization. They know that the tenets of coaching will reveal themselves in ways that are surprising and rewarding. They understand and promote Cognitive Coaching^SM becoming fractal in nature within their organization. They know that their experiences have become an interesting example of field theory at work. They expect and embrace the influence of Cognitive Coaching^SM on the field of education and comprehend that coaching holds limitless possibilities for the future.

The "Tale of the Hundredth Monkey" and the experiences of District 155 will hopefully encourage others to explore Cognitive Coaching^SM within the context and framework of their own organizations. The tales also are intended to lead those who wish to innovate to a realization that changing any culture is hard work that can only begin with those who are strongly committed to advancing innovative practices. The payoffs can be immense and joyful, but only if individuals in the organization pay attention to the values and vision of their organization. . . . and then toil to provide requisite resources, skills, incentives, and action plans vital for meaningful change to take place.

And so this tale ends. There are new islands to visit and sweet potatoes to wash!

Chapter 2

Coaching Principals for Increased Resourcefulness

By: Jane Ellison

Introduction

When Cognitive Coaching[SM] is a priority with the principal of a school, he or she surpasses the concept of the principal as instructional leader and becomes the organizational developer of the school. As such, the principal's focus is on developing: (a) shared norms and values; (b) knowledge of principals of learning and teaching; (c) collaborative decision-making structures; and (d) processes that provide for ongoing growth, efficiency, and effectiveness. Principals who use Cognitive Coaching[SM] with teachers and teachers who use it with each other do so because it increases the resources within and self-directedness of others. With all the support the principal is providing for others, who is providing support for the principal? Many recognize the principalship as a potentially isolated and lonely position. What might happen if someone were providing the kind of coaching support to principals, that principals are providing to staff?

This chapter describes an action research project Jane Ellison conducted to determine whether or not regular, brief sessions of

Cognitive Coaching[SM] would support principals in feeling more effective and more satisfied with their work. In Cognitive Coaching[SM] language, she wanted to help principals feel more resourceful. The outcomes exceeded expectations—the data showed that principals and assistant principals, as well as their staffs and supervisors, saw increases in the building adminstrators' resourcefulness.

Principals are overstressed, overwhelmed, and experiencing burnout at an unprecedented rate. In a recent conversation with an elementary principal, she said there were 10 programs/projects at her school that were not there 5 years ago. With increased accountability and legislation, the job of the principal is becoming more demanding and more stressful (Hall & Hord, 2001; Fullan, 2001); the resulting pace often causes principals to either leave the profession or feel less than efficacious about their work. An additional concern is that fewer educators are seeking the challenge of being building administrators (The Denver Post, February 3, 2002).

When Art Costa and Bob Garmston developed Cognitive Coaching[SM] in 1984, it was a way in which principals could support teachers in planning, reflecting, and problem-solving. It has been shown to increase both personal and professional efficacy in teachers (Edwards, 2001). Why would it not hold potential for building both personal and professional resources needed to handle the tough job of a principal? A project was undertaken to determine whether or not Cognitive Coaching[SM] would work for principals in a way that would allow them to be more effective and feel more satisfied with their work—in other words, to feel more resourceful.[1] The project involved twelve principals and four assistant principals from the Cherry Creek School District in Englewood, Colorado, who received weekly Cognitive Coaching[SM] for a 4-month period. The idea was to determine whether or not regular, brief sessions of Cogntive Coaching[SM] with school leaders would cause greater resourcefulness. As a researcher I sought answers to two main questions: (a) How might Cognitive Coaching[SM] allow districts to support principals under stressful conditions? (b) What specific skills do principals need in order to support their own and their staff's resourcefulness?

Background

As a principal for 15 years, I am fully aware of the pressure and stress that go with the job. When I learned Cognitive Coaching[SM], it changed the way I interacted with teachers and increased my own feelings of resourcefulness. Instead of "pre-observation conference," I held more informal planning conversations with teachers. Stress was reduced for both of us. What had been formal "post-observation conferences" became more useful reflecting conversations. Cognitive Coaching[SM] gave me more flexibility in my "supervision" functions. This flexibility led to gathering data that teachers felt was important and reflecting conversations that focused on student learning and were perceived to be valuable by teachers.

When I became a director and moved to the central office, I was given the responsibility for supervising principals. As a former principal, I wanted to be sure I provided them with support—I wanted my interactions to increase, not decrease their resourcefulness. Knowing that Cognitive Coaching[SM] was the way to do this, I struggled with how to both coach and evaluate principals, until I realized that as a principal I had done both with teachers. The key was being close to their work and understanding what they were dealing with on a day-to-day basis. I made it a priority to visit the principals under my supervision once a week. The feedback from the principals let me know that Cognitive Coaching[SM] was an important resource to them.

Later when beginning to train others in Cognitive Coaching[SM] on a full-time basis, I found that the stress and pressure experienced by principals had magnified. When asked about the support they were getting, most principals reported that they felt isolated and alone. Believing that Cognitive Coaching[SM] would make a difference to principals, I planned an action research project.

Action Research Design

I approached a school district with a proposal that principals and assistant principals would receive weekly Cognitive Coaching[SM] on a volunteer basis over a 4-month period. A variety of questions came to mind. Could Cognitive Coaching[SM] support principals in these times of increased accountability, high-stakes testing, and multiple demands—sometimes conflicting on principals' attention? What skills do principals need to be self-directed in contributing to staff and personal resourcefulness? How does a principal find time to reflect in an already overbooked day? What might happen if the principal had a weekly, 30–40 minute appointment with a Cognitive Coach?

Reflective practitioners, particularly those who develop collaborative cultures, flourish in such stressful settings (Costa & Garmston, 2002; DuFour & Eaker, 1998; Garmston & Wellman, 1999). Could Cognitive Coaching[SM] support a principal in becoming more reflective?

Sixteen building administrators volunteered to participate in the project in which they would receive weekly Cognitive Coaching[SM] from me. The participants comprised a diverse group:

> Years of experience: 1 to 14 years
>
> Gender: 4 men, 12 women
>
> Levels: 15 elementary, 1 middle
>
> Positions: 12 principals, 4 assistant principals
>
> Knowledge of Cognitive Coaching[SM]: 10 had attended the Foundation Seminar®, 6 had not had formal training

The first week's meetings were scheduled. It took 2 days of back-to-back conversations to connect with each of the 16 administrators. Before ending each conversation I scheduled another appointment, trying but not always able to meet with each administrator once a week.

The Coaching Process

Each administrator received 6 to 8 hours of Cognitive Coaching[SM] over a period of 4 months. The number of sessions with each principal ranged from 10 to 13, not including the final, videotaped reflecting conversation. The sessions lasted from 20 to 60 minutes, with the average length of a session being 34 minutes.

Total time in conversation	6–8 hours
Time spent consulting or collaborating	4–31 minutes
Number of conversations	10–13
Length of sessions	20–60 minutes
Average length of session	34 minutes

Figure 2-1. Administrator Coaching

At each session, the administrators determined the content of the conversation. Sometimes they started with a topic from the previous session, and at other times they started with something new. I followed the lead of the administrator and based on what the administrator shared, navigated between and among support functions (Cognitive Coaching^SM, collaborating, and consulting) and maps to guide mediational interactions (Costa and Garmston, 2002, pp. 14, 15).

Occasionally I decided to "step out" of coaching to either consult (provide expertise to the administrator) or collaborate (co-plan or brainstorm). The decision to change from the support function of Cognitive Coaching^SM was made when it appeared to me that the administrator's resources were low or not apparent. In such cases, I signalled the administrator that I was switching support functions by first asking for permission (e.g., "Would you like some options?") and second by shifting my body to indicate nonverbally that the support function had changed. In each case, I was able to return to the support function of Cognitive Coaching^SM and ask a question such as "So what do you think might work for you?" or "What meaning do you make from that?" Sometimes the administrator asked me for an opinion or advice. In such cases, I first asked the administrator what he or she thought, then responded to the question. My intention was always to support self-directed learning.

Support Function	Intention	Strategies Used
Cognitive Coaching^SM	Support self-directed learning	Pause, paraphrase, probe, inquire
Consulting	Provide knowledge/expertise	Offer alternatives from which to choose, model, research
Collaborating	Develop shared knowledge/expertise	Brainstorm

Figure 2-2. Support Function Strategies

An analysis of the times when I switched support functions revealed a pattern. In the 181 coaching sessions, I switched to consulting a total of 97 times and to collaborating 3 times. The total amount of time spent in consulting or collaborating ranged from 4 to 31 minutes (out of the total of 6 to 8 hours spent with each administrator). Collaborating took the form of co-brainstorming or co-planning. In two cases, it was to brainstorm ideas for supporting a teacher who was struggling; in one case it was to develop an agenda for a staff meeting. Consulting took the form of a menu of ideas, modeling, sharing of research, and/or observations (Lipton & Wellman, 2001). The two topics on which I most often shared research and offered ideas were Cognitive Coaching[SM] tools (e.g., paraphrasing, rapport) and content from The Adaptive School: A Sourcebook for Developing Collaborative Groups (Garmston and Wellman, 2002; e.g., decision-making process). Of the 97 times I consulted, 31 concerned Cognitive Coaching[SM] and 19 concerned Adaptive Schools.

Journals

In addition to the regularly scheduled coaching sessions, participants responded to an e-mail journal prompt after each session. Two questions were asked: How has the coaching session affected your thinking/perceptions? How has the coaching session affected your behavior/actions?

Each week the journals were independently read and rated by Carolee Hayes and Jane Ellison, Co-Directors of the Center for Cognitive Coaching[SM]. The Co-Directors identified what States of Mind were present in the journals; the analysis of the journals indicated that the most frequently identified States of Mind were consciousness and craftsmanship. There was a .95 reliability between the Co-Directors when identifying consciousness in the journals and a .75 reliability with craftsmanship.

The journal entries served to encourage reflection in the administrators, as well as provide visible evidence of increased resourcefulness. As indicated by the samples below, thinking was modified as a result of coaching sessions. The journal entries below were printed with permission of the administrators:

Entry # 1

How did our session affect your thinking/perceptions?

Wow! What a session. I thought it was a fantastic hour that altered my thinking profoundly. Our one conversation about how to present information to the G.T. teacher took an amazing turn. Instead of my presenting the information to the G.T. teacher, we presented the information in a way that builds the interdependence of teachers and teams. What a wonderful way to help promote a learning organization! Also, our time spent in dialogue about a professional growth continuum will leave my brain working overtime. A long-term plan clearly defined which indicators would bring a much deeper purpose and meaning to the evaluation process. How to implement? Where to begin? Ouch, my head is hurting!

How has our session affected your behavior/actions?

Actually, we have started planting the seeds already. Today in a meeting we were able to seize a moment and ask teachers about advanced kids and how they are seeing the support from the G.T. teachers. However, we did not form agreements or talk about specific numbers. . . . our next step.

Thanks for you time. I'm sure after 15 or so sessions each week topics must be a little repetitive. . . . but I always feel you are right there with me. Thanks for helping me dig deeper!

Entry # 2

How did our conversation affect your thinking/perceptions?

This process, not just yesterday's conversation, has helped me to focus on my leadership style. As we talk, I realize that my natural style is very effective with 4 of the 6 teams. Yesterday's conversation helped me to focus on the best approach to my work with first and fifth.

How has our conversation affected your behavior/actions?

Our conversations have helped me to differentiate my leadership style for these two teams. I am finding that I am much more direct with both first and fifth. I made up my mind before meeting with first grade this week that the recess issue was not up for discussion, but I knew that if I just walked in and gave that directive without data it would not have worked. My natural inclination is to think through a problem, I rarely leap without looking. This trait allowed me to wait for the data necessary to support my request. Our conversations on the importance of data made this work.

Data Collection

Two sources of data were used to determine whether or not administrators increased resourcefulness as a result of the coaching sessions: my observations and surveys. The administrator, three of his or her staff members, and the supervisor of the administrator completed pre- and post-surveys. The survey instrument assessed resources in the Five States of Mind: consciousness, craftsmanship, efficacy, flexibility, and interdependence. There were 40 questions, 8 in each State of Mind. Using a Likert scale, a point value was assigned to each response: 4—Strongly Agree, 3—Agree, 2—Disagree, 1—

Strongly Disagree. Figure 2-3 lists some questions from the survey, each one focusing on a different State of Mind:

I usually consider several ways of doing something before deciding what might work best.	SA	A	D	SD
My communication with others rarely needs clarification.	SA	A	D	SD
I feel like I make a difference in the district.	SA	A	D	SD
On most days, I take time to reflect on my work.	SA	A	D	SD

Figure 2-3. State of Mind Survey Questions

This instrument was adapted from one developed by the Co-Directors of the Center for Cognitive Coaching in 1998 to support teams in diagnosing group States of Mind.[2] Internal energy and resourcefulness are observable, but difficult to assess; the survey provided a cross-validation of my observation data.

Results

At the end of 4 months, and after studying the results of my observations and the surveys (self-, staff, and supervisor), the following conclusions were reached:

1. Principals/assistant principals felt an increased sense or internal resourcefulness in the areas of efficacy, consciousness, craftsmanship, flexibility, and interdependence. This was validated in the data collected from their self-, staff, and supervisor assessments.

2. Weekly Cognitive Coaching[SM] contributed to resourcefulness in the following ways:

   • It enabled participants to be more reflective and thoughtful by providing structured time to think.

   • Regular sessions ensured that reflection was a part of each week, thus habituating the behavior.

   • It provided a "sounding board" for issues that could not be discussed with others.

Following are some of the comments of principals and assistant principals at the end of the study:

> "Better focus on process and procedure; better forethought and reflection."

> "Time together helped me broaden my to thinking for self-coaching."

> "I feel more confident in my current position."

> "Making time, 30–45 minutes, for systematic reflecting and coaching allowed me to think and clarify situations, to explore options of action and to plan steps."

> "These meetings have helped me determine my goal for the next years."

> "As a first year principal attempting to build a collaborative professional community, the coaching helped me to clarify my thinking around all issues, but especially around process and clear communication."

> "The weekly sessions enabled us to get to the heart of my leadership style versus a hit and miss problem format."

> "The reflection and planning I have done regarding my interactions with staff has increased. My listening to and accepting input from staff has increased."

> "Ultimately this means I am growing into a better leader, better planner, better principal."

The supervisor of four of the principals said, "It has been extremely valuable to the participants, and I have seen some real growth from those involved."

The results of a written survey, completed by each administrator after the last reflecting conversation, revealed that

1. All but one participant felt it was important that their Cognitive Coach was not their supervisor.

2. The coach's experience as an elementary principal was valuable to all participants.

3. Trust was important to all participants.

Data Analysis

A summary of the data from the States of Mind pre- and post-assessments is presented in Figure 2-4. For each survey (self, staff, and supervisor), the number of administrators whose survey results revealed increases is reported. Although there were 16 participants in the study, some surveys were not returned thus resulting in a smaller number of participants for whom survey data was available.

	Increased Consciousness	Increased Craftsmanship	Increased Efficacy	Increased Flexibility	Increased Interdependence
Self	13/15 (87%)	13/15 (87%)	9/15 (60%)	13/15 (87%)	12/15 (80%)
Staff	11/15 (73%)	10/15 (73%)	11/15 (73%)	9/15 (60%)	11/15 (73%)
Supervisor	11/13 (85%)	10/13 (77%)	12/13 (92%)	9/13 (69%)	12/13 (92%)

Figure 2-4.   States of Mind Pre- and Post-Assessment Summary

What Important Points Seem to Stand Out?

One point that stands out is the predominance of increases in resourcefulness. Additionally, the few number of decreases (not reported in Figure 2-4) are much smaller than most of the increases. However, it would not be accurate to use numbers alone to determine the increased resourcefulness of participants. Responding strongly agree to every item on the survey would yield a score of 32 in each State of Mind. A participant who was rated higher before the survey might have a lower increase than one who was rated lower before the study. Another example of the numbers not telling the whole story is that there were some 1's (Strongly Disagree) given on the pre-surveys, but no one was assigned a 1 on any of the post surveys. All one can say as a result of looking at numbers is that most of the principals felt and were perceived as having increased resources (as measured by the survey) at the end of the study. This data validates my knowledge of the participants and confirms that there was significant growth in almost every participant's resourcefulness.

What Seems Significant?

Given the purposes of this study, perhaps the most significant data comes from the self-assessment. If participants felt more resourceful, that in itself would contribute to being more effective. One participant even remarked that she was coaching her staff more, as a result of being coached.

Probably the second most important data are that of the supervisor's assessment of the administrator's resourcefulness. If a supervisor believes an administrator is and treats an administrator as more resourceful, that might contribute to greater effectiveness on the part of the administrator. This category of data contained the least number of decreases in comparison to the staff and self-data.

What Are Some Interrelationships of Data?

Overall, the self- and supervisor data are more closely aligned than the staff data, with one exception. Efficacy and interdependence showed the smallest increases in the self-data, but the largest increases in the data collected from the supervisors. The staff data revealed the lowest percentage of increases, with flexibility increasing for only 60% of the administrators.

Earlier I suggested that the numbers do not tell the whole story, and two sets of data from staff support that. The two participants who were rated lower by their staff in all five States of Mind had surveys that looked very different. On one's survey, the range on the States of Mind was from 30 to 32; the range on the other's was from 21.5 to 28. The lowest a person could be rated on a State of Mind was 8 and the highest was 32.

One other point to make is that 5 of the administrators asked their supervisor if they could continue having me conduct regular Cognitive Coaching[SM] conversations with them after the 4-month period ended. As a result of that request, they received 13 additional weeks of Cognitive Coaching[SM]. I noticed one point that might separate this group from the others—none had any decreases from their staff's assessment. From the two other data sources, one had a decrease in the self-assessment, and two had decreases from their supervisor. Perhaps this suggests that it's not the quantity, but the quality of coaching that is most important.

What Might Be Some Patterns or Trends?

One pattern was that of increased resourcefulness from the beginning of the study to the end. Focusing on the self-assessment data, there is a pattern in the States of Mind. The highest increases were in the States of Mind of consciousness, craftsmanship, and flexibility. Another pattern is the self-assessment data from the assistant principals; some of the highest individual increases in resourcefulness occurred for these participants. In addition, each of them, at some time during the study, told me that this was one of the most valuable professional development experiences in which they had ever engaged.

One participant remarked that the coaching sessions were more like one long conversation, in that she could pick up each week with the threads of the previous week's conversation. This feature, she said, differentiated the Cognitive Coaching[SM] sessions from any other type of mentoring she had experienced. Without regular meetings, each conversation is more like an isolated experience, lacking the cumulative effect she experienced in this project.

Recommendations

It is important to recognize that the participants in this project volunteered. Their verbal comments, along with the data from the surveys, indicated that weekly Cognitive Coaching[SM] did make a difference in their resourcefulness. In addition to the nonjudgmental coaching, it was the regularity of the scheduled (on the calendar) support that was notably different from other kinds of mentoring administrators had received.

My recommendation is simple—districts should be mobilizing their resources to determine how they can provide Cognitive Coaching[SM] support to principals (and assistant principals) on a regular basis. Administrators want, need, and deserve the same support they are striving to provide with their staffs. Probably few people in any district would disagree; the main objection would be that it is too expensive. One finding from this study was that all but one participant felt that it was important that their Cognitive Coach was not their supervisor. Even if a district did not hire additional personnel to provide the coaching, there would be cost in terms of reassignment of responsibilities of district staff. However, if a district were to look at providing coaching support to principals as an investment in their future (both the administrator's and district's), might not the money be better spent there than on other resources. That is, if principals felt more resourceful in their jobs, maybe they would not "burn out" as quickly and perhaps more educators would be interested in pursuing the job of principal.

Endnotes

1. For the purposes of this study, resourcefulness was defined as having internal capacity in the Five States of Mind, as defined in Costa, A., and Garmston, R. (2002). *Cognitive Coaching: A Foundation for Renaissance Schools.* Norwood, MA: Christopher-Gordon.

2. *Team Assessment Survey* available from the Center for Cognitive Coaching, Highlands Ranch, CO, 303-683-6146.

References

Costa, A., & Garmston, R. (2002). *Cognitive Coaching^SM: A foundation for renaissance schools.* Norwood, MA: Christopher-Gordon.

DuFour, R., & Eaker, R. (1998). *Professional learning communities at work.* Reston, VA: Association for Supervision and Curriculum Development.

Edwards, J. (2001). *Cognitive Coaching^SM: A synthesis of the research.* Highlands Ranch, CO: Center for Cognitive Coaching.

Fullan, M. (2001). *Leading in a culture of change.* San Francisco: Jossey-Bass.

Garmston, R., & Wellman, B. (1999). *The adaptive school: A sourcebook for developing collaborative groups.* Norwood, MA: Christopher-Gordon.

Hall, G., & Hord, S. (2001). *Implementing change: Patterns, principles, and potholes.* Boston: Allyn and Bacon.

Lipton, L., & Wellman, B. (2001). *Mentoring Matters.* Guilford, VT: Pathways Publishing.

Stanton, Billie. (2002, February 3). *Where are all the principals going? The Denver Post,* p. 1E.

Chapter 3

Building Trust
in the Trusteeship

By: Barbara Cape and John Dyer

Introduction

Conflict on boards of education and among trustees is a common phenomenon across the United States and Canada. Superintendents typically dedicate hundreds of hours trying to build collaborative working groups, often to no avail. The result is high board turnover, unproductive meetings, and frustration of employees charged with leading schools. Dysfunctional boards leave the public with cynical views about the credibility of the schools charged with serving today's students. Faith in public education gradually erodes.

Barbara Cape, a school trustee, and John Dyer, an external consultant, provide insights into alternative ways of thinking about board and trustee leadership using the tenets, principles, and concepts of Cognitive Coaching[SM]. Their dual voices speak to diverse perspectives and provide a vision for collaboration in examining new ways of working in the context of deeply embedded patterns of practice. Their shared journey is both a challenge to readers in considering operating mental models and a template for redefining patterns of practice.

Prologue

This case study describes a 2-year process using Cognitive Coaching^SM concepts to support and develop the school board in St. Vital, Manitoba. It documents some of the events, activities, and learnings that resulted in significant improvement in the board's effectiveness. Two perspectives are taken in the article. John Dyer was the facilitator; Barbara Cape was a board member. The two voices reflect their unique perceptions related to board processes and decisions. The contrast is intended to provide insight into different ways of thinking about a group's work.

> **School Board:** 1. a group of people usually elected, who manage the schools in a designated area; 2. a collection of individuals who get together weekly to argue about their differences; 3. a decision-making body in a school jurisdiction that frequently suffers from an identity crisis; 4. an elected board of educational governance that rigorously supports "change" as long as it applies to somebody else.

BC: In the fall of 1995, our board and administration began, somewhat unexpectedly, a journey of renewal. This voyage changed our views about our purpose and our role as a board and as trustees. At that time, the board was ineffective and nonproductive in an environment of distrust, power struggles, and paranoia among its members and with the administration. In a conscientious attempt to establish some harmony during the last remaining months of a 3-year term, we organized a single day trustee/administrative team workshop and hired an external facilitator, John Dyer.

> **Facilitator:** 1. one who facilitates; 2. an interpersonal teflon-ator; 3. a person who borrows your watch and then tells you what time it is.

BC: The first workshop with John Dyer was the beginning of a process that changed the character and operational style of the Board of Trustees. The decision-making process became more positive, more productive, and more effective than it was in 1995.

JD: As a facilitator retained to work with the St. Vital Board of School Trustees, I began by having a personal discussion with each of the members of the board. From those discussions three dynamics were evident: (a) each trustee was a dedicated, well meaning, conscientious individual who was committed to providing quality education for the students in the School District; (b) there were diverse perceptions of the origins, specifications, and possible resolutions of the major issues and problems which they faced; and (c) each individual was highly autonomous, but personal agendas were interfering with the potential of their collective experience, insights, knowledge, and wisdom.

On completing my conversations with the trustees, I identified three primary outcomes: (a) to build and maintain trusting relationships through the development of interpersonal awareness and understanding; (b) to reach agreement on fundamental issues of purpose, roles, and outcomes; (c) to explore the intricacies of decision-making. These outcomes would contribute to establishing the trust and good working relationships necessary for the Board to enhance its effectiveness.

States of Mind

JD: The workshops with the trustees were designed to apply the concepts developed in the Cognitive Coaching^{SM} work of Dr. Arthur Costa and Dr. Robert Garmston (2002). Cognitive Coaching^{SM} acknowledges five significant "States of Mind" that influence our thinking, our decision-making, and our capacity for high performance. They are efficacy, flexibility, craftsmanship, consciousness, and interdependence. These mental dispositions have an impact on what we are able to accomplish. One major objective of the workshops was to raise the levels of these "States of Mind" with board members to enhance their performance both individually and collectively. One of the challenges of designing a program was not only to address the issues identified by the board members, but to identify the low-level States of Mind connected with the issues and to explore the high-level States of Mind that would support the resolution of the issues.

Workshop #1

JD: A starting point for this pilgrimage was the surfacing of "limiting" States of Mind, attitudes, emotions, and feelings. Prior to embarking on a journey, individuals customarily select the appropriate luggage; they carry only those items that will be most helpful. This requires a conscious decision to leave behind those items that would be an encumbrance. When I reviewed the situation with the school trustees it was evident that they were carrying a load of baggage that was preventing them from moving forward.

> **Baggage:** 1. the trunks, bags, suitcases, etc., that a person takes when travelling; 2. a container that proves that nonliving things

do reproduce; 3. a travelling case which contains items that impede progress; 4. a metaphorical reference for camouflaged neurosis.

JD: The first activity was a process designed to purge the emotional residue that was contaminating the board's effectiveness. The group used flip chart paper to record past events and situations that were negatively affecting their work. When the list was completed, we performed a ritual that concluded by throwing the "baggage" in the trash. The process physically and symbolically represented a commitment to move away from the past and accept the challenges of the future. The ritual gave the group a fresh starting point.

BC: I remember the "Ritual for Ending" because it had such a dramatic impact. The very process of recording the "negatives" that were getting in the way of our working effectively together was revealing. It allowed everyone to see the effect our negative behaviors were having. We felt defensive, unsafe, and distrustful. By having our feelings brought to the consciousness of the whole group, we collectively owned the pain and frustration of our past together. We had to let go of the notion that *we* wouldn't have a problem if *they* would only behave differently. We had to assume responsibility for the problems we had created and to realize that we were all responsible for finding the solutions.

When John suggested that we take our lists of grievances and "burn the past," I questioned how this gesture would make any difference. As we took the lists off the walls, folded up the paper, and put it in the trash, I experienced a sense of physical relief. A tremendous weight had been lifted from my body. We were free to start afresh.

JD: The passage towards "new beginnings" formally began when the group was invited to respond to the question: "If a board of trustees wanted to fail, what would they do?" A "paradoxical intention" is an approach advocated by consultant Gary Philips (Frankel, 1985, pp. 146, 147), who says, "Never try to improve something until you look at what it would take to make it worse." We were developing a prescription for failure.

The list generated by the group contained 28 items including power struggles; unwilling to compromise; implement change by edict or mandate; politically driven, not value driven; don't trust other board members; personal agendas and form conflicting cliques.

BD: There was a disturbing moment of truth as we reviewed the list and reflected on some of our past behaviors. We realized that our biggest deficit was not related to budget, but related to our individual and collective conduct. We were following a path that would guarantee failure. It was obvious why there were tension and dissatisfaction in our work.

A Person First

Trust: 1. a firm belief in the honesty, truthfulness, justice, or power of a person or thing; faith; 2. an invisible adhesive that cannot be purchased commercially; 3. an essential constituent in the construction of interpersonal monuments, the absence of which will inevitably result in the collapse of even the most spectacular human structures.

JD: Building trust takes time. This is one of the biggest challenges for a facilitator working with a group. There are no shortcuts to trust. Trust takes place over time and is based on, among other things, character and conduct. This is not a situation where one can combine the ingredients, add water, stir, and wait five minutes. Elected officials do not always have the opportunity to give undivided attention to the importance of this issue. Workshop retreats provide an ideal environment (nonthreatening and nonpublic) in which activities can be structured to support trust building.

To initiate the focus on trust, I engaged the participants in a series of human development activities. I began with an interpersonal communication activity and continued with the exploration of educational belief systems. We also investigated the cognitive styles that existed within the group. What clearly emerged was an appreciation that individuals within a group have some identifiable commonalties and, at the same time, some significant differences. Having differences does not imply that the group is nonfunctional. In fact, it is the commonalities that bring groups together, but it is differences that keep them together. Strength comes from diversity.

These exercises emphasized the importance of open communication and allowed the group to focus on a taxonomy of trust-building. A degree of self-disclosure established a basis of awareness—a foundation for trusting. This helped the group to understand the decisions people made and their behavior. With that understanding it was easier to accept other points of view, and acceptance led to trust.

BC: It was not uncommon for me to feel that the time spent on "getting to know you" activities was a waste. I felt impatient and wanted to spend our time dealing with "important issues." The interpersonal activities that John included in our workshops changed my thinking. One particular communication activity was dramatic in demonstrating how little time we had invested in our relationships with each other. For this exercise I was paired with one trustee with whom I constantly disagreed. I had an assumption that he and I saw the world differently, that we had dissimilar values and beliefs. Little trust existed between us. We only tolerated each other. In the exercise we took turns responding to open-ended statements concerning our individual reactions to different situations. The statements were designed to gradually become more personal and revealing in a non-threatening way. As we progressed through the statements, it was shocking to discover that we shared many of the same feelings and reactions to situations. There were numerous areas where we were in agreement. What was more dramatic was the realization that we had worked together for six years and this was the first time that we had sat together and talked about ourselves as people. It was little wonder that there was such little trust between us.

JD: The State of Mind of *efficacy* is a dynamic component of the "trust" issue. When one is fearful and insecure, it is often a self-fulfilling prophecy. We attend to those things that support our belief that we have reason to be fearful. This low state of personal *efficacy* results in behaviors such as making negative assumptions or jumping to erroneous conclusions. This State of Mind distorts our world and confirms our perception that the real "power" is outside of us. When we are convinced that we are victims, we resort to being cautious, defensive, and protective.

It is also difficult to be open and receptive to other points of view when one feels threatened and is preoccupied with fear. Little trust exists when people are protective and defensive. When people are secure and confident, their sense of self is independent of external forces; and they have a high degree of personal *efficacy*. They make positive assumptions, think the best of others, and see the positive element in all situations. Being secure means that one has energy to intentionally listen and respond to others. This increases the understanding and acceptance of others, which contributes to the building of trust.

BC: At the time of the first workshop, trust among board members and with senior administrators was low. Our behavior was defensive, fearful, and protective. We were also dealing with some difficult community issues that added to our stress. As these negative feelings intensified, we no longer consulted with each other nor provided each other with emotional support. We responded by distancing ourselves, feeling rejected, and hurt. In our self-imposed isolation, we were unable to share our feelings and reactions. This resulted in a growing sense of distrust and betrayal. We doubted, questioned, and were suspicious of others' positions including any recommendations from the senior administration.

It was unfortunate that we didn't have a better understanding of how our reactions were contributing to the deterioration of our working relationships. With this knowledge, we could have pursued other strategies to promote openness instead of jumping to negative conclusions and reacting defensively. The changes and stresses we were experiencing could have been an opportunity for trust and effectiveness to grow, rather than resulting in serious damage to our ability to work together.

I have learned that the time we take to deal with each other as people is an important part of working together. Hearing about each other's personal lives, interests, challenges, and successes helped us to appreciate the richness of experience that each person contributes to the group. When we came to understand each other, we built a firm foundation of trust. This provided stability and confidence when making difficult and stressful decisions. Activities and social situations that allowed us to get beyond our roles as trustees or administrators were crucial for creating positive relationships. These relationships contributed to high levels of performance and decision-making. Far from being a waste of time, they were an investment in effectiveness and trust-building.

Clarity of Vision, Roles, and Responsibilities

BC: The next step in our development as a board was to develop a shared vision and to clearly define the roles and responsibilities of the board and administration. The very nature of the decision-making process that occurs at board tables does little to build on people's trust in each other. This process, as defined by Robert's Rules of Order, is one of promoting and defending a point of view, pitting one position against another. It relies on debate and argument to arrive at a decision that is supported by a majority of the membership. Because of the mindsets that accompany the use of parliamentary procedures, "majority rules" was definitely not a process that could be used to develop a collective vision statement. We trusted that the facilitator would use an alternative strategy for accomplishing this goal.

> **Vision:** 1. the power of seeing, sense of sight; 2. the power of perceiving by the imagination or by clear thinking; 3. what Moses experienced when he wandered too long in the desert; 4. that which auditory learners sometimes hear about.

JD: It was my perception that we needed to revisit the group's notion of personal and political identity. Some precision was needed in the articulation of what the board felt it was trying to accomplish and to clearly define its role in the process.

Using a "managing by consensus" process developed by Bob Chadwick (1994), I invited the group to explore the question "What are the best possible outcomes if our board works effectively together?" Individuals recorded their perceptions quietly and personally. I recorded every individual's response. . . . without debate, without challenge, without argument. The statements were then compiled into a collective statement.

Each individual's words were retained. The document was a form of vision statement in which each trustee's contribution was included. It was an extremely positive document and was filled with optimism and promise (see appendix A).

BC: I felt skeptical about the "best possible outcomes" activity. How could individuals with such diverse priorities and beliefs come up with one statement on which we could all agree? It seemed that we were always in a power struggle. How could it be possible that one collective statement could encompass our vast differences? I expected that the resulting document would be superficial, patronizing, meaningless, and a collection of contradictions.

I was amazed at the final product. It contained everyone's contribution and everyone's goals. Yet it made sense and had cohesion. It did articulate the vision we had of an effective board. It was our collective vision as individuals and as a group. Even more remarkable to me, we all agreed on the content and wording. Without debate, argument, or the need to assert, defend, or belittle, we had created a common vision; one that reflected the beliefs of each individual and was owned and supported by the entire group. By using this process, we had discovered the value of interdependence.

Workshop #2

BC: During the time between the first and second workshops, three new trustees were elected to the board due to a municipal election. In addition, a new superintendent and three new assistant superintendents had been appointed. The composition of both the board of trustees and the administrative team had changed significantly. Because of the benefits derived from the first workshop, there was a strong commitment to starting out on the right track. The new leadership group was enthusiastic about working effectively and wanted to explore resourceful ways of achieving this aspiration.

As an elected Board, part of our craft is to be effective. In our sincere desire to improve our performance as a group of trustees we wanted to gain skills and understanding of processes that would enhance our ability to work together and make good decisions. Workshop retreats are an essential part of developing our individual and collective craftsmanship. A second workshop was planned.

> **Role:** 1. a performers part in a performance, play, opera, etc.; 2. a part played in real life; 3. the integration of who you are and what you are doing while simultaneously trying to avoid being psychotic.

Responsibility: 1. obligation or duty; 2. obliged or expected to account for; 3. a strategy of evasion that can be used to blame the innocent.

JD: The clarification of roles and responsibilities was the objective of the second workshop. I wanted each individual to affirm that their personal mission as trustee was legitimate, to acknowledge that each individual might have a somewhat different perception of their role in the governance process. In an environment of *interdependence* these differences are to be expected and respected. The initial process provided an opportunity for the trustees to talk in pairs. One was designated as speaker, the other as listener. The task of the listener was to listen, to restate or paraphrase to ensure understanding, and to ask for clarification when appropriate. There was no debate. The speaker did not have to defend his or her feelings about his or her personal mission. Through a rotation process every individual had an opportunity to talk with each of the other trustees as speaker and as listener. This not only allowed individuals to clarify their thinking, it created an appreciation for the value of their colleagues. In addition, the understandings that emerged contributed further to the development of trusting relationships—a continuous goal.

The senior administrators joined the group for the second half of the workshop. The group wanted a written statement of roles and responsibilities by the end of the day. To develop this text, individuals were provided with personal reflection time in order to consider the role of an elected school trustee in St. Vital. They personally recorded their reflections. In a serial process, each individual presented one of their perceptions and it was recorded on flip-chart paper. The contributions continued in sequence until every individual had contributed his or her ideas. The collective statement that was developed can be found in appendix B. The original words used by the board members are in regular type. The words in italics were added during the revision process.

Our second focus revolved around the issue, "The responsibilities of the elected board of trustees are . . ." Brainstorming generated a list of responsibilities. The group then developed categories/headings under which the items could be classified. Items were added and deleted as we progressed. The final list provided a clarification of trustee responsibilities as perceived by the group (see appendix C).

The time spent on these two activities could be perceived as redundant. This information is documented and is readily available from most trustee associations in North America. The difficulty with prewritten text in board handbooks and school acts is that the group has no ownership for the information. By collectively and *interdependently* developing the material, the trustees understood the reasoning behind the thinking. The personalization of the material made it meaningful and relevant to the group who had a 3-year commitment to work together. It accessed another important State of Mind by increasing the *consciousness* of each individual.

One of the major challenges for school trustees is to understand the separation of governance and administration. The concept of the elected role can be simply stated "to establish policy and to give direction." The role of the senior administration is to implement the directions of the board (Thomas, 1994). However, when elected to office the reality of public pressure becomes evident. Trustees are exposed to telephone calls, complaints, requests, demands, criticism, social conversations, proposals, and submissions from various stakeholders including parents, community members, students, business, and other politicians. It is easy to be seduced by the power of decision-making, the temptation to tell the administrators what to do. After all weren't trustees elected to represent the concerns of the public? This confusion of responsibilities can be a major source of conflict for elected school trustees. It was this potential enticement that I wanted to dispel from the onset.

BC: When this workshop began, I was aware of some very different feelings concerning my expectations of both process and outcome. Other retreats were stressful because of the ongoing politics among the group. It seemed that we spent time setting goals and objectives, but we weren't able to carry through with our plan once we returned to the board table and our regular meeting format. Because of the previous workshop with John and what had been achieved, I began our second session with more confidence to trust the process. Having been used to operating with Robert's Rules of Order in which one's position must be debated, it is a relief to experience a process where everyone's view is listened to, honored, and included. Free from having to design arguments to support or defend my own position, I was able to really listen to my colleagues. In addition, I felt very supported in being honest about my own views. This sense of mutual respect was evidence that we were evolving into a caring team.

At the intellectual level, it was quite easy to articulate the trustees' role of establishing policy and monitoring the system. It was not complicated to understand that the administration is responsible for implementing the policy decisions. However, as an active member of the community we saw, heard, and experienced things that demanded attention. As conscientious elected officials, we responded. It was tempting to meddle, interfere, intrude, or invade the territory assigned to administrators. This can be a spontaneous reaction when new trustees are elected and a recurring enticement for those reelected. To combat this phenomenon, it took time for the Board to talk this through—not for debate, but for clarification. It is an issue that we have to constantly revisit.

BC: Beginning a new term of office was an important time to revisit our role and responsibilities as trustees. The perceptions of the role and power of the board from a community member's perspective must be refined to be congruent with the reality of the position. This can be a difficult area for trustees and superintendents when there is not clear understanding and agreement. These workshop activities gave us the opportunity to define, for ourselves, the roles and responsibilities of our position. This allowed us to make a personal commitment to our collective vision of how we conduct our business as individual trustees and as a collective board. We created a common understanding to which we can refer when we need to be reminded that *we are not administrators.*

JD: Consciousness is a critical State of Mind for trustees in dealing with roles and responsibilities. I wanted the trustees to address internal locus of control and be willing to restrain impulsivity. To further emphasize the importance of consciousness and listening to other points of view, I concluded the day with an activity acknowledged in Robert Kegan's (1995, p. 50) book *In Over Our Heads.*

BC: To bring closure to the workshop, John had us participate in a dramatic, metaphorical demonstration of the negative impact of debate, argument, and contradiction. Each trustee was given an electric lamp. All the lights in the room were shut off. John invited one of us to turn on our light and present an idea to the group. Turning on the light indicated that we were illuminating the others.

One of the trustees presented an idea that he had. We were all invited to respond. When we spoke we could switch on our light. When we contradicted the suggestion or made a counter proposal, we could keep our light on but the original speaker had to shut off his light. This resulted in us alternatively turning lights on and off, as we contradicted the previous speaker or advocated for our own idea. We only had one light turned on at a time.

The atmosphere changed when one of the trustees built upon a previous idea and extended the thinking. John allowed both those lights to stay on because we were increasing our illumination. We were expanding our insights rather than shutting them down. The next person who spoke paraphrased what was previously said and then asked a question for clarification. Now we had three lights turned on. The next person asked a very negative question that put everyone on the defensive. All the lights were turned out except the one who asked the question. The message became very clear. We have an opportunity to build understanding, to share meaning, to be enlightened if we listen, support, extend, paraphrase, and ask questions that extend thinking.

John had us repeat the exercise, and we started the entire process from the beginning. The original speaker presented his idea again. It was only a matter of minutes before the light of every trustee was turned on. We were excited when we realized the power of dialogue and suspending our own individual ideas for the moment.

States of Mind and Board Decision-Making Processes

BC: An important by-product of the workshop activities and the formulation of these documents was that our consciousness concerning decision-making processes was raised considerably. We had the opportunity to experience making group decisions, using processes that were different from the traditional parliamentary process used at our board table. These alternative processes were more efficient, more comfortable, more productive, and more unifying than Robert's Rules.

> **DECISION-MAKING:** 1. deciding or settling of a question, dispute, etc., by giving judgment to one side; 2. to make up one's mind without being confused by the facts or distracted by a different point of view; 3. talk 'till you drop.

When one reviews the history of decision-making in a community setting, this process of decision-making based on "majority rules" served us well at a time when changes occurred slowly. The main objective was to ensure that there was support from a majority of community members for the decisions made and the actions taken.

The authority of an elected council or board was defined by the position itself. Decisions were accepted because of the belief in the hierarchy of power positions. The process of reaching a decision was through the use of influence and persuasion (debate) to "win" majority support for a particular viewpoint. Historically, power positions have been an accepted part of many roles and relationships in the family, community, or workplace. People have been accustomed to accepting the "rule" of someone else even if they didn't personally agree with the position. One was expected to accept the authority of someone in a position of authority.

Parliamentary procedure relies on argument and debate to arrive at a decision; a power struggle to determine which point of view will get the support of the majority. The adversarial nature of this process separates people into opposing sides, either for or against an idea. It does not contribute to making the best decision. Instead, a decision is made based on its popularity with the majority.

In the political world in which we live today, there is an indication that community members have lost confidence in their elected representative's ability to make good decisions. The disappointment and cynicism with politicians and the political process is often accompanied by questions about the character and integrity of the politicians themselves. By blaming the politician have we ignored the real cause of our frustration and distrust in politics—the decision-making process itself?

In our communities, schools, and workplaces, we are learning that it is important to work collaboratively. There is value in the skills, talents, and wisdom of all members. In our multicultural communities we benefit from the diversity of beliefs and approaches. It is understandable that we are distrustful and frustrated by a decision-making process that is exclusive, adversarial, and limiting.

It is possible that the traditional process of decision-making that occurs at board meetings is undermining and destroying the very trust that is required to work effectively together. If this is the case, then the exploration of alternative decision-making processes becomes not only desirable but also absolutely necessary. Breaking from the chains of convention requires the engagement of another critical state of mind, *flexibility.*

JD: The tradition of parliamentary governance is so deeply embedded in communities that it requires a major shift in thinking to explore other options. Learning new decision-making strategies is not so difficult. What is difficult is developing an internal and collective confidence that alternative approaches are not only legitimate but can be both more effective and more efficient. Changing mindsets is a prerequisite for changing the behavior. The State of Mind of *flexibility* provides the openness of attitude that allows us to explore others' ways of doing things.

Workshop #3

Budget: 1. an estimate of the amount of money that can be spent and the amounts to be spent for various purposes, in a given time; 2. a mythical god that only has the power that others bestow upon it; 3. a financial whip used to beat a dying horse; 4. when in doubt, the place to place the blame.

BC: The third workshop with John Dyer was planned to look at how we would include the community (particularly parents) in the annual budget process. This had been a source of frustration during the previous couple of years. Active parent councils and staff wanted to become more involved in providing input and feedback to the board throughout the process. Although the board had attempted to increase the opportunities for involvement, there was widespread frustration with the process and a perception that the board was only going through the motions. A feeling persisted that it did not take other stakeholders' viewpoints seriously. The purpose of this workshop was to design a new approach.

JD: The intention of the third workshop was to demonstrate a variety of decision-making processes in dealing with a real and current issue, the budget. I wanted to break down the rigidity in thinking that boards are limited to a single process for decision-making. The objective was to alter the habit of mind that parliamentary procedure and decision by vote is the only option available to those who are elected to political office. Our goal was to develop practical skills and usable tools that would enable us to extend the repertoire of decision-making processes.

BC: We began the workshop by celebrating our accomplishments of the past year. This was done by listing month by month our activities and successes. I remember initially feeling some frustration in wanting to get on with talking about the budget. Even though I know these *grounding* activities are important, I still instinctively want to get to the business. I need to constantly remind myself that these exercises are an integral part of working effectively together and are "business."

As a new board, we had been together for 9 months. It had been a busy time, but I would not have described it as unusually productive. Putting to paper a listing of our work and our outcomes forced me (and the others) to recognize and appreciate how much we had achieved as a group. There was a great sense of accomplishment, satisfaction, and pride in being a member of this board. This was the first time I had experienced these feelings in my 10 years as a trustee. In hindsight, the reasons for this are significant. Although in the past the board had set goals, these goals were mostly for the organization. Through our work with John, we set goals for ourselves. We articulated the way we wanted to function and what we wanted to accomplish during our term. More importantly, we had taken time to reflect on our goals and to acknowledge our progress together recognizing and celebrating the outcomes already reached. At the conclusion of the activity, the positive energy was obvious. We concluded that evening's session socializing together, trustees and administration, as a cohesive and successful team.

Assumptions, Dialogue, and Suspension

JD: To focus on alternative decision-making processes the trustees built an "assumptions wall." This is a process that invites the participants to record their assumptions about a particular topic. These notions are stated briefly and concisely, on strips of paper approximately 14 x 17 in size. They are written large enough with felt pens so the group can read them. Then they are attached to the wall. When all have been posted, they are read and discussed at two levels: (a) questions for clarification, and (b) data or evidence on which the assumption is based. There is no debate about the "rightness or wrongness" the "correctness or incorrectness" of the assumption. It is a revealing process. People's assumptions are a reflection of what they believe to be true. If 2 individuals have different assumptions and both individuals believe their assumptions to be right, how do we determine what is true? Is it by arguing, contradicting, and refuting the other point of view? Our suggestion is that it would be more valuable to listen to each other carefully and respectfully to present our observations without being defensive. Trustees need not spend their time searching for "who's right," but to invest their time developing "shared meaning and understanding."

BC: Our focus on the "budget process" began during the next activity of building an "assumptions wall." I recall the moment when it occurred to me that my beliefs about the process and parents' involvement were based on assumptions that I held for which I had little actual evidence. There was an identifiable shift in my thinking. I experienced a new level of awareness. It became a meaningful activity to search out and discover just how many assumptions we all held concerning this project. The wall soon filled up with our contributions. When it came time to review our work, no one was put in a defensive position. We listened to each person's items and the data explaining the assumption. We realized that we all hold our beliefs for legitimate reasons. As we listened to the reasoning of others, adjustments to our own thinking occurred. New questions arose and new assumptions were exposed. With each person's contributions, our individual and collective thinking became clearer.

This was another example of the importance of the States of Mind of *consciousness* and *interdependence*. We became aware of what was going on in our own minds and how that influenced others; we also understood what others were thinking and how that impacted our behavior and decision-making. Also the very act of sharing our assumptions created an opportunity to consider other viewpoints and to be influenced by them. Operating at high levels in these States of Mind allowed us to accomplish three things:

(a) we were willing to give up some traditional forms of decision-making and explore new alternatives that worked more effectively for us; (b) we abandoned defending of our personal points of view and listened carefully to perceptions and perspectives of the others; and (c) we didn't start with a pre-conceived idea of what the end result would be. Instead we were open to considering all possibilities in the best answer that we created together.

JD: The second activity addressed the issue of *dialogue.* This focus is based on the work of David Bohm (1990). It involved a formal discussion of the concept of *dialogue* and the critical importance of "suspension." The word dialogue comes from the Greek word *dialogos. Logos* means "the word" or in our case meaning of the word. *Dia* means through (not two). This suggests that the meaning of the derivative is "stream of meaning" flowing among, between, and through us. Following the presentation we conducted a *dialogue* applying the concepts. It reinforced the importance of the State of Mind of consciousness. Before we can use *dialogue,* we have to be aware of what it is. As we engage in *dialogue,* we have to be consciously aware of what is going on in our minds. We must remain aware of what we are thinking as well as make conscious decisions about how to focus our attention.

     In his book On Dialogue, David Bohm (1990, pp. 12, 13) clarifies the concept of *suspending.* Group members will bring their assumptions; and as the group continues meeting, those assumptions will surface. What is called for then is to *suspend* those assumptions, so that they are neither accepted or suppressed. Members don't believe them, nor do they disbelieve them; they're not judged as good or bad. The goal is to simply see what they mean—not only one's own, but those of others as well. The goal is not to try to change anybody's opinion. When this meeting is over, somebody may or may not change his or her opinion.

     Assumptions will come up. And if you hear somebody else who has an assumption that seems outrageous to you, the natural response might be to get angry, to get excited, or to react in some other way. But suppose you suspend that activity. That means that it is sort of there in front of you. You are not suppressing it, not carrying it out, not believing it or disbelieving it, you are simply seeing the meaning of your assumption along with the other person's. You may not even have known that you had an assumption. It was only because someone came up with the opposite one that you found out that you have one. You may uncover other assumptions, but we are all suspending them and looking at them all, seeing what they mean. . . . That is part of collective thought—people thinking together. At some stage we would share our opinions without hostility. We would then be able to *think together*; whereas, when we defend an opinion we can't. An example of people thinking together would be that somebody would get an idea, somebody else would take it up, and somebody else would add to it. The thought would flow—rather than there being a lot of different people, each trying to persuade or convince the others.

BC: What I remember clearly as John presented the information about dialogue and suspension is that it made so much sense. Peter Senge (1990, pp. 246–248) observes that when people contribute and surrender their individual ideas to the group for exploration, development, expansion, and refinement, the group owns the outcome. It becomes a new creation shared by everyone. I gained an appreciation for many of the problems the board had experienced in the past. We were so busy arguing for our point of view that we never gained an appreciation for what else was being said. We had limited ourselves to making a decision based on one or two people's thinking. We didn't have the capacity for *suspending* and as a result were not *thinking* together or establishing shared meaning. We did not create a solution involving everyone's ideas and efforts.

> **Mind Maps:** 1. using visual graphics to exhibit the dimensions of a concept or situation which display the connections and linkages between the parts; 2. a valuable tool in a journey of the imagination; 3. a dirty, wrinkled, improperly folded document found in the glove compartment of the brain.

JD: Having completed our attention on *suspending,* the last step was to apply these principles to the budget process. The senior administrators and the trustees were divided into two mixed groups. They were provided with large sections of flip chart paper (36" x 48") and felt pens. Using the skills of *dialogue* and *suspending,* the task was to develop a mind-map or concept-map which represented all the components of the budget process. Visually indicating the relationships between the components is also an important dimension of the concept map. Through the use of dialogue, all members of the group were expected to reach agreement on the design and content of their concept map. This process took almost 3 hours of concentrated thinking, sharing, explaining, comparing, suggesting, reflecting, illustrating, and connecting.

BC: By the time we had arrived at this activity, we had a half-day left at the retreat. I was beginning to feel some frustration, because we had yet to start developing the actual budget process. When John explained that this activity would have us create a concept map, I felt discouraged and questioned how drawing a web would assist us in this very critical task that had been the primary objective of this workshop. In hindsight, I am amazed at how difficult it was for me to let go of my notion of how the Board "should" do its work. My State of Mind of *flexibility* was low. I had reverted to rigid thinking that the way we had always done things was the way that we should continue to do things. My lack of flexibility was blocking my openness to this process.

It took some time for our group to become comfortable with the mapping process. Hesitantly, we committed a few of our ideas to the chart paper. Soon we began generating numerous ideas and factors that needed to be considered in the budget process. As the map started taking shape, we added depth and detail to the various segments of the web. Ideas generated more ideas. The web became more complex and interconnected. There was a moment of insight when all the details of the picture created a pattern for me. I suddenly realized that what we were drawing was a planning process that encompassed everything we did as a school division. The annual approval of the budget was only one component of a much larger and more comprehensive process of goal setting, planning, and decision-making. It had been exhausting work, but the satisfaction that came with having a concept map showing the big picture; and the relationship of the pieces to the whole instilled a high sense of accomplishment. Applying the tools of *dialogue* resulted in universal participation and common understanding. We had produced agreement without fragmentation. It demonstrated to us the potential that we had when we worked together and abandoned our previous practices of arguing, defending, or trying to "win."

In concluding our work at the third workshop, we realized that there is a profound interconnectedness in the work that is done by our board. We can't deal with any individual part of our work without considering the total context. The budget should not be driving the decisions about programs, but the decisions about programs should be driving the budget. The budget planning process is not a separate topic; it is part of a systemic planning process.

Although we were unable to finish the task during the retreat, we had completed enough to allow our administrative team to continue working with the maps we had jointly created. They returned to the board a few weeks later with a well-articulated, year-round planning process for involving staff, community, and the board. The application of this process lead to the approval of the budget. It was a process that was highly successful, fully supported by the stakeholders, and for which the Board has received positive feedback and encouragement.

JD: As an external observer, I noticed visible changes in the group's style of interaction. Individually they exhibited behavior that indicated that they were functioning at high levels of the "States of Mind" that resulted in high performance and high productivity. The trustees were

- attending to one another (*interdependence* and *consciousness*)

- extending each other's thinking (*flexibility*)
- searching for clarity (*craftsmanship*)
- exploring all possibilities (*flexibility*)
- consistently refining (*craftsmanship*)
- contributing ideas and suggestions (*efficacy*)
- sharing their meaning and their understandings (*consciousness* and *interdependence*)

In the time allocated, the maps were not completed. The participants were exhilarated and simultaneously mentally fatigued. However, the experience had profound short- and long-term impact.

BC: In reflecting on the culmination of the three workshops, the following observations about group processes and decision-making were evident:

- A trusting environment is a freeing environment.
- We make better decisions when we search for understanding rather than argue for our vested interests.
- None of us is as smart as all of us.
- The "States of Mind" are the critical dimension of trustee success—individually and collectively.
- Alternative decision-making processes are more effective and productive than debate and discussion.

Although we did not complete our thinking on the budget process by the conclusion of the workshop, we accomplished something much more important. We built a foundation on which our future decisions could be constructed. We developed a framework on which a planning process could be built. We cemented our relationships with each other so that we could continue as an entity, knowing that there would be differences and disagreement but that there would always be respect, co-operation, and the search for the best answer. One of the major additional benefits is the generic nature of the process. We have a model for decision-making that provides a high degree of inclusion of stakeholders. This process has many applications at many levels throughout the district.

Epilogue

BC: A year after our last workshop with John Dyer, the impact of the time we spent learning new ways of thinking about our roles and the way we work together is still evident. We begin every board meeting with time alone as trustees to ground ourselves as a group and to reconnect as individuals, as human beings. We go around the table sharing what is going on in our personal lives and expressing concerns we have about items that we will be dealing with on the evening's agenda. We do much of our decision-making in "committee of the whole" so that we are free to use the alternative decision-making models that encourage us to make use of all of our experiences and creativity.

There is a high level of trust among the group; and we feel safe to put our ideas forward and allow the group to develop, refine, build, and create solutions. When there is a problem, we take a step away from it. We question what we could be doing differently that might help us to arrive at a more effective solution. We listen to and honor each other's viewpoints, seeking out a course of action that includes the contributions of each person. We have grown to appreciate our differences and to see how they enrich our decision.

During the past 2 years, I have learned that the group's wisdom is greater than any one particular viewpoint. Creating solutions together results in a decision that is far more effective. I look forward to meetings as an opportunity to share my own thoughts, ideas, and experience. In the process, I am confident that I have a unique contribution to make; but I am also aware that other viewpoints are equally valuable. It is challenging and rewarding to work together to create outcomes that include everyone's ideas. The Board room has become a place where tension and frustration have been replaced by creativity and synergy. I appreciate and enjoy the laughter and good humor that has become a part of our working together. Being a trustee has never been more productive, creative, or satisfying. I feel a part of an effective team.

The board and administration recently had a retreat. For the first time since our voyage of renewal began, we did not have an external facilitator. It was interesting to observe that the lessons we had learned were evident. We celebrated our past accomplishments; we listed our goals and put them in an order of priority. The group *thought together* about what it wanted to accomplish. We listened to each other. What evolved was a further refinement of the planning process. More importantly, the focus was not on resolving conflict between trustees and administration; the focus was on curriculum and how we can improve the learning that children experience in our schools. Isn't that what trusteeship is all about?

References

Bohm, D. (1990). *On dialogue.* Ojai, CA: David Bohm Seminars.

Chadwick, R. (1994, December 10–11). *Beyond conflict to consensus workshop, Learning the process—Exploring conflict: A learning manual.* Paper presented at the National Staff Development Council Annual Conference, Orlando, FL.

Costa, A., & Garmston, R. (2002). *Cognitive Coaching^SM: A foundation for renaissance schools* (2nd ed.). Norwood, MA: Christopher-Gordon.

Frankel, V. (1985). *Man's search for meaning.* Washington Square Press.

Kegan, R. (1995). *In over our heads.* Cambridge, MA: Harvard University Press.

Senge, P. (1990). *The fifth discipline: The art and practice of the learning organization.* New York: Doubleday.

Thomas, L. (1994). *School board member handbook.* Vancouver, British Columbia: EduServ Inc.

Appendix A

Best Possible Outcomes
A Collective Statement

Developed by the St. Vital Board of Trustees
August 23, 1995

The following statements were developed from the exact comments generated by the St. Vital Board of Trustees on August 23, 1995. The words written in *"Italics"* have been inserted to facilitate the flow of the concepts and to make the statements grammatically appropriate. The tense of some verbs has been changed to keep them in the active voice.

It is important for trustees to remain focused on what is best for kids. We are value driven, have a clear mission, and live by it. *Effective trustees* are proactive, rather than reactive *and* place kids first rather than playing politics. *As a board of trustees* we stand united during the best of times as well as during the worst of times.

Effective school boards have a clear expression and articulation of goals, roles, and responsibilities. The clearly defined roles are respected and *individuals* stay within the role of trustee. The role/function of the board is distinct and separate from administration. We take responsibility for that role and do our job well. Policy is established, and the administrators are permitted to implement such *policy. The board* should not be afraid to trust administration's advice to the board. *It is recognized* that the chair is chosen as a spokesperson *for the board* and always represents the views of the group to prevent dissension.

We use an inclusion approach: taking ideas from all partners in education and encompassing them in decision-making. Process*es* would be in place to solicit information from all areas before making decisions and setting goals. *There is* open communication with staff. Board members keep in touch with community pulse *and are willing* to look at all sides of an issue. *It is also essential that trustees* not interfere with channels of administration communication.

Board members are aware of what is happening in the system *and* are in schools regularly. *In addition,* students and parents are included to have a voice in the board; *and* there are regular barometer checks with our community. *It is essential* that we regularly evaluate our behavior and our performance.

To be effective, trustees are respectful, thoughtful, and nonpolitical. *They maintain* a high degree of integrity and do not wash their dirty laundry in public. *The board is* open to change and innovation. We celebrate success and learn or build from failure. We remain open to suggestions and new ideas.

Communication *in the board* is honest and appropriate. Problems are handled and directed to the people closest to the area of their responsibility and role. *There are* high levels of trust, commitment, listening skills, problem-solving techniques, *and* understanding of each other. There is open, respectful discussion at board meetings even when no one is watching. *Individuals* use paraphrasing *to ensure clarity and understanding.* Board members are able to share their concerns openly and know that they were heard. Board members *also* respect each other's positions and understand them. *There is* no grandstanding discussion in public meetings; the focus is on problem-solving.

School board meetings are energizing, respectful exchanges of ideas. We build on each other's views/beliefs. Input from others is welcome *as a means* of reaching the best decision that is respected and supported by community and system. Meetings are for us to do our unique job and not rehash, accept, or reject decisions made by administration. There are regular discussions of educational issues, not the "bus stop" issues.

Meetings are held in a business like manner, and decision is well thought out. *Trustees* come well prepared for meetings. *There is* full commitment and participation by every board member.

The board of trustees works in an atmosphere of mutual trust and respect. We treat people the way we want to be treated. For good decision-making, each viewpoint is valued, encouraged, and supported. We listen to all with an open mind. We do not prejudge others' motives, *thereby,* building on each board members strength. *Board members* are accountable, supportive, and positive to each other and all staff.

Trust *exists* at all levels. Staff (teachers and administrators) and parents articulate support for the board and *display a* willingness to work together. We express our appreciation for all staff, and are respectful of each other and those in our system.

Appendix B

St. Vital Trustee Retreat

November 10, 1995

Role of the Elected Board of School Trustees

The role of the board of school trustees is to advocate for students, to ensure that the best quality of education is available to all students in St. Vital, *and* to ensure that the needs of the students are met.

The board is responsible for developing, promoting, and protecting the mission statement. *They are* the "creators" and the "keepers" of the dream, *by* ensuring that the system has stated values and that those values are adhered to and reflected upon. *It* articulates values and beliefs of the community and ensures that the system operates within them. *The school board* represents both community and education needs and goals. *It* is the link between professional *educators* and the community. *They* safeguard the framework of public education—its policies and values. They provide leadership in *establishing* direction for education.

Trustees establish long-term plans and directions *and* facilitate and support the work of the system through appropriate policy and budget allocation. Priorities are set in the areas of programming and budget. Broad frameworks and broad outcomes are set, and *the board* delegates to others the responsibility for carrying them out. Deliberations *are conducted* in a productive and open manner. Decisions are made fairly and openly.

The board of trustees has an obligation to consult with the community and respond to the community. *It* facilitates the exchange of information brought by stakeholders, decides/reflects on functioning, and adapts as needed. *They* orchestrate and conduct the contributions of stakeholders.

Appendix C

St. Vital Trustee Retreat

November 10, 1995

Responsibilities of the St. Vital Elected Board of School Trustees

- **ADVOCATE FOR STUDENTS**

  Advocate for children, promote partnerships, advocate for public education, ensure all activities are student centered, model standards of quality of interactions, recognize each student is individual in development, and support innovation.

- **ESTABLISH MISSION AND GOALS, ARTICULATE VALUES AND BELIEFS**

  Communicate the vision, long range planning, act with integrity, listen in a nonjudgemental manner, promote partnerships, advocate for public education, project image of professionalism and solidarity, act as a corporate entity, model standards of quality of interaction, promote morale, role model for best practice, and support innovation.

- **SET POLICY**

  Set and establish policy, long range planning, ensure that policy and process (regulations and procedures) are established and followed, delegate the implementation of policy, evaluate the effectiveness of policy, gather information, be proactive, advocate for public education, guard the trust, and allow administration and staff to do their day-to-day activities (job) without interference.

- **ALLOCATE RESOURCES—BUDGET**

  Stewardship of resources, develop budget, set budget to achieve goals, set education tax levy, manage resources, and represent the community when dealing with contracts.

- **ALLOCATE RESOURCES—HUMAN**

  Allow administrators and staff to do their day-to-day activities (jobs) without interference, manage resources, and hire the best administrators and staff.

- **HIRE THE CHIEF EXECUTIVE OFFICER (SUPERINTENDENT)**

- **COMMUNICATE**

  Educate, inform parents/public on policies/procedures, share information with stakeholders, assess information, represent needs to government, represent community when dealing with contracts, work together, delegate implementation of policy, promote partnerships, advocate for public education, guard the trust, promote morale, and celebrate achievement.

- **SELF-REFLECT—EVALUATE**

  Act as a corporate entity, evaluate effectiveness of policy, evaluate the effectiveness of board meetings, function as a member of a team, respect the persona of the board and individuals, act with integrity, listen in a nonjudgmental manner, and assess information proactively.

Chapter 4

Public Coaching

By: Carolee Hayes and Jane Ellison

Introduction

Cultures are created over time through human interactions, negotiations, and conversations. The weaving that occurs through these conversations creates unique patterns and textures in the fabric of the culture. Ellison and Hayes describe a specific application of Cognitive Coaching[SM], public coaching. Public coaching provides a unique strategy for creating meaningful conversation by key organizational members. This process assists groups in accessing the thinking of their leaders, mediates the thinking of the leader, and intertwines the threads of understanding across the organization.

The chapter describes the intentions of public coaching and explores the conditions that need to be in place to effectively utilize it. The authors also consider cautions in using the process. Specific examples of applications of coaching are also explained.

Generally, Cognitive Coaching^SM has been utilized as a one-on-one process to mediate the thinking of an individual. In exploring other applications, a powerful discovery has been made—when an individual of key significance to a group is coached in front of that group, the group has a unique opportunity to access the internal thought processes of this individual. This process is called *public coaching.* Public coaching is defined as,

> one-on-one coaching with a significant individual, in a setting observed by others in the organization, for the purpose of giving the audience access to the thinking of the person being coached, as well as the opportunity to consider how the individual's thinking can assist the organization's development processes. (Hayes, 1995, p. 44)

One important value of public coaching is its impact on *both* individual growth and organization development. As a strategy, it is inherently holonomous. Public coaching mediates the thinking and resourcefulness of the individual leader who is coached. It also assists the audience in accessing how the person thinks as an individual leader who is simultaneously contributing to a larger system. Parallel to the impact on the leader's thinking, each audience member is making individual meaning of the coaching and the group is making collective interpretations about its work.

Public coaching was an incidental discovery by one of the authors, resulting from modeling coaching techniques with a principal in front of his staff. At the end of the model, the staff seemed more intrigued with the content of his thinking than the coaching processes used to mediate his thinking. Rather than looking at the failed outcomes, an examination of the unanticipated outcomes became an interesting exploration. In following up with the staff, the author discovered that even a month later the staff was still analyzing and reflecting on the principal's thinking. It was clear the staff had never had such exquisite and explicit access to their principal's thinking. They were fully engaged, appreciative, and responsive to the new insights. Staff responses were not as focused on the topic and content of the principal's thinking but on his metacognition—how he considered key issues, assumptions he held, and values that were evident in his internal processes and decision-making. Without any intention to do so, the principal became a model of thinking aloud, reflecting publicly, and sharing a journey of personal inquiry and problem-solving.

Public Coaching—What It Is, What It Is Not

Public coaching is based on willingness and intention to externalize and share internal thought processes. One value of the process is to support an individual leader by mediating the five states of mind to greater capacity and resource, serving the leader in becoming more effective and self-directed. That is a well-known impact of coaching an individual. A second value added outcome is to provide public access to the thinking of a leader, allowing all members of an organization to access and consider the cognitive processes of a key player in an interdependent system. Public coaching develops trust through increasing communication with a group that would not ordinarily have access to an individual's thinking. Because of the critical role of a leader in supporting and facilitating an organization's goals, the leader's shared metacognition can impact group states of mind, especially group consciousness.

In public coaching, one goal of the coach is to mediate the leader's thinking. A second goal is to assist the group in understanding the thinking of the leader. The simultaneity of the two goals attends to both individual and group needs. Successful public coaching requires that both the coach and the leader have a shared understanding of the purposes of public coaching, including specificity about what it is *not* intended to do. Public coaching is not an interview to provide staff access to specific information about a person's stance. Public coaching has no intention to provide a public platform for a leader to "speech-make," advocating one stance or position over another. Public coaching is spontaneous and unrehearsed. However, the coach may consider in advance whether the conversation should be planning, reflecting, or problem-resolving in response to contextual understanding and agreed-upon focuses between the coach and the person being coached. The coach might also consider which States of Mind to explore in order to serve the dual purpose of meeting—the individual and organizational needs.

The name *public coaching* implies a purpose greater than private one-on-one coaching. The coach needs to be prepared to use the structures of the coaching maps with thoughtfulness and responsiveness in the moment, always cognizant of the thinking of the individual. Simultaneously, the coach is attentive to the needs of the audience, respecting that some territory may be useful to explore for either the leader or the audience but not serving both. There is emphasis on serving a personal need and a public need. The coach's work is challenging because it has the tensions of holonomy intertwined in the process. The coach is expected to mediate an individual's thinking, to serve the thinking of the group, and to integrate the needs of both into a holonomous purpose greater than either.

To clarify the specific purposes of public coaching, consider this example. A newly hired principal is holding a first staff meeting in a new school. A public coaching session is planned as a means to connect to the new staff and to share the thinking of the new principal. The coach and the principal meet prior to the meeting to clarify goals for the coaching. Both agree that the coaching session will be unplanned and will evolve naturally. As they talk about the principal's entry into a new system, there is agreement that the focus of the conversation will be planning, with some additional reflections on the principal's understanding of learning from prior leadership experiences. The principal agrees to respond to questions in a thoughtful and responsive manner in-the-moment rather than through a prepared and rehearsed set of words. They both see it as an opportunity to have a meaningful and productive conversation that gives the audience access to authentic thinking about important work. The coach and the principal consider norms for the session. They agree to not broach territory that is confidential or more appropriately held as private (e.g., individual issues, private conversations). Each agrees to honor the in-the-moment decisions by either, as each sees fit to meet the individual and group needs The coach agrees to set the stage with the staff explaining that the session is spontaneous and unrehearsed with an intention to provide access to a leader's thinking. The coach prepares for the meeting by reviewing the elements of the planning conversation and thinking about which states of mind might best serve the principal and the staff.

Skills of the Coach

Public coaching is something that requires a broad range of skills on the part of the public coach because the stakes are high. It is the coach's responsibility to set the stage to ensure the success of the process, much like it is the responsibility of the teacher to set the conditions for a successful classroom. Attention must be given to assessing the system and its readiness for this level of vulnerability by the coachee. The public coach must assess the total system's readiness for the process of public coaching. Is the culture one which values reflection, and is it one that supports risk-taking in individuals? The public coach must also assess the individual's strengths. Is he or she efficacious enough to be vulnerable in a public setting? Is the coachee a person who can think on his/her feet? Does the individual understand the power of the process of public coaching? Without employing both individual and organizational assessment, more harm than good can easily be created.

The public coach is working to manage one of the tensions of holonomy—to serve the needs of the individual while also working to support the needs of the group. This requires some data collection about the group prior to the coaching session. This might be based on prior knowledge or on some actual formal or informal data collection such as interviews, surveys, spending time talking with staff members in the lunch room, and so forth. Failure to do some type of assessment of the group can result in asking questions which seem irrelevant to the group or in asking questions which are overly sensitive to the group that could be better dealt with in a different forum. The more the coach understands the group, the more likely the coaching questions will serve the group. The coach is well served by thinking about the states of mind of the group as a whole. For instance, if the group is known to have low efficacy, the coach may want to ask the leader questions about how he or she plans to empower group members.

The public coach is also responsible for knowing the person being coached well enough to be able to create a coaching environment that is safe, targeted, and genuinely supportive. Some prior relationship with the coachee is often beneficial, such as having been colleagues in another setting or having worked together on a project. The coach and the leader must have prior trust in their personal relationship that allows them to know at a deep level that neither will lead the other into a discussion that is too risky or too intimate. The relationship should be based on shared values that have been explored. Some of those might include a shared belief in risk-taking, open communication, values-based learning, and the use of data to think collaboratively. The coach and leader should engage in open dialogue prior to the public conversation about risks and beliefs in order to enhance trust and alleviate surprises.

A prior relationship is not an absolute requirement, but it is recommended for providing a foundation for trust. The audience will quickly assess that the coaching session is not comfortable or natural if the two participants are using the session to establish a relationship. Without some basic trust, the group's needs may be easily sacrificed by energy going to developing a relationship between the coach and coachee.

The coach should have knowledge of the job focus of the coachee in order to ask questions that target key issues in the context of the group listening. Also, some knowledge of the states of mind of the coachee may serve the coach in making connections between the leader's thinking and the group's needs. For example, if the leader has high craftsmanship and low interdependence, the coach will want to utilize this knowledge in developing questions for the conversation.

Efficacy
What are some of the skills you bring from past experiences as a leader that will assist you here?
How do you know when you have done everything you can possibly do?
Flexibility
As you consider the perspective of your community, how will you be certain you understand their viewpoints?
What are some issues you might not have planned for or considered?
Consciousness
What are some things you know about your own leadership style that will be important to consider in the next months?
How will you monitor the effects of your decisions?
Craftsmanship
What criteria are you considering for making decisions about . . . ?
What seem to be the greatest priorities for your attention right now? How might that change over time?
Interdependence
What are some resources that are available in your staff that might assist you?
What might be some goals of your staff and community that interface with your goals?

Figure 4-1. Examples of Generic Public Coaching Questions

The public coach brings thorough knowledge of the four Cognitive Coaching[SM] Capabilities (see Figure 4-2) and uses them with high craftsmanship and consciousness. The coach knows the intention is to mediate the individual's thinking while serving the larger audience. All of the skills of coaching are required to stay grounded in this intention. The coach matches the style of the coachee while sometimes stretching the coachee out of natural zones of comfort. The coach consciously navigates within and among maps as the conversation proceeds.

- Know one's intentions and choose congruent behaviors.

- Set aside unproductive patterns of listening, responding, and inquiring.

- Adjust one's style preferences.

- Navigate within and among coaching maps and support functions.

Figure 4-2. Cognitive Coaching Capabilities

Finally, the coach is aware of his/her own states of mind. Public coaching requires interdependence in order to serve the individual and the audience. The public coach must be highly conscious and craftsmanlike. The coach's attention must be directed to multiple considerations. The coach must listen with full attention, paraphrase, pause, and question. Simultaneously the coach must monitor time, audience energy, use of the coaching maps, and states of mind of the coachee. Public coaching is enhanced by the coach's efficacy related to coaching skills. Flexibility also serves the public coach, allowing the coach to ask questions that serve both the leader's needs and the audience's perspective.

- Audience Information

- Leader Information

- Coach Information

Figure 4-3. Preassessment Areas for Public Coaches

Conditions for Successful Public Coaching

Costa and Garmston's (2002) work regarding levels of trust provide an initial framework for assessing an organization's readiness for public coaching. Four levels of trust are considered as essential—trust in self, trust in relationship, trust in process, and trust in the environment. The person being publicly coached must trust him/herself to be capable of expressing his/her thinking in a manner that serves the organization and sustains the potency of the leader. The relationship between the coach, coachee, and audience must also have some foundation of trust. Both participants must value the process of Cognitive Coaching[SM]. Finally, the environment must be one in which thinking and reflecting are valued. That valuing includes a culture that accepts inquiry as a way of working, knowing that answers to educational issues are complex and sometimes unclear.

Organizational health is another necessary condition for public coaching. Organizational health means that common goals are shared and processes are in place for airing differences in a manner that keeps the focus on issues, not on personalities. A healthy organization is one that places high value on learning and sees learning as an ongoing and conscious target. Diverse perspectives are sought out in healthy organizations as sources of learning. Individuals take responsibility for their actions and don't place blame elsewhere in healthy organizations. Members of high-functioning organizations feel they make important contributions to the organizational mission and are intrinsically rewarded for doing so. If an organization is highly polarized or dysfunctional, public coaching is probably not appropriate.

The intention of public coaching needs to be clear to all parties. The public coach is deliberately using one of the coaching maps to support individual and organizational growth and consciousness. The audience understands the purpose of the coaching session is to mediate a leader's thoughts, and the leader is clear that the coaching is designed to provide a window to his/her mind. Skills for processing of the coaching need to be in place. The group needs to have time to reflect on what they heard in a way that allows them to interact and make meaning.

Possible Applications

What are some ways that public coaching has been utilized? A new superintendent was publicly coached after attending training on Adaptive Schools (Garmston & Wellman, 1999) with his administrative staff. He reflected on his learning and considered how he might lead collaborative efforts in the future. Many times we have used public coaching to give a new principal a unique way of entering a new school. The coaching of a new principal is often a planning conversation.

Diane Smith, principal of Fox Creek Elementary in Colorado has developed several unique uses of public coaching

- She was publicly coached at a staff meeting to introduce her staff to her thinking regarding moving the school away from being a year-round, four-track school.

- She utilizes public coaching of teacher candidates as an interview strategy. After having a planning conversation with Diane in front of the hiring committee, the teacher teaches a lesson that is followed by a reflecting conversation. The hiring committee believes it gets far richer data about the candidate's thinking than might be gained in a traditional interview that can be rehearsed.

- She held a public reflecting conversation with each teacher in a grade-level team regarding how they taught writing conventions. Diane reported that every teacher spoke to the power of the process.

Nearly every teacher indicated that this was a powerful experience. Most of them had never taken the time to simply listen to what each other does in any area of instruction. The teachers who had been feeling discounted had the opportunity to share their expertise without interruption. They felt very validated. The discussion following these conversations was far richer because everyone had heard several strategies they had not used as well as the affirmation that they had many strategies in common. (D. Smith, personal communication to Carolee Hayes, September 12, 2002)

We have used public coaching to ask leaders to reflect on survey data regarding the climate of the school and school improvement goals. This can precede goal setting processes or further analysis by the group. The leader of a curriculum committee that was struggling was publicly coached on her reflections, which then lead to a problem-resolving conversation. The committee used the insights from her coaching to do their own rethinking and planning.

A very sophisticated form of public coaching is to coach a group in front of an audience. We have used this with leadership teams at the district and building level. Another application was to coach the grade-level team where state testing occurred. The other teachers got insights into the pressures the team was experiencing as well as ideas for supporting their colleagues.

The applications of public coaching are only limited by our imaginations. What is most important about the strategy is that the audience gains exquisite and rich access to the thinking of the person being coached in a way that could not be communicated as well in some other format.

Time for professional conversations in schools is limited and, therefore, a precious resource. As schools work to become truly collaborative cultures, professional conversations become critical vehicles for developing shared meaning and understanding. The challenges of holonomy require thinking in new ways about how colleagues can effectively communicate. The quality of professional conversations is a significant variable in the collective thinking of an educational staff. Public coaching is one strategy that can facilitate an integration of individual and group needs by inviting open communication. It supports the growth of leaders, facilitates group development, builds common understandings, and develops trust. It is a process to support thoughtful, reflective, trusting cultures.

References

Costa, A., & Garmston, R. (2002). *Cognitive Coaching[SM]: A foundation for renaissance schools* (2nd ed.). Norwood, MA: Christopher-Gordon.

Garmston, R., & Wellman, B. (1999). *The adaptive school: A sourcebook for developing collaborative groups.* Norwood, MA: Christopher-Gordon.

Hayes, Carolee. (Spring 1995). Public coaching as a tool for organization development. *Journal of Staff Development, 16* (2), 44–47.

Chapter 5

Cognitive Coaching^SM in Business and Industry

By: John Dyer

Introduction

Cognitive Coaching^SM has been widely applied in educational settings. Its application has been more limited in the private sectors of business and industry. Do the processes that are known to be effective in one culture transfer effectively into another culture? This chapter addresses that question from the perspective of business participants in Cognitive Coaching^SM training.

John Dyer shares insightful journal entries to illustrate how noneducators receive Cognitive Coaching^SM practices. He explores the commonalities and differences between the worlds of education and business related to coaching issues. Dyer addresses how core values related to competition and profit affect coaching efforts. The chapter further examines the relationship between individual coaching outcomes and organizational outcomes. The reader is left with important insights about how the most basic mental models of a corporation impact innovative practices.

Cognitive Coaching[SM] was originally developed as an alternative form of supervision for teachers and educators. Over time, the Cognitive Coaching Foundation Seminar® has been delivered in a variety of settings including educational, business, and industrial environments. This chapter represents a compilation of some of the relevant insights gained from those experiences. It gives testimony to the impact that these skills have in diverse situations both in personal and in work environments. Reviewing the extensive impact of the Cognitive Coaching[SM] training, it is evident that individuals respond to different parts of the experience. One strength of Cognitive Coaching[SM] is that individuals internalize the skills and concepts in an adaptive fashion. Each seeks personal and professional applications congruent with his or her character, personality, identity, and the context and the relationship with the person being coached. There is no one way to coach. The unique artistry of the coach applying a set of Cognitive Coaching[SM] skills, tools, and maps with professional discretion defines a coaching interaction.

In working outside of the educational domain, I have taught coaching and witnessed its successful application in a broad range of fields including heavy oil mining, supervision of a hair dressing school, human resources, environmental sciences, natural gas transmission, nursing, and manufacturing. Impact has been dramatic and meaningful at both an organizational and individual level. In exploring this application of Cognitive Coaching[SM], consideration will be given to differences in the goals and cultures of educational agencies and business and industry. Concrete examples of specific aspects of Cognitive Coaching[SM] from participant journals will be shared.[1] Finally, impact will be addressed.

New Roles, New Rules, New Tools

In comparing the intentions of Cognitive Coaching[SM] to other business models, I have identified some of the distinctions presented in Figure 5-1.

The mental models regarding leadership in education and the corporate environment have contrasting features that are critical to consider as one implements Cognitive Coaching[SM]. One of the significant principles of leadership in the corporate environment is that individuals are appointed to a position as a result of their experience and decision-making capacities. This results in a predominance of top-down leadership styles. The identity of business leaders frequently parallels their responsibility for "being in command." When introducing Cognitive Coaching[SM], the first challenge is to explore the question, "What is leadership?" Although participants can be in a hurry to get to the skill development of coaching, considerable time needs

Cognitive Coaching^{SM}	Historical Mindsets Prevalent in Corporate Coaching and Supervision Models
Communication tools that a coach uses to help others think for **themselves,** make good decisions, and solve their own problems.	A process for helping others do what **the supervisor or organization** wants them to do.
An approach to personal/professional growth, development, and learning.	One aspect of a system for evaluating others or appraising performance.
A way of supporting.	A way of giving advice and/or suggestions.
A set of skills, tools, and structures that provide a means for building capacities in others.	A leadership strategy for influencing others.
The mediation of another person's self-directed learning, problem solving, and self-modification.	The imposition of personal beliefs, strategies, decisions, and behaviors on other individuals.
Supporting others in the achievement of their goals.	Facilitating others to help you achieve your goals.

Figure 5-1. Distinctions Between Cognitive Coaching^{SM} and Other Business Models

to be spent clarifying contextual issues, particularly the issue of identity. It is encouraging to realize that there are contemporary trends in leadership that include recognition of the need to acknowledge and promote the capacities and skills of subordinates. Part of the "Total Quality" movement is based on that premise.

Cognitive Coaching^{SM} redefines essential leadership skills for many members of the corporate world. The testimony of Jake, one of the program's participants, articulates his insights about leadership as not a static process. Jake explores the meaning of transformation and connects it to the process of coaching:

> Jake: Cognitive Coaching^{SM} is transformative for leadership. Leadership is talked about but the "how to" is elusive. I have discovered good listening creates leadership. People have a need to be listened to. Good listening lets people know you care to take the

> time to understand the person. They look to you as a leader. I am convinced of the connection to leadership. A good leader listens to people, understands them. People are willing to follow this leader because he understands them. It takes a leader to take the time to listen. This course (Cognitive Coaching[SM]) is connected to empowerment—empowerment of followers and leaders. In coaching, the person leaves the problem-solving conversation with a higher level of support, choices, resources, and consciousness. They are empowered. Note that the problem is rarely solved within the conversation but the person is empowered to make progress. They are unstuck. . . . unsticking yourself from a problem by changing how you view the problem.

Another contrast to the educational environment comes from differences in fundamental values. The corporate system is based on economic competition. This is a driving force at the organizational level. The objective is to beat the competitors and earn the greatest revenue. This paradigm can be internalized at the individual level and becomes a mental model for personal decisions and behaviors within the organization. Employees compete with one another for clients, customers, commission, advancement, promotion, or salary increases or bonuses.

I was invited to do some team-building workshops for a major oil company. In the initial exploratory conversation, inquiry into the symptoms suggested some work in team-building was desirable. The corporate liaison commented that members in a team were not cooperating with one another, that they often sabotaged the work of other team members, that important information was often withheld, and that the team members preferred to work in isolation rather than collaboratively. The culture of this company included promotions, salary increases, benefits, and perks all being awarded on individual performance. In terms of immediate rewards there were no obvious, personal benefits for working with the team. I declined the contract. The situation demonstrated that there needed to be organizational readiness for the introduction of a Cognitive Coaching[SM] philosophy. The work culture and leadership must support the principles and practices of Cognitive Coaching[SM]. Because schools are not profit driven, there is often an inherently higher level of support for collaborative practices than one might find in the corporate environment.

In addition to values, which may differ from educational contexts, the corporate world operates from different goals. In education, the overarching goal is learning. In business it is profit. The principles of coaching are congruent with learning as an end. In the business domain, learning is a means rather than an end.

Time is the devil of productivity deadlines. In business and industry, deadlines are the perceived stepping stones to higher profit. Employees are pushed to produce more and produce it faster. When an individual feels something has to be done immediately, there is no time to listen. Directions are given and commands are followed. Then it is on to the next task.

Cognitive Coaching^SM takes time and requires a high level of listening skills. Prior to development of the skills, there has to be a philosophical conviction that the wisdom, experience, and intelligence of coworkers and employees are valuable resources. When conducting the training, this mindset may not be present at the beginning of the training but it definitely might emerge as a result of the training.

> Chris: The patience and attentive listening attributes are very interesting. In the past I have often interrupted with my "solutions." When they were adopted I felt useful but I also owned the problem. Letting others develop solutions may seem an easy way out of having to have all the answers but that is certainly one of the benefits. I think I always knew others also had the answers but I wanted to be first. However, it is not always good to expose yourself that way.

> Mitch: My purpose should be to try to help team members learn, explore alternatives, work through and/or achieve a transition, or take action when appropriate. I cannot do this without actively listening to what the other person is truly trying to say. In the situation I mentioned earlier, I initially made the presupposition that the team was reluctant to address their peers because they simply did not want to and they did not think it was their role to play. After actively listening to what the team members had to say, and by asking questions rather than giving answers, it became evident that they were willing to manage their manpower responsibilities once they knew how to. My impressions from our first encounters were completely changed.

In the previous examples, there is a major shift in Chris, as he moves away from a practice of disempowering others by offering his perceptions first, to a realization that he can honor the speaker's potential through patience and attentive listening. This is important because the organizational culture in Chris's work site has traditionally promoted people based only on their levels of expertise. This process instills a hierarchy that supports top-down directives. When persons are promoted to positions of authority they are expected to give directions, advice, suggestions, and perspectives. To break a pattern of such historical precedence requires a high degree of self-confidence *and* a significant fluency in Cognitive Coaching^SM skills. This is one of the major training challenges in working with participants from the world of industry. In Mitch's case, he applies the listening skills in a group context and realizes how his previous patterns have led to misunderstandings and false assumptions.

In implementing Cognitive Coaching[SM] in a business environment, unique cultural factors must be considered as well as the inherent goals and values of the organization. If these are not aligned with those of Cognitive Coaching[SM], the implementation is unlikely to have systemic impact. It may also be difficult for individuals to feel success in implementing the process.

Trust and Rapport

Traditionally, leadership has been viewed as being in command or being the authority; the relationship with employees has been seen as secondary to efficiency and high productivity. When the boss is in command, trust and rapport are not necessarily relevant. If, I, the boss, have something to say, you listen! There are strong messages sent about status. There has sometimes been a mindset in business that rapport is an example of "warm fuzzy" or "touchy feely" thinking and has no place in the corporation world. However, the following testimony suggests that rapport does have a place in a business environment.

> Dave: This (Cognitive Coaching [SM]) really works. I had two recent situations where I actually thought about the techniques (of rapport) as I used them. The first one was with a very quiet and shy lady at work who is easily embarrassed. She came to me with a work-related problem and instead of dealing with it right there on the floor, I asked her to come to my office. Once at my office, I sat with her at my table and quietly asked what I could do for her? She very quietly outlined the situation. I quietly asked her some more specific questions. She quietly gave out more and more information. While this was not totally a coaching situation because she actually wanted an answer, I know she preferred this approach because she's been back several times.

> The second opportunity to knowingly use some of these new skills was in a sales situation in my store. A young man came in off the street, whom I had never met before. He was very excited to find the store and couldn't get over our selection of books. . . . He was very animated in his hand motions and body language and I found myself caught up almost instinctively in his actions. I'm not really sure if I would have done this naturally or if by thinking about as I was doing it as a conscious effort.

> What I have noticed is that at least now I'm aware of when I'm not using the techniques to their best advantage. When this happens I feel I've somehow shorted the other person and myself of a more in-depth understanding. I guess if you are aware when this is happening it allows for correction.

Dave's comments are encouraging because he was able to consciously use rapport in two diverse work situations. In the first instance he supported a colleague by matching her quiet reflection. Dave is not a quiet person by nature. By intentionally reflecting his colleague's gentleness, she was comfortable in extending her communication with him.

In his second opportunity, Dave discovers that he is building a relationship with a customer by authentically reflecting the person's animation and excitement. His conclusions are impressive and sincere as he notes that he has "shorted" the "other person" and "himself" of more "in-depth understanding." This is not a self-serving motive; it is very altruistic.

Rapport can also be used in a group context such as team meetings. As Jake comments the rapport (or lack of it) sends strong messages to the other group members and/or the team leader. When one understands the messages, the nonverbal information can be used to facilitate meeting effectiveness. This can be a significant understanding in those organizations that have restructured and expect self-directed teams to work effectively.

> Jake: I have been noticing the powerful effect of maintaining rapport. Here are my thoughts. In problem solving meetings held on January 27 and February 2, and 5, the group of 13 people were focused on solving a big problem. The rapport with the group broke several times when more then one conversation started at once. The meeting became very chaotic and unsettling. This started with people turning away from each other to have a private conversation. Someone had a cell phone that kept ringing. They were talking in low tones on this phone. Some people started drifting, they just sat there as if they were in suspended animation. This is a deeper awareness for me. I felt very uncomfortable. There was no congruence among us. No wonder we don't accomplish much in some meetings. I suspect this is a key factor in highly effective group interactions. There is good rapport among the members of the group. You leave with a greater sense of congruence.

We know that trust develops over time. One of the paradoxes of Cognitive Coaching ^{SM} is that you need trust to coach and that coaching builds trust. Even when the organizational culture is not fully trusting, the coaching process can have significant impact at the individual level.

Paraphrasing

An observation that is frequently repeated by those who participated in the training is the appreciation for the power of paraphrasing. Its power is underestimated. The use of the paraphrasing seems to be minimal in many business organizations. After participating in Cognitive Coaching ^{SM} training, Colleen made the following comment:

> Colleen: No one paraphrases anymore. I observed that when someone in the group said something no one made any attempt to follow through. The people in the group didn't even respond until I paraphrased! I noticed that people became involved only after I acknowledged the speaker. . . . People started to validate each other, and the quality of thoughts, feelings, beliefs shared was incredible.

She also noted the powerful impact that her use of paraphrasing had on other people in the group. The predominant resistance to paraphrasing in the corporate world makes the acceptance and internalization of the skill a definite challenge for the trainer. If the individual's identity and beliefs are incongruent with the common practice, it is almost unreasonable to expect that the skills will be evident in subsequent behavior. The tragedy is that when used appropriately, paraphrasing is a complimentary skill that extends thinking and builds rapport. It is a significant leadership behavior and is as appropriate in the business environment as it is in any other environment. The following testimonies give tribute to the impact that this skill has in communication situations. Each of the individuals who commented is in a leadership capacity within his or her respective organizations.

> Jake: Peter and I check in regularly with each other and I would say we are both on a similar journey in many ways. We have created an ongoing open forum, which focuses on behaviors and actions of others' and ours, our interpretation and learning from them, and a check to see if our behavior is changing. This example involved paraphrasing back to Peter his thoughts about trying to motivate people to take an active interest in helping each other out when the work place gets busy. He is somewhat disappointed that people don't help out more then they do. I focused on listening skills, paraphrasing and questioning. Stating back to him what I heard him say seemed to help him reflect on his situation. He continued with several insights. This conversation seemed to bring richness to the information he was processing. He went away thinking some new thoughts about the situation. There was a definite shift in his thinking. This was confirmed in later conversations. Most importantly, I did not get involved in his thoughts.

Bill: At this point I summarized her concern, her emotions, her resources, and her alternatives. When I finished paraphrasing, she thought for a while and then stated which alternative she was going to take. She felt good about her decision and devised a plan to execute her decision.

When I asked her how she felt about the coaching session, she had these comments:

1. It gave her the opportunity to articulate to another human being exactly what her problem was. Up to this point, she had never completely done that.

2. She heard her problem stated back to her. It gave the problem reality.

3. She had to stop and actually think of solutions to the problem.

4. She felt good about having her emotions understood by another person.

5. It relieved her tension. She felt at peace.

Jake: In a small group meeting involving several of the people I work with, two of the people are usually on opposite sides of an issue. The conversation was getting heated. This was a good listening experience for me. I paraphrased what each person, one at a time and really focused on whom I was talking to at the time. This helped diffuse the situation. We were able to move to a common place to start working on the problem. Afterwards, a third person commented on how the two people visibly were calmer after the paraphrasing. The third person was surprised we were able to move past the issue in the group. Usually we wouldn't. I saw this as well. I am convinced of the positive effect on people of being heard and understood. It helps deal with the emotion.

Probing for Specificity

We are aware that as individuals we filter information received through our senses. Our brains cannot possibly hold all the data that could potentially be delivered to it. As a consequence humans generalize, delete, and distort information. These filters are reflected in our language. The ambiguity in language is necessary because we cannot possibly express everything about everything.

One pattern in individuals in positions of authority is it to make presuppositions about employees and the effects of communication. The assumption holds that when a leader speaks, the employees internalize the language to a mental model that parallels that of the speaker. This is not always the case. Another assumption is that the mental model that is generated in the leader's head as he or she listens to an employee is congruent with the mental model held by the employee. This pattern of assumptions results in misunderstandings and visible inefficiencies.

In Cognitive Coaching ^{SM}, business leaders learn that language expresses the mental model that the speaker is holding. If the model lacks clarity the potential for high performance is limited. There is also the danger of poor communication and misrepresentation. The practice of "listening for" unspecified language and then "probing for" specificity supports the person in minimizing his/her generalizations, deletions, and distortions and provides an opportunity to develop a much clearer and shared mental construct.

> Thomas: Probing for specificity is all-important to get to the root of whatever is being sought. . . . but I have not yet learned to always challenge or question the speaker's generalizations. They seem so normal in conversation that they pass me by. It is only upon reflection that I often realize that an opportunity was missed. In our work environment there exists a barrier between those folks that represent management and those that are considered non-management. In discussions between members of both groups generalizations abound that continue to promote an adversarial environment.

Questioning

Marilee Goldberg (1998) contends, "All knowledge comes from questions." In working with individuals in business and industry, the author has observed that the use of questioning is limited to the notion of the questioner collecting data. For a supervisor who maintains an identity as boss, the acquisition of information is congruent with the role of boss:

> "I need this information to ensure that I make the correct decision."

> "I require this information to be assured that you are doing things correctly."

> "I am asking questions as a way of demanding an explanation from you."

> "I am using questions to investigate your performance so that I can write an evaluation."

In the identity as boss, this type of questioning may be legitimate. When talking with employees, it is clear that this type of questioning is perceived as a type of interrogation. The result is that they are intimidated, they are stressed and anxious, they maybe resentful and bitter, they feel put down and insulted, and their self-confidence and self-esteem is reduced. The impact is that the boss minimizes and inhibits the effectiveness of his/her subordinates. He/she does not get to learn of the best thinking of the employee.

When providing Cognitive Coaching^{SM} training in an industrial environment, instilling an understanding and an appreciation of a different paradigm in questioning is essential. As participants understand questions that extend and enhance thinking are an incredible resource for the coach, their appreciation for the art of questioning is increased. Cognitive Coaching ^{SM} develops a richer valuing of employees as intellectual capital. Employees are not viewed as mechanical tools to achieve a corporate objective. Rather the employees are seen as dynamic, organic, intelligent beings who, when intellectually engaged, contribute to the resources and culture of the organization. Employee thinking is the essence of a "learning organization." Organizations don't learn, people do. Once this shift of thinking occurs, the value of well-formulated questions becomes indisputable.

> Dave: The elegance of subtle questioning has always eluded me. I'm like a bull in a china shop: I rush head long to the let's fix it stage every time. What's worse is my responses are almost always loaded with suggestions or (negative) presuppositions. . . . Gently probing for specifics is another new approach for me and I've had some success using it. I've always liked to get all the data on a subject I could handle before making a decision or helping someone else make up their mind. I thought that it was part of the job as coach to help convince them. The new method you (John Dyer, Training Instructor) gave me lets me off the hook, in a manner of speaking. In coaching situations helping someone find their own answers has far more value.

> Mary: I found it very interesting when we were discussing the questioning techniques in order to move towards a more critical thinking pattern—"what might, what do you think, what, how." I have begun to use these more often, with a lot of success. I have been getting comments such as "I hadn't thought of that," "Hmm, that is making me look at this differently" as the "coachee" starts to move towards their own solution. As was said in class though "I have tooth marks on my tongue." It would be so easy to revert back to the so-called "expert" response, as so many times people seem to be looking for an answer. An insight for me from these types of questions is that often what the other person is looking for is validating of the answer they already have, but may not realize. If they hear it verbalized in a response it is validated. How much more validating for them it is to have the same "answer"

come directly from them. This process is so much more natural; I have never really liked to be seen as the "expert" or giving advice.

Thomas: Asking good questions is not such an easy thing to do. Even with this awareness I still often find myself starting a question with "do you . . .", "is it . . .", "are there . . ." and others that result in a yes or no answer. I should know better. Also, I have found starting a question with "why" invariable puts the listener on the defensive that is then not a productive or supportive environment. I have found it easier to cut the word "why" from my repertoire. A good example for a change in attitude . . . when not using "why" as a start to a question is with my son. I can see very readily in that personal context, which has historically been competitive, that the "why" implies judgment. That can be demeaning. However, when I start with "What are the things you considered . . ." He is very eager to share his knowledge and imagination.

The previous comments articulate the conceptual understanding that the participants learned about questioning. The following examples of changed questioning behavior are particularly significant when one realizes that English is a second language for Rene, who is in a supervisory position in a private training institution that provides certification in beauty culture.

Rene: When questioning we need to pay attention to the tone of voice and choice of words. The questioning patterns that we learned are very challenging. By learning the questioning skills, I can apply them in my coaching. Situations I practiced on questioning,

A new teacher decided to quit after spending four weeks in class as an assistant/observer. She found that it was too stressful and overwhelming. I asked her questions like

- What are your goals?
- When you say you are under stress, what made you stressful?
- What do you want to achieve in your career?

At the end of our meeting, she felt much happier and relieved. She identified what she wants and she decided to stay part-time to try again. I felt good because I helped her think and choose for herself.

New teachers feel that their trainer is not friendly and is intimidating. The trainer feels that some of the new teachers do not meet her expectations no matter how hard she tries to support them. Some of the questions to the trainer were

- What have you tried to give them your support?

- How are they doing compared with what you had planned for them to do?

My friend's supervisor asked her to use the new textbook published by a different company. She is not sure what to do because she disagrees with him. I asked her some questions like

- When you said that you disagreed with him, what comparisons have you done between the two books?

- If you have to change the textbook, how does it affect your lesson plans?

- How much time does he give you to prepare for the class?

- How do you measure to see if the existing textbook is better than the new one?

Planning Conversations

In addition to the power of the coaching tools, participants from business and industry frequently comment on the use of structures to ensure focused conversations. The depth and quality of dialogue is acknowledged along with the value in using conversation time in the most efficient manner. The basis of effective operations in any enterprise is good planning. In an industrial setting, the planning process can resort to a debate as to whose ideas or suggestions are going to be used. It can be an argumentative and confrontational practice. If esteem, reputation, status, and promotional incentives are linked to success of the project, then individuals revert to competitive debate and advocacy for one's personal proposal. In providing a planning structure and combining the structure with effective communication tools, the planning process takes on an entirely different dynamic. The impact has been startling.

As training participants gained confidence in using a planning model, the most profound insights resulted when they used the process with other individuals. The practice of encouraging speakers to develop their own plans and explore those notions that had the greatest appeal to them changed the relationship and resulted in enhanced performance. As the nature of the plan and the ownership for the plan remained with the speaker, the implementation of the plan was assured. Because the plan had been thought through, was clear and precise, the likely success of the plan was enhanced.

Gary: I asked questions and let him do most of the talking. "So where will you start?" "How will you know what should be included in this material?" What other sources of input can you get?" Etc. I was able to remain neutral despite having opinions, which were screaming to get out! But I found that by paraphrasing it kept me concentrating on his words and idea's and not my own. I also found that my paraphrasing and questioning actually kept Dave on track. He usually wanders about a lot while talking, after referring to previous experiences and all. I often came right in on his comments with paraphrasing and further questioning; it went well. Dave wanted to take some notes as we were going along; he took a lot of notes actually. He ended up with a plan and a fairly clear idea of what he wanted to ask them to develop.

Carolyn: Today I had an opportunity to try out a planning conference in a natural setting. . . . The situation was that three colleagues and I had been given a one time chance to hire a temporary assistant to help us accomplish some work we had been unable to get to. I used the planning conference map to guide the meeting with my colleagues to figure out what we should do to proceed. In this case we started with articulating which goals and objectives we were trying to achieve by hiring the assistant. I used questions such as "What does each of you see the assistant focusing on?" "What are our highest priority issues that need to be addressed?" Once we had some ideas on the table about that, I moved the group to consider our indicators of achievement. Again I tried to use open-ended questions to get at these thoughts. My "best" question was "What will it look like six weeks after our assistant has been working?" One of the biggest challenges I had in coaching this session was having three people at once—there were so many ideas and differences of opinion generated!!! I tried to use paraphrasing skills to ensure clarity and to encourage the ideas to be quite specific. I noticed that my colleagues were also using paraphrasing and questioning with each other and me. Coaching must be contagious. From there I used the map to come up with a work plan that addressed what we would need to do to help our assistant be successful and what information we would need to gather for her. Overall this conversation was very productive in that we came up with a concrete, specific plan that was satisfactory to each of us (imagine four happy nurses in one room).

Colleen: Second planning conference—The second conversation went from when and how she would approach her husband to schedules, finances, classes . . . all very logical in her options. Having listened and coached up to that point I said (after I summarized), "What does your heart tell you?" Wow! It was like a flood! All this stuff came out and she became excited. She said she was going to go home, talk to her husband, ask what he wanted to do, give him her ideas re: Mexico, money, schedule, and discuss feelings . . .

Two days ago there was an envelope slid under my office door with a thank you letter from her. I had to chuckle because she thanked me for suggesting she look at the problem via what her heart was telling her. AMAZING! I only asked the question!

Colleen's testimony acknowledges the extended benefit of using the tools of Cognitive Coaching^SM when discussing personal issues with employees.

Reflecting Conversation

Reflection in business is a common practice. Most organizations have review procedures or requirements in place to assess the success of initiatives and to do an analysis of personal, team, or project progress. Sometimes lacking is a clear process or structure that develops the higher level thinking in the review process. A common reaction in participants when presented with the "Reflecting Map" has been an enthusiasm for the simplicity of the design for keeping the conversation focused and the potential for ongoing learning.

Carolyn: I used the reflecting conversation today to help bring closure to a very stressful work situation. Two days ago a young patient died unexpectedly on one of our nursing units. Upon investigation of events leading up to her death, it was evident that the nurses' documentation was incomplete and lacked detail. . . . To deal with this situation the nurses met with the hospital lawyers and went through the situation and the chart line by line. . . . After this meeting, the nurse manager (PCM), the nurse educator (CNE), and I met to debrief the situation. I used the reflecting conversation map to guide us through this discussion, but my role was one of both coach and participant as I was very involved in the meeting with the staff.

We started our debriefing with our individual impressions of the staff meeting. As a natural part of this discussion people shared what specifics they saw and heard that supported these impressions. This was a very informative part of the debriefing as each of us was positioned in a different place in the room and could see the reactions of different staff members. While we all had the overall impression that the meeting with the staff had "gone better than expected" our reasons for this were quite different. . . . What became clear in our discussions is that none of us had specifically defined strategies or outcomes for the staff meeting—we had left that up to the lawyers. We spent a long time talking about

> what the staff and we learned from this experience and how we could use that to improve our practice and prevent similar occurrences in the future. If I am ever in this situation again, I think it would be important to sit down with the lawyers ahead of time and hear from their perspective what is important to achieve and how that will be done. While this was not a "typical" reflecting conversation, once again I did find the map helpful for providing structure and keeping the discussion on track.

If one is in doubt about the power and potential of Cognitive Coaching[SM] in business settings, reading the following testimony will dissolve that hesitation. Although the paragraph is short, the results are significant and meaningful because the individual being coached suffers from autism.

> Colleen: Today I conducted another formal reflective conference with a client who went on a job interview on Friday. . . . The client I coached is high functioning autistic. This is the first time I observed him truly exploring himself and taking ownership. Normally he would answer only some questions. Today his eyes were up to the ceiling, sideways, looking down and he never said, "I don't know." Which was something he used to say quite often.

States of Mind

The five states of mind are a pervasive force in all coaching interactions. They separate high performance from low or adequate performance. Participants immediately understood the concept of using coaching to improve performance. Repeated connections were made between high or low performance (in self or in others) and high or low states of mind.

> Bill: My strategy was to use the Planning Conversation to bring him to a higher state of mind. He has lots of self-confidence, so I tried to focus more on flexibility, consciousness, and interdependence.

> Colleen: Today I sat down with a client and my objective was to mediate from powerlessness to efficacy. Client identified she wanted to be working ASAP. Client identified stumbling blocks and things that kept her away from achieving her goals.

>> Me: You want things to change for you, yet somehow the thoughts are becoming stuck somewhere.

>> Client: Yes—fear and my attitude are holding me back so I'm spinning my wheels and my school work and my work here is suffering.

>> Me: Nodded and said, Overwhelming.

> Client: Yes.
>
> Me: What would happen if you were able to break things down?
>
> Client: Eyes looking up and down to the right. Eyebrows lifted. Client looked at me as if to say tell me more.
>
> Me: "What are you trying to accomplish at school?"

The dialogue continued with paraphrasing and questioning and concluded ...

> Me: I continued to coach her and help her solve her own problem. When she smiled at me it was like a light bulb went on for her. Even her body language changed and she went from powerlessness to taking responsibility for her own actions. By the time she left, she came up with ideas to maintain a successful job search as well. Today was magic!

One of the signs of an emerging coach is the capability to be conscious of the States of Mind that are operating in one's self.

> Steve: The problem with being flexible is that I don't always bend in the direction that I want. Or at least that is what I thought would be a problem. I've since encountered some new and exciting philosophies since allowing myself to bend. I always thought this would threaten my own beliefs but have since found that I can strengthen and expand my thinking. I find this happens when I'm asked questions in a nonthreatening manner. A manner that allows me to explore what I believe in, incorporate new ideas and yet remain solid as an individual. I am convinced that I can do this for other people as well.

> Susan: As a coach, one has to realize that getting the person you are coaching to higher levels of the states of mind can be a difficult job in some situations, but what might be even more difficult is getting yourself (the coach) to a higher level and maintaining those levels.
>
> Knowing who you are, what our beliefs are, and knowing that you have the capability to act on those beliefs without overshadowing another's identity takes a lot of thought and consideration on the part of the coach.

> Mitch: I needed to reach a higher level of consciousness in order to understand that the team was trying to get me to see that they were lacking in craftsmanship. By exploring the five states of mind I found they were high in efficacy (they truly wanted to succeed),

they were flexible (even though they did not fully agree with teams managing manpower, they were willing to do it), and they were interdependent (they could not see themselves doing it alone and requested support and training). We were all in need of trying to understand each other better and, as we found out, all in need of improved skills.

Problem-Resolving Conversations

The third structure in Cognitive Coaching[SM] is the problem-resolving conversation. In many ways the skill to supporting others' thinking through a difficult problem is the most practical of all the coaching training. To internalize it with confidence is also very demanding. This map provides the coach with a structure to engage the speaker in high levels of cognition, productive states of mind, and enhanced levels of resourcefulness. It is not a surprise that people in industry appreciate the potential of this approach in enriching the intellectual capital of their organization. I have noticed an intellectual appreciation for the potential of this map, while also observing it as the biggest leap in thinking with which the corporate trainees are faced.

The difficulty of moving to an internal process of problem-resolving is that habits of mind are so engrained. The corporate world has historically developed internal expertise. When decisions need to be made or problems need to be solved, the "expert" is consulted and solutions, directions, or suggestions are offered. It is a way of life. It is part of the culture. It is the way things always have been done.

The most common concern expressed by business people in the training program is the inability to listen objectively. Their thinking goes immediately to offering solutions or advice and to suggesting to the other person what he or she should do. Even when these individuals are convinced of the importance of coaching someone to solve his or her own problems, the previous patterns are so indelible that they surface without invitation.

Based on the following comments, it is evident that individuals can replace previous habits with new skills and approaches. The positive results of using the coaching skills reinforced these new behaviors. Over a period of time, the developing coach integrated the practice as part of a natural communication repertoire.

> Gary: Rob approached me with a time and work prioritizing issue—what to do when and what about other things. . . . It seemed to go real well. I listened and paraphrased and listened some more. It really came down to what he wanted to do and the competing priorities. I asked him what he thought was the right balance and how he might achieve that, and it just seemed to flow. I

followed that up with some how will you know you are successful questions, and he described every thing he needed to watch and do. When we were winding up he looked at me and said, you know I really need to know if you are OK with this, cause I've been doing most of the talking. I took that as a compliment, but said yes I am quite all right with it. I told him he knew as much as I did with regards to our project, so I trusted he would do what needed to be done. He thanked me, and said he felt a lot better having talked it through and off he went. Nice feeling on my part!

Dylan: She had a crisis in a nonprofit association. She was calling for advice on process in her role as President.

The course was useful in that I used a lot more paraphrasing and questioning than I normally would have otherwise. The issue is an emotional one and is affecting her Board, a coach, and a referee (quite messy actually).

My old habits are to be "telling" or "demonstrative" when dealing with these types of questions. I think she appreciated my softer approach this time around. A single benefit of Cognitive Coaching^{SM} is that "the coach" tends to spend much more time with a person, rather than a rush to judgment.

The result of this coaching is that Marg has laid out some rational steps and avoided a particular high risk/volatile situation. Without my coaching help, I'm sure she would have become quite bogged down.

Stan: I have been transformed. . . . undergone a cognitive shift of my own. In the class yesterday and today we talked about states of mind and of being conscious of what state of mind you and your "subject" are in. Once you have identified the state of mind (of coach and the subject), you can think about where you want to be and work to get there—to work towards peak performance. Now I know why this stuff is so important! I was wondering about what it had to do with the course and now I realize it is the essence of the process (Cognitive Coaching ^{SM}). In pace and lead you want to move your subject from a position of weakness or uncertainty to a higher state of mind, clearer thinking, deeper reflection. This is so beautiful, so elegant, so profound, so respectful, and so powerful!

Comparisons to Other Training and Coaching Experiences

Businesses invest a great deal of money in training and developing their employees. Not being a part of those experiences, I have relied on the testimonies of the participants to identify the differences in Cognitive Coaching[SM] compared to other skill development initiatives in which they have participated. The pattern that emerges in their expressions is an appreciation for the power of using a cognitive, mediative focus in working with others. The significant shift from giving solutions and "working outside-in" is evident. Participants expressed appreciation for the strategies for "working from the inside out." The external focus of the past has been replaced with a more productive internal cognitive focus. The journal entries are congruent with the inside-out nature of learning. Each person internalizes and applies that which is meaningful to him/her, congruent with his/her belief systems, compatible with his/her character, and appropriate to his/her environment.

> Colleen: I went into Cognitive Coaching[SM] hoping it would give me the skills I needed to cope and be the best I could be so I could administer/create an environment which would allow my clients to succeed! Fine! However, that's not what Cognitive Coaching[SM] is all about. Cognitive Coaching[SM] is not about what I want (or my stake in it). . . . It's about what the other person wants! I am currently working with people on social assistance helping them get back into the work force. As my current group consists of high barriered participants, I was hoping to find the answer to "how do I get them to change their behavior from inappropriate to appropriate so they can not only find work but be able to maintain it?" In terms of using Cognitive Coaching[SM] skills, I realized when we discussed Dilt's Levels of Learning/Change that if my "identity" is who and what I am about, then identity for my clients is their belief in who they are and what they're about in a moment of time! . . . As a life skills coach, so they can realize the impact of their behavior and beliefs, I not only show them how to conduct themselves in an interview, etc., but allow them an opportunity to explore their own beliefs and invite and encourage them to challenge the messages they receive from themselves and others which are harmful and destructive. Although I model attending behaviors, facilitate in a safe environment, and honor everything I spoke about in the first few pages, I realize that the application of Cognitive Coaching[SM] is most effective when they reach the point where their identity changes and they want to help themselves. . . . I have discovered (through constant evaluation/reflection this week, re: questioning techniques & planned coaching) this does work

and fits when my clients have come to the point where they truly want to make changes and explore options, when they are ready and have worked through crises, gained confidence, and they want things to be different.

Dave: The difference for Cognitive Coaching ^{SM} is that its essence is drawing out those factors from others, causing them to see for themselves. The key factor is that "the need" comes from within (the speaker) and brings about a change to one's (the speaker's) state of mind.

Steve: When I saw how this man from Southern Alberta, who knew nothing about our work, talked to and asked questions of one of the class participants and brought the problem this person was experiencing to a workable solution, my jaw hit the floor. I knew enough about the participant's work to understand why he was experiencing his difficulty and had actually encountered similar situations, but to have some guy from outside the company sit back and effortlessly talk the participant to a workable solution was a profound experience for me. This was the tangible that I had been searching for.

Jake: I like the idea of working at higher levels of learning in an organization (Robert Dilts). I have experienced many company programs designed to motivate people, improve quality, improve performance, organize work, manage time, and develop teams. Most in my experience are based on good intentions but suffer from undercommittment and are characterized by large amounts of work and limited success. Finding a stronger leverage point to create change fits with the "working smarter, not harder" axiom.

Cognitive Coaching ^{SM} supports the speaker by going to where the speaker is. This fits with learning principles discussed by Peter Senge where the "Learner learns what they to learn." I see strong value in Cognitive Coaching ^{SM} to help the learner become more aware of what they want (and need) to learn. The process of helping a speaker move from an existing state of mind to a desired state of mind through a cognitive shift creates a gap between existing and desired. Once the gap is identified, the speaker is motivated to do something about it. Thus, the speaker now recognizes a need to learn something in order to change their existing circumstances. The important distinction here that applies to organizations and the value of Cognitive Coaching^{SM} is the motivation of the speaker. What appears to happen most often in my experience is a manager perceives the person wanting to change and proceeds to tell them what and how they should go about it. This method is more likely to create compliant resistance then the open embracing of change. Cognitive Coaching^{SM} provides an

option for the manager/coach to help the person to discover what
they should do for themselves. This fits nicely into the new style of
participative management, which is much touted today.

Impact of Cognitive Coaching^{SM} Training

The real test of the impact of a teaching endeavor is not so much in what
people say, but more so in what they do. Does the training in Cognitive
Coaching^{SM} actually have an impact on business peoples' behavior? To what
extent are the skills appropriate and to what extent are they applied? Five
areas of impact on individual behaviors are evident in the anecdotal evidence provided by Cognitive Coaching^{SM} participants:

- Validation of Thought Processes

  The coaches are intentional in hearing and responding
  to the thought processes of their colleagues. As para-
  phrasers, they accept the internal thoughts and facilitate self-insight regarding thought processes. They have
  skills for drawing out the internal thought processes
  enhancing the consciousness of their employees about
  internal influences on behaviors.

- Focus on Thought Processes, Not Just Behaviors

  Behaviors are examined as products of thought processes and as choices related to the focus on the internal. Colleagues are given greater control of their own
  behaviors through access to their own metacognitive
  processes.

- More Effective Listening

  Participants in Cognitive Coaching^{SM} appreciate their
  new ways of listening and strive to develop higher craftsmanship and consciousness regarding how they respond
  to colleagues. They value listening as a critical skill of
  leadership and embrace its ability to empower others.

- More Effective Use of Data and Questioning

  The anecdotal data suggests that business people are
  valuing the power of sharing data and asking questions
  to assist their colleagues in making meaning of data.
  This is a shift from giving judgments and advice. It rep-

resents mediating thinking for personal construction of learning as opposed to giving external feedback.

- Capacity–Building

    There is a shift from managing employees' behavior to seeing one's work as developing the thought processes and self-directed learning focus of employees. This is a mental model of leadership that redefines how one works.

Mary: I was part of the coaching demonstration with John, I gained a closer look and "feel" as to how to set this kind of experience. What became important to me during this was not just to respond, but examine how I was responding, and why. I noticed how John was paraphrasing and validating my thought processes; his listening skills, body language, eye contact, etc. The question "How are you going to use this as an opportunity to learn?" made me realize that I need to do more than just have a "coaching" session. I need to reflect afterwards—"What went well, what did I learn" on paper as well as mentally, in order to continue to grow in my coaching skills. As we continued our introduction to Cognitive Coaching^SM, I realized how much of the "talking" in coaching I had done (let the speaker do the talking). . . . Another insight for me, when discussing Performance Appraisals, was that we need to focus on the thought process rather than the behavior. Too often in Performance Management we focus on the behavior, and then wonder why the behavior does not change or why the change is not sustained.

John: This course has been a valuable step in learning about myself. I often ask many questions for clarification; however, this can have the appearance of an interrogation. This is a cognitive shift for me. I recognize my need to change how I go about obtaining information. I am learning to change the pace and format of my questioning to remove the interrogation flavor. I am using paraphrasing to change the pace of the questions. This slows the conversation and gives the person a chance to confirm the information discussed. I find using wait time takes the place of some questions. The person provides more information, often the answers to the questions I was going to ask.

Steve: I've since had to re-evaluate my entire communication strategy which was to ask questions which lead to a predetermined answer. You know, help the other person figure out what they were trying to say. The section on Attributes of Good questions helped me immensely in formulating effective questions. Drawing information from questions rather than getting predetermined answers was new and sometimes frightening because I never knew what the answer was going to be. What a wonderful change this has been for me. Talking to people is like reading a new book instead of scripting what people are going to say. It still takes a lot of effort but is far more rewarding. . . .

Another thing I have learned is that my style of questioning conflicted with my preferred state of mind, which is to be flexible. How can I be flexible yet ask questions that have predetermined answers.

Thomas: My past coaching has invariably been a "helping" with my ideas and solutions. I often received much satisfaction from seeing my ideas implemented. The resentment observed in other people, I thought, was a display of jealousy of my success. I accept that may have been part cause of the resentment. It may also be that I did not allow and involvement in the process of problem: I "forced" a solution; I displayed impatience and probably made others feel unvalued, inferior, and uncommitted to the enterprise. Another negative result was when I offered a solution, I then also inherited or owned the problem.

The gem I received from this discussion is that most individuals or groups usually have all the skills to develop the solutions or help they need. My role as a coach then is to provide the path or conveyance (coach) to a solution so that they feel non-threatened, feel equity, and feel like they own the problems and the solutions.

Mitch: I reviewed a performance appraisal with one of the employees that work for our group. When he first arrived in my office, he was livid with contempt for his fellow workers. He felt that they had been unduly harsh on him, they had not one good thing to say about him and were picking on him for no valid reason After about 15 minutes of his venting frustration, I paraphrased what I though I heard him say and probed for specificity. The dialogue went something like this:

> Mitch: No one on the team had anything good to say about you and there were no areas that you can see for self improvement?
>
> Employee: Yes, that's what I'm saying.
>
> Mitch: When you say, "No one" does that mean every co-worker that had input?
>
> Employee: No, just some of them.

> Mitch: Of the ones whose comments you found offensive, were all their comments negative?
>
> Employee: No, but most of them were.
>
> Mitch: So . . . what I understand so far is this . . . Some of your coworkers provided some feedback that you do not agree with. This feedback has you upset and you do not agree with those negative things that they said.
>
> Employee: That's correct.

We then reviewed his appraisal forms individually, line item by line item, and discussed each one in detail. We discovered that of the eleven areas that they had appraised him in, seven reflected high performance observations from his teammates while only four areas suggested improvement. I had him explain to me what his thoughts were on what a high performer would look like in each area. Then I asked him to compare his present performance to what he considered to be high performance. The resulting conversation produced a list of things that he could see himself doing that would bring him to a higher level of competency. We agreed on an action plan that would enable him to perform the duties and a means of self-measurement that would be indicators to him on how successful he was doing.

This was probably one of the longest performance reviews that I have held to date, but it was definitely one of the most rewarding. By the time he left my office he had changed his own perception of his coworkers from contempt to appreciation. . . . Paraphrasing, summarizing, probing for specificity, and clarifying are powerful tools for effective coaching!

Dylan: An informal Coaching Experience—I was asked to chair the selection committee for the new Children's Services Board in our area. This was a one-month project, which fell squarely with the timeframe of the c.c. course. Therefore, I applied a lot of the C.C. techniques—and with considerable success.

My two committee colleagues were aboriginal and francophone. None of us knew each other prior to the project. The cross-cultural differences, the tight timeframes, and our collective lack of prior history made it especially important to establish trust.

I spent considerable time allowing us to get to know each other. We created a climate of listening and respect. The aboriginal woman had a depth of knowledge and insight. At the same time, she was not naturally forthcoming. C.C. techniques were a sensitive way to draw out her wisdom. As a result, the whole committee and our results were strengthened.

The positive rapport and trust was important as we got into the decision-making part of the project. Our task was to put recommendations forward to the Minister (note—this is a cabinet member in the legislature, not the local clergyperson). This involved the ranking and screening of candidates. This is when the "going got a little tougher." If it were not for the identity we had established as a group, the whole process could have been stymied.

It was useful to use paraphrase in the interviews with the candidates. This was an effective way to prompt additional information.

Jane: The first coaching situation occurred with one of my staff, who for the purposes of this paper will be called "Mary." Mary had approached me with a concern that some employees in another area of the organization were not treating the employees in the area she worked in with the respect and value that she felt was owing to them. I asked if she wanted to talk about this issue in further detail and try and identify some ways to deal with the issue.

She was highly emotional about this concern, and I acknowledged the emotion in the situation by making an observation. I said, "You are feeling very strongly about this issue, and you want people to respect you and your colleagues." We were meeting in a coffee shop away from the work place, and I was concentrating on establishing rapport and building trust. I was very focused on her body language, and tried to match the way she was sitting leaning forward with my own body language. Building trust was not really a problem in this example, as we had worked together for several years and had a good level of confidence and trust with each other to start with. I asked her to tell me about the situation, and she started describing several examples of the type of behavior exhibited by the employees in the other area that she characterized as disrespectful. I paraphrased her examples and her comments to ensure that I understood what she was saying and to ensure that she felt I was actively listening to her. I concentrated on providing appropriate amounts of wait time between paraphrasing or questioning to allow her to formulate her answers or opinions. I found that the paraphrasing alone acted as a means to draw out her thinking and to have her speculate about how she could better deal with the behaviors of others in the department. The types of questions that I asked her as our coaching session went on were ones that tried to get her to think of alternatives. Examples of these questions included "What are some strategies that you could use to communicate with the other people in the department about your concerns?" and "If you were to follow this strategy, what are some possible outcomes?" This session was successful in that it assisted Mary in identifying a plan and some strategies for dealing with her concerns.

Susan: In a recent "interpersonal skills" training class that I facilitated for our employees, I had the opportunity to see how difficult it can be for some folks to view "coaching" as a positive experience. The session I was facilitating was called "Coaching for Optimal Performance." The participants (mostly department managers) were to think of an employee who works at a better than average performance. The process was to "coach" this good employee to look for opportunities to achieve even higher standards. Two of the participants in my class had great difficulty understanding the process. Comments I got from them were: "Why would I try to get someone to come up with ideas to do better? If I know what they need to do why can't I just tell them? It would save a lot of time." In our industry where there is a lot of pressure to meet production standard, it's easy to understand their thought process.

We talked a bit and I tried out some of the process from Cognitive Coaching[SM]. I first paraphrased by saying, "so you felt it would be more efficient to just tell your employees what they should do, to possibly save time." They both responded, and we continued. The turning point seemed to come when I asked a question following a statement that one made about lack of consistency in the employee's work performance. My question was, "Consistency of performance is one of your main concerns; how might you work towards improving that?"

From that point the two of them started talking about encouraging others to offer suggestions, acting on the employees ideas, giving employees responsibility, and feeling confident that the employee will follow through.

Colleen: Observations at work—When clients come in distraught, feel cornered, angry, etc., when I verbally identify the state of mind they are in, through paraphrasing, I see all kinds of BMIRS happening. When I use phrases like: "You fell stuck" or "You have no choice"—they respond "Yes!" "Exactly!" "Finally, someone understands! "With the skills and awareness I have developed I can create an environment which allows them to move to a higher level of efficacy or flexibility. I've also noticed that the saying, "The mind once stretched never reverts back to its original form," is true. I see my clients become empowered again! Some clients have shared that this is a first for them!

Conclusions

As a result of working in a variety of corporate and industrial environments, some new conclusions and insights about the application of Cognitive Coaching^{SM} in the business community are becoming clear.

1. Coaching skills are a valuable asset in any environment as long as individuals use them with integrity and clarity about intentions.

2. Although some prevailing practices at the organizational level in business may sometimes seem incompatible with the paradigm of Cognitive Coaching^{SM}, significant changes can occur at the personal level that ultimately have an impact on the corporate culture.

3. In educational environments, learning is the mission of the organization. Life-long, self-directed learning is an expectation that may or may not be stated. When Cognitive Coaching ^{SM} is offered in an educational institution it is inherently congruent with the intentions of the organization. Although learning is frequently identified as important to business organizations, it may be interpreted as the installation of skills and practices that are important to the organization. The notion of developing the intellectual capabilities of employees, to enhance the thinking and decision-making of others would not be rejected in the business environment. However, it is not celebrated at the same level of priority and value that has been observed in educational environments.

4. Extensive attention is currently being paid to the concept of coaching in the corporate world. The term *coaching* has many meanings. The sports model of coaching is prevalent—the boss is seen as the coach of the team. Directive coaching is when the role of a coach or mentor is to provide advice and direction. Technical coaching is approved when individuals are acquiring new skills and practices. The *expert* shows another person how to do something and then monitors them and corrects them as they apply the new skills. These variations in the use of the term *coaching* demand that time is pro-

vided at the beginning of the Cognitive Coaching ^SM training and throughout the course of the training to ensure that the conceptual understanding of the terminology of *coaching* is being interpreted and understood in an appropriate way.

5. Given the traditional bureaucratic structures of business and industry, some patterns of leadership that contradict with Cognitive Coaching^SM may be deeply embedded in organizational cultures. This may mean that it is a more demanding challenge for the participants to overcome some unproductive patterns of listening, responding, and questioning because old behaviors are reinforced and valued.

6. Conceptually there is a high degree of support for the theories and practices of Cognitive Coaching^SM. Participants respond to the training with enthusiasm, but the challenge of changing well-learned behaviors and practices can be discouraging. This observation is consistent with my observations about the reception of Cognitive Coaching^SM in educational environments.

7. Businesses and corporations could richly benefit from extensive Cognitive Coaching^SM training. It is a program that contributes to the success of the individual, extends thinking, complements good decision-making, and develops the intellectual capital of the organization.

8. The instructional language has to parallel the everyday language that is used by the participants. The development of a corporate manual[2] for the training was essential. This manual eliminated and replaced all of the educational references and examples. It also changed some of the vocabulary to be more compatible with business.

9. All of the Cognitive Coaching^SM tools, skills, maps, and approaches are appropriate for noneducational environments. The exception is the section in "Filters of Perception" that focuses on "Educational Belief Systems." This section has been replaced in the corporate manual with an instrument and discussion relating to a "Leadership Style Matrix."

10. There are highly skilled people who work in business and industry. They are keen to learn and are committed to self-improvement. They want to be effective in their jobs, and they want to contribute to the company's success.

Final Word From a Participant

Colleen: Through shared discussions, practice of acquired skill, and gained knowledge inside and outside the classroom, I have been a part of that process. (Cognitive Coaching℠ to build a learning community). More importantly I have had an opportunity to "work the soil," "sow some seeds," "remove the weeds," encourage growth, and enhance the quality of my life and help build a helpful learning community in the garden around me with people I respect and care about. What a beautiful gift.

Endnotes

[1] With exception of some typographical and spelling errors, the journal entries of participants have been presented exactly as written to ensure that the tone and character of the reflections are maintained.

[2] More information about this manual can be acquired from John Dyer, 1230 Varsity Estates Road N.W., Calgary, AB, CA. (403) 247-0408. email jadyer@attglobal.net

Reference

Goldberg, Marilee C. (1998). *The art of the question.* New York: John Wiley & Sons.

Chapter 6

Cognitive Coaching^{SM} Online: Benefits and Challenges

By: Jenny Edwards, Jane Ellison,
Laura Mitchell, and Yaso Thiru

Introduction

As school personnel communicate increasingly through electronic means, the question emerges about the possibility of online coaching. Can the interpersonal skills of acknowledging, listening, and questioning be communicated electronically? Might it be possible for two people to engage in a Cognitive Coaching^{SM} conversation and not be in the same room, the same city, or even the same state or country? If Cognitive Coaching^{SM} were effective online, it would open a multitude of possibilities for expanding the influence of coaching throughout systems around the world.

Two pair of educators decided to find out how a Cognitive Coaching^{SM} relationship might play out online. One person in each pair, Jenny Edwards and Jane Ellison, are experienced Cognitive Coaches. One of the coachees, Yaso Thiru, was familiar with coaching through her graduate school experience; the other coachee, Laura Mitchell, has been using Cognitive Coaching^{SM} in her work as an assistant principal. Although the circumstances of their coaching relationships were different, their findings were similar. The most important ingredient in an online coaching relationship is the same as in a face-to-face coaching relationship—trust.

Think about how you communicate each day—in person, on the telephone, in writing, through e-mail. Now, think about how much time you spend in each type of communication. For many people, e-mail is the most frequently employed type of communication in day-to-day interactions with others. It is both efficient and effective, especially when geographical distance is involved. Many people in the Cognitive Coaching^{SM} community have wondered whether or not it would possible to coach online. Such a possibility would eliminate the need for 2 people to be in the same place at the same time, saving a great deal of time and increasing the long-distance relationships that could be established.

This chapter chronicles the experiences of four educational professionals who engaged in Cognitive Coaching^{SM} through e-mail. One pair, made up of a professor experienced in Cognitive Coaching^{SM} and a graduate school student new to coaching, chose to use a chat room. The other pair, a co-director of the Center for Cognitive Coaching and an assistant principal with a year's experience with Cognitive Coaching^{SM}, corresponded through regular e-mail. Although the circumstances were different, the experiences proved to have a great deal in common.

Coaching Through a Chat Room: Jenny and Yaso's Experience

"Would you be willing to coach me in a chat room on the Internet? I understand that you are trained in Cognitive Coaching^{SM}. I have heard of it, it sounds interesting, and I have some things that I would like to receive coaching on."

This was an invitation offered Jenny Edwards by one of her doctoral students, Yaso Thiru. Jenny teaches in Fielding Graduate Institute's doctoral program in Educational Leadership and Change, and her students are dispersed around the United States, as well as in other the countries. Jenny thought the challenge of coaching online sounded interesting and provided an opportunity to explore yet another venue for Cognitive Coaching^{SM}.

The process began slowly, as Jenny had never used a chat room. When the time came for their first online coaching conversation, Yaso set up a chat room at Alaska Pacific University that was totally dedicated to their coaching chats. After finding a time when both were available, they logged on at the same time. Their first conversation was filled with comments such as, "Now how do I do this?" "In which box do I write the message?" "How am I doing?" "Testing." "Testing again." "Are you there?"

In using the coaching maps online, Jenny soon realized that the maps did not have to be followed exactly; and she could spend more or less time in the different neighborhoods of the conversation, depending on Yaso's needs and the flow of the conversation. Jenny's insight from the first conversation was that she was going through the same process of implementing and refining her coaching skills online as she had done when she learned to coach in person. She could not apply all the skills at once; learning to coach online was a process of implementing one coaching skill at a time, continuing to add skills until all were in place.

With regard to coaching tools, Jenny found that paraphrasing was even more critical online than in-person. In the absence of nonverbal cues, paraphrasing was the main way in which Jenny let Yaso know that she was listening and that she understood and cared. Paraphrasing was also the way that Jenny could reflect the emotion as well as the content of what Yaso said. Empathic paraphrases went a long way toward helping the conversation seem more natural. By paraphrasing and mirroring back to Yaso both the content and the emotions involved, Jenny demonstrated that she understood 100% of the message.

Another tool that Jenny found to be important was pausing. She used pausing online just as effectively as she did in person. Pausing and not responding immediately to Yaso's message provided both Jenny and Yaso with time to expand even more on a thought or to generate additional thoughts. In addition to intentional pauses, sometimes pauses occurred because one party was not sure of what to say. Either way, the outcome was the stimulation of thought processes.

Jenny found that the essential coaching pattern of pausing, paraphrasing, probing, or inquiring was again equally effective online as in person. After paraphrasing, Jenny asked questions that were designed to mediate Yaso's thinking. Since she was not able to use an approachable voice, Jenny found that plural forms, exploratory language, and especially positive presuppositions were key elements in supporting thinking.

Trust is the basis for any coaching relationship, and Jenny and Yaso consciously used strategies for building trust. One strategy was to begin by sharing something about themselves before beginning each coaching conversation. A 5-minute "warm-up" went a long way toward building trust. By doing this, both parties were saying, "I'm human. I have lots of things going on in my life." Over time, as they shared with each other, they developed even greater trust.

Another way that Jenny and Yaso developed trust was by being trustworthy. This meant being on time for the coaching conversation. If something came up and one party needed to log onto the conversation late, a call to the other was made. It also meant keeping what the other party said in confidence. In order to be able to openly share thoughts and feelings, both parties had to know that the coaching partner would not divulge what was said.

Another way they developed trust was for Jenny to focus totally on Yaso and be supportive of her thinking during the coaching conversations. Jenny monitored her intentions by continually asking herself the question, "Am I saying/asking this for the benefit of my coaching partner or for my own benefit?" If the statement or question was for her benefit, then she left it unsaid.

Rapport was another key ingredient in their coaching relationship. The only element of rapport that could be mirrored online was language. Jenny matched the language, the words, the phrasing, and the terms that Yaso used. For example, if Yaso said, "I plan to revolutionize the thinking of my colleagues," Jenny picked up on the word "revolutionize" as being important to Yaso and began using it. "So what might be some indicators that the thinking of your colleagues has been revolutionized?" "What might be some strategies you will be using to revolutionize their thinking?"

Yaso's language also gave Jenny clues about the representational system she was using. Jenny listened for words that indicated whether Yaso was processing information visually, auditorally, or kinesthetically. When Yaso said, "Help me visualize the skills I need to become a Cognitive Coach," Jenny responded with, "What might be some skills you have seen effective coaches use?" Later in the conversation, Yaso asked, "What would I be hearing in an effective coaching conversation?" Again, Jenny matched her auditory language and responded, "What types of questions might ring a bell for you?" Kinesthetic language was used in their exchanges when Yaso said, "I want to get a feel for a good coaching conversation," and Jenny responded by saying, "What have effective coaching conversations felt like to you in the past?"

As Jenny and Yaso developed rapport and got into a conversation flow, Jenny was aware of Yaso's response time as an indicator of thinking. In face-to-face coaching, the coach knows that he or she has asked an effective question when the coachee gives behavioral manifestations of internal response states (BMIRS), which are nonverbal and verbal indicators of thinking before answering. With the absence of BMIRS, Jenny found herself using the amount of time it took Yaso to respond as an indicator of her thinking

Nonverbal acknowledging, such as nodding one's head, leaning in towards the person, titling the head, raising the eyebrows, and smiling, could obviously not be done online. Thus, verbal acknowledging became even more important. Jenny used verbal acknowledging by writing comments such as, "uh, huh," "hmmmm," "okay" in a message by itself or before a paraphrase.

These types of verbal acknowledgments helped the conversation seem more natural.

When working with Yaso online, Jenny focused on crafting questions in order to come across in a true spirit of inquiry. Jenny wanted to ask questions designed to expand Yaso's thinking. By paraphrasing after every statement Yaso made and by asking questions with the elements of an invitation, Jenny was able to create a climate of inquiry.

The Five States of Mind were an integral part of every coaching conversation. The written responses gave Jenny an even greater opportunity to analyze the states of mind. In each conversation, Jenny consciously crafted questions and paraphrases to increase Yaso's resourcefulness in one or more of the states of mind. In addition, Jenny's craftsmanship and consciousness increased as she honed her coaching skills online.

At the end of each session, Yaso and Jenny took time to reflect on their conversation. This gave Yaso an opportunity to be aware of how the coaching was supporting her thinking, and it gave Jenny feedback on how the Cognitive Coaching^SM was affecting Yaso's thinking. This feedback helped Jenny become aware of how she was growing as an online coach.

Coaching Through E-Mail Messages: Jane and Laura's Experience

Jane and Laura's online coaching relationship was an extension of in-person coaching in which they engaged during the Foundation Seminar®. Laura had shared with Jane some issues as an assistant principal and was interested in putting those issues into a coaching setting. As Laura learned Cognitive Coaching^SM, she saw the benefits of discussing important topics in a coaching session rather than just complaining about them to a friend or colleague. When the suggestion was made to engage in coaching online, Laura agreed to participate. She thought the online process would be great to try because of the limited resources of time and because of the distance between them (Denver and Houston).

Critical to the success of Laura and Jane's experience was Laura's understanding of and trust in the process of Cognitive Coaching^SM. Laura knew that if she were honest with Jane through her responses, Jane would respond back with honesty and recognize Laura's openness to trust. If she had not trusted the Cognitive Coaching^SM process, she might not have been able to trust Jane with many of the situations that they discussed. Laura trusted that each question that Jane asked would mediate her thinking.

Laura and Jane established rapport during the Foundation Seminar®. In addition, they had a coaching conversation during the training that started the development of their trust. Trust grew as they conversed online and understood the limitations of online coaching, especially in making inferences and interpretations. Laura learned to ask for clarification when she was not sure what Jane was asking and also to tell Jane some of the emotions that she was experiencing, rather than leaving it up to Jane to read between the lines of her writing. They talked about the difficulty of coaching online and agreed to let each other know when there was confusion or emotion that would be evident more in an in-person coaching session.

Laura found the tools of paraphrasing and questioning as well as the three conversation maps to be particularly effective in online coaching. She was initially surprised at the power of paraphrasing online. "When Jane gave a paraphrase back to me that was just right, it felt as if she was the only one who was listening to me that day." Laura's understanding of questioning allowed her to trust that a question could mediate her thinking, even though she might not understand why Jane was asking it.

When Jane worked with Laura through a highly emotional event in which Laura was stuck, Laura's understanding of the role of the coach was important. There were times when Laura wanted answers instead of more questions. She wanted Jane to tell her what to do or to solve her problems for her. She knew that as a cognitive coach, Jane did not have an agenda for or with her. Her efficacy grew as she realized that Jane was asking her to find the resourcefulness to solve her own problems.

Challenges of Online Coaching

Both pairs who coached online encountered similar challenges. The major challenge was the absence of face-to-face interaction. Since 65% of a message is communicated nonverbally (Burgoon, Buller, & Woodall, 1989), there is a risk in online coaching that the words might be misinterpreted. Without being able to see a person's facial expressions and gestures or hear the tonality in their voice, it is difficult to know how effectively one is communicating. Another challenge is the speed of typing of both parties. If both type quickly, then the chat room coaching conversation will go more rapidly than if they type more slowly. Also in the chat room setting, the boxes that are provided in which to type the message only hold a limited number of letters. Jenny and Yaso developed a process in which they typed until they ran out of room. If they still had more to say, they would type ellipsis points (. . .) to indicate that more was to come in the next message.

In the case of the e-mail coaching, a challenge was the time it took to respond to a message. Sometimes it was several days or a week before there would be a response; several times responses passed each other in cyberspace. Frequent checking of e-mail and taking time to respond when the message was received helped Jane and Laura overcome this challenge.

Another challenge to consider is the public nature of e-mail. If online coaching is to be effective, both parties have to be open and honest in their communication. This might be difficult, depending on the likelihood that others might be able to access one's e-mail.

Benefits of Online Coaching

Online coaching benefits both the coach and the coachee. One benefit for the coach is the increased craftsmanship that comes from having a written record of one's coaching to examine. For example, the coach can see what types of paraphrases and questions are most frequently used and what types of responses the different paraphrases and questions elicit from the coachee. As Jenny said, "Coaching helped me learn, validate my ideas, explore, and discover."

Another benefit of online coaching is that both coach and coachee can take longer to respond. They can look at previous entries, take time to formulate questions, or even revise questions before sending them. Online coaching allows the luxury of time to think, craft a response, reflect on the response, and then send it.

Learnings and Applications

Jenny and Yaso found that no matter what the obstacles were, the time they spent coaching online was definitely worth it! Laura and Jane agreed that the benefits outweighed the hard work and some of the ambiguity that occurred. Both pairs learned that the establishment of trust was the most critical element in the success of the online coaching. In addition the coach's craftsmanship with language, paraphrases, and meditative questions helped ensure that messages were being understood as they were intended.

Laura summed up her learning from online coaching when she said,

> I compare the growth that I had from my first year to the second year as an assistant principal [AP]. The difference in the two years can best be measured by my confidence to take risks. In my first year as an AP, I was learning my role and what would be

expected of me. I focused more on doing what was expected of me. I worried about doing the right thing. I did not want to get into hot situations that I could not handle or control. I wanted to be able to work in my role as an AP without causing too many problems. Throughout this past year, I was willing to take risks. I found myself in difficult situations, and I had the confidence to take on those situations. Because of that, I did not see myself as taking risks that could lead to failure. I found that instead I had the confidence to step out into new and different situations with the tools and strategies that I needed to be successful. I think that the best way to measure my growth as an assistant principal was to say with confidence, "Yes, I can do that!" and knew that I could.

Online coaching can be used by anyone who lives at a distance from or has limited access to his or her coaching partner. Universities are increasingly implementing distance-learning programs, and coaching online gives professors the opportunity to coach their students rather than solely give information. In the new distance-learning culture, on-line coaching can become the principal tenet of learning and exploration. Distance learning is for motivated, self-directed learners. For this type of learner, coaching can be a valuable tool for learning because of its potential for encouraging exploration as a way of knowing

The ultimate goal of coaching is for the coachee to begin to internalize the process so that he or she automatically asks the Planning Conversation questions when planning, and the Reflecting Conversation questions when reflecting on past events. Cognitive Coaching[SM] online provides the coach with the opportunity to practice and refine coaching skills, while providing the coachee with time and space for thinking. With the Internet, Cognitive Coaching[SM] can happen anywhere at any time.

The process of Cognitive Coaching[SM] is an invitation to think. A person's thinking can be mediated from either written or spoken text. Developing skill in coaching online can be especially beneficial in our fast-paced world.

Reference

Burgoon, J. K., Buller, D. B., & Woodall, W. G. (1989). *Nonverbal communications: The unspoken dialogue.* New York: Harper & Row.

Part 2

School Applications

The critical day-to-day interactions that affect student learning occur at the school level. This section addresses structures that allow the principles and practices of Cognitive Coaching[SM] to become an integral part of each human interaction in a school. In addition, it is at the school level that Cognitive Coaching[SM] can begin to impact parents and the community.

The chapters in this section describe varied approaches to developing school culture—from interviewing to hiring, to supervising, to designing and constructing the school. When Cognitive Coaching[SM] is in all the fibers of the school culture, the fabric becomes one of adaptivity, changing form and continually clarifying the essence, identity, and direction of the school.

Chapter 7

Developing
Adaptive Schools

By: Robert Garmston and Carolee Hayes

Introduction

Cognitive Coaching[SM] was developed to support leaders and colleagues with processes for mediating self-directed learning in others. Inevitably, questions emerged about how Cognitive Coaching[SM] might be applied with groups and organizations. Pursuing this line of thinking, Robert Garmston and Bruce Wellman (1999) developed a comprehensive approach to school improvement called Adaptive Schools. Its aim is to model the adaptivity found in biology, in which organisms react to changing environments by changing form while remaining consistent with a core identity. Garmston and Wellman envisioned schools that could provide a meditative environment, in which all the players contribute to the organization's practice of being self-managing, self-monitoring, and self-modifying. The ultimate goal of such schools is continuous self-directed improvements in student learning.

This chapter describes how principles and tenets of Cognitive Coaching[SM] inform the Adaptive Schools framework. The authors provide examples of how principals and other leaders have translated the concepts and tools of Cognitive Coaching^SM into organizational practice. They link those practices to results for individuals, groups, and organizations and challenge leaders to consider how to utilize mediative strategies to support both individual and organizational development.

To borrow from Charles Dickens, in regard to education, this may be the best of times and worst of times. It is the best of times in relation to quantum advances in knowledge about and technology for learning. It is the best regarding an intensified focus on student learning. It is the worst regarding the incessant demand for change without regard to the heroic job most teachers and administrators already perform. It is the worst in that over simplified schemes of accountability are mandated without provision for improving internal capacities. School staffs today are overwhelmed and fragmented. Burnout is not unusual. New programs abound and school boards and legislatures seem anxious to adopt innovations that promise to quickly impact standardized test scores rather than examining the deeper issues in student achievement. Schools today are expected to respond to an ever-changing environment, be accountable, and continuously improve. Assumptions about current practice must be reexamined in order to survive and serve in such a demanding climate.

Richard Elmore (2002) asks if teachers and principals can be bullied, intimidated, or punished into producing better test scores for students. We think not. What we do know is that it is the collectively focused quality and skills of the teacher that most impacts student achievement (Marzano, Pickering, & Pollock, 2001). Furthermore, the conditions of work place culture inform what teachers actually learn and do. Programs, high stakes testing, and initiatives may be added but without thoughtful teachers, working collaboratively and committed to using their expanding understanding of the teaching-learning process, quick fixes are doomed to failure.

This chapter addresses how leaders use principles and practices of Cognitive Coaching^SM to develop collective momentum—for staff and students—toward self-directed learning. Studies reveal that teacher behaviors, attitudes, and cognition are influenced more by the workplace culture than the skills, knowledge, training, and biographies of individual teachers. Leaders in Adaptive Schools know that reculturing toward communities of collaboration and shared responsibility for student learning is essential. Restructuring may or may not be useful. These leaders also know that capable groups are made, not born. In schools applying the principles of adaptive schools, working communities grow, learn from experience, and become more productive. In less effective schools, things stay the same, group learning is episodic, and the capacity to work together to improve teaching remains relatively static. Many leaders are finding Cognitive Coaching^{SM} to be an excellent resource for accelerating the development of collaborative groups. In fact, staffs skilled in Cognitive Coaching^{SM} acquire the skills and orientations of Adaptive Schools perhaps three times faster than those without prior coaching work.

It is not any one reform that impacts student achievement. Instead, the climate and culture of the school, teachers' instructional competence, and the daily interactions with adults are the greatest influences for student achievement gains. In a study of eight elementary, eight middle, and eight secondary schools, researchers found conditions in which school-wide achievement gains were made. The central features of these "professional communities" were collaboration, a focus on student learning, reflective dialogue, clear values and norms, and overcoming teacher isolation. Cognitive Coaching^{SM} can contribute to the emergence of each of these features in a school community. Studies (Edwards, 2001) have found Cognitive Coaching^{SM} to have genuine impact on the collaborative culture of schools. Additionally, a coaching repertoire includes the verbal and relationship skills for trust, reflective dialogue, analysis of student work, and the cognitive capacities for self-directed improvement.

Without conscious attention to developing a collaborative culture, professional efforts are disjointed and unfocused. Individuals may excel, but the school as a whole is not producing together, learning together, developing new approaches and gaining greater collective knowledge from individual achievements. The leader of the future sees his/her work as developing a collaborative culture focused on student learning. The following are some examples of how leaders live this vision:

- Chris Monachino, former principal of Harrison Elementary School in Lakewood, Ohio, saw the potential of developing greater collaboration and ownership for student learning by applying the skills and processes of Adaptive Schools. She wrote grants to train her staff in Adaptive Schools and modeled and monitored the use of the skills in all aspects of her school staff's work. Along with other best practices utilized by her school, Chris attributes the gain—in just three years—from less than 50% to 100% proficiency of the Harrison students on the Ohio State reading proficiencies to the staff's increased collaboration and use of Adaptive School practices.

• Another leader who values the potential of using Adaptive Schools' principles in her work is Cindy Stevenson, superintendent of Jefferson County Schools, the largest school district in Colorado. She knows that the processes she uses with her board of education are critical to impacting her commitment to focusing on student achievement. In a recent board meeting to determine a process for making major budget cuts, Cindy utilized the Circle Map (Hyerle, 2000) as a tool for assisting board members to view the issues from multiple perspectives. Stevenson consistently uses the principles of Adaptive Schools to mediate the thinking of all of her stakeholders, valuing the basic premises of Cognitive Coaching^SM. She sees her job as a leader to mediate thinking of her constituents to support the best possible decision-making for students.

• As teacher leaders, a team of staff members at Ponderosa High School in Parker, Colorado, was also trained in Adaptive Schools work. When charged with developing a site-based decision-making council, they used the skills and tools learned in their training to dialogue before finalizing a charter for their site council. The discipline shown by the group was remarkable, dialoguing over a 6-month period to ensure all of the perspectives were heard and nuances considered. Seven years later, the charter still is honored and is utilized to lead the school's decision-making processes. Student achievement has continued to grow and develop under the thoughtful decision-making processes of the site council.

The challenge for leaders who understand the contributions of one-on-one Cognitive Coaching^SM is to transfer that knowledge and skills to a systems focus. "All groups struggle to achieve a successful balance between managing and adapting to external relationships and maintaining harmonious and effective internal relationships" (Schein, 1992). So schools, to deliver the best for students, understand themselves as parts of a holonomous system and manage themselves as well as interact successfully with their external environments—district office, parents, unions, school boards, and beyond.

Adaptive Schools provide the conditions in which teachers can reinvent practice to increase student learning. Leaders envision conditions within six domains of group development that facilitate such improvements: getting work done effectively, doing the right work, working interdependently, managing systems, developing the group, and adapting to change. Two prevailing orientations are (a) whatever the degree of accomplishments, groups can always get better at their work, and (b) that both individual and group capacities are necessary to produce and implement innovations.

Figure 7-1 describes the specific application of Cognitive Coaching^{SM} concepts related to Adaptive Schools work. Each element will be described as it is applied in Adaptive Schools.

- States of mind

- Seven norms of collaboration

- Four functional areas of shared leadership

- Group member capabilities

- Using data for instructional decisions

- Three coaching questions for groups

Figure 7-1. Cognitive Coaching^{SM} Concepts Applied in Adaptive Schools

States of Mind as Collective Energy Sources

As in individuals, there are sources of energy in groups (Garmston & Wellman, 1999). (See page 142 in the chapter on Cognitive Coaching^{SM} with Small Groups for the manifestations of group States of Mind). While efficacy, craftsmanship, consciousness, flexibility, and interdependence propel individuals toward excellence, so, too, they serve as catalytic forces in groups. A State of Mind lives uniquely in an individual and varies over time according to contextual conditions. In a group, the states of mind live collectively as energy sources. Although a group may have many efficacious individuals, it may not function as a whole in a manner that demonstrates a sense of empowerment. Take for example, the group who responds to a district request for input with a statement like, "What difference does our opinion make anyway; they've already made up their minds about the decision." The group's efficacy is low. The thoughtful leader will structure, teach, mediate, model, or initiate group monitoring to increase group efficacy.

Structure

Adaptive schools manage the physical environment in ways to promote certain awarenesses and levels of learning. Advanced Cognitive Coaching^{SM} seminars address a model of intervention conceived by anthropologist Gregory Bateson in which identity influences all other levels of learning. The notion is that learning occurs at different logical levels, each is related to the others, the higher ones (identity, values, beliefs, capabilities) will influence the lower ones (behavior and environment), and a lower one may influence the one above it. So the leader wishing to structure, say for interdependence, will use the principle of diversity to organize subgroups for a task.

Teach

This level of intervention is best for the behaviors and capabilities of collaboration. Teaching paraphrasing or providing instruction on the metacognitive skills of being a group member (capabilities) are appropriate foci for this level of intervention.

Mediate

Mediation may occur with individuals or with groups when planning, reflecting, or problem-solving. Mediation skills draw extensively from Cognitive Coaching^{SM}: paraphrasing, pausing, probing, presuming positive intention, and inquiring.

Model

Leaders and group members model when they display certain skills or dispositions as part of their regular work performance. As Julie Versaw said in the chapter on coaching third graders—be careful what you model. With adults too, modeling is a powerful device of teaching and expressing what is important.

Monitor

Leaders invite group monitoring of behaviors, capabilities, values, and beliefs. Some adopt a process-task ratio in which, at the end of every meeting, a few minutes are protected for staff reflection about the processes and quality of participation in the meeting. This is similar to the reflection period used at the end of a planning or reflecting conversation and has the same intent—to learn from the current experience and be better prepared to seek refinements that will make the next event even more productive. A pair of monitoring questions directed at capabilities is: "What were some of the decisions you made about when and how to participate in this discussion? What were some of the effects of those decisions on you and others?

So effective leaders in Adaptive Schools utilize the five states of mind of Cognitive Coaching[SM] to promote energy enhancing a group's ability to deal with challenges. Providing a group with knowledge of the five energy sources is one road into its increased consciousness. A survey for assisting individuals and groups in assessing their energy sources is another strategy that is non-evaluative and allows them to self-assess.[1] A leader can also ask a group to periodically examine its goals and to ask such questions as, "Which energy sources will best serve us in our current work? How might we tackle these challenges from a more efficacious position? What might be needed in order to support our interdependence in this work?" Leaders grow in influence by developing a repertoire of group intervention strategies to enhance the five energy sources.[2]

As a group becomes more and more adroit in using energy sources to analyze its work, the transfer can be easily made to examining learning issues. A school might ask such questions as, "How can we support growing efficacy in our students as readers and writers?" "What level of consciousness and craftsmanship are required for our students to perform at high levels on performance assessments?" "How can we build that level?" "How can we develop greater flexibility in our students' problem-solving skills?"

Consciousness may be the critical state of mind for leaders wanting to utilize coaching skills in an organization. The leader seeks ongoing awareness of internal decision-making processes that influence his/her behaviors. That awareness serves to inform other states of mind operating to influence the leader. For example, the leader who reflects on decisions s/he made in a stressful meeting is using consciousness as a pathway to evaluate other states of mind. As a result of reflection, greater flexibility may develop in considering responses to feedback from the staff. The constant attention to the leader's consciousness enhances efficacy, flexibility, craftsmanship, and interdependence. Simultaneously, the leader collects data on individual and school performance, analyzes the data, and chooses a course of action as a conscious response to the analysis.

Jody Younkin, principal of Sierra Avenue Elementary School in Thermalito School District, Oroville, California, began her tenure by collecting data on the energy sources present in her staff.[2] She has thoughtfully presented the data to the staff and is using it as a guide for team self-reflection and self-analysis. Bill Powell, when Superintendent of an international school in Dar Es Salaam, Tanzania, used the states of mind in induction processes to help new staff adapt to the school and the Tanzanian culture.

Seven Norms of Collaboration

Groups working over time develop patterns of behavior that persist and become internalized ways of working. These "norms" can be either productive or counterproductive. Often norms live at an implicit level. Members new to a group learn the norms inferentially through experiences where behaviors are positively or negatively reinforced. For instance, the new teacher who does hallway duty on a regular basis receives messages from staff and administration about the group's expectations. In one school, a colleague may voice appreciation for the visibility of a colleague in monitoring student behaviors. That acknowledgement in another school may be labeled "brown-nosing the administration." A person new to the culture quickly internalizes expectations and ways of working.

Adaptive Schools draw on the language tools and values of Cognitive Coaching[SM] to assist groups in making collaborative behaviors overt, explicit, and intentional. Seven norms of collaboration are taught and practiced. Groups are encouraged to post the norms, monitor the norms, and develop feedback loops on use of the norms. The seven norms are

- Pausing
- Paraphrasing
- Probing
- Putting Ideas on the Table
- Paying Attention to Self and Others
- Presuming Positive Intention
- Pursuing a Balance Between Advocacy and Inquiry

Pausing, paraphrasing, and probing are three of the response behaviors taught in Cognitive Coaching^{SM} seminars. When utilized in group settings, they mediate both individual and group thinking, even if only one member of the group is using these tools. Interestingly, as groups monitor their use of the first three norms, they sometimes discover that although these are common activities in coaching interactions, the transfer has not been made to group applications. Groups who are pressed for time and who have a high task focus often lose awareness of processes that increase efficiency, effectiveness, and satisfaction. Simple attention to the pausing, paraphrasing, and probing can elevate a group's productivity and efficacy. Passions of individuals in groups can often lead to advocacy for an issue that becomes redundant and repetitive. The simple act of using a summarize and organize paraphrase can assist the group and the individual in understanding the thinking and allow the group to move forward.

One district group reported that consciously using these norms caused the following outcomes:

- Listening for understanding instead of for advocating only
- Focused listening with attention to key tasks
- More efficient use of time
- More willingness to hear other points of view
- Increased complexity in thinking about issues

Presuming positive intention is a norm linked to the skill of embedding positive presuppositions in questions and paraphrases. A group that operates on an assumption that members come with resources to contribute and intentions which are honorable works differently than a group that sees one another as having limited contributions and self-serving intentions. Developing the attitudinal part of this norm is much like assuming the best of students in a classroom. Expectancy theory supports us in behaving in the way we would like others to be. The group members use the same tools in communicating with positive presuppositions as with individuals in a coaching relationship. In group meetings one might hear such a question as, "What resources do we need to reach consensus on this decision?" The statement assumes that resources are available, can be garnered, and that the group has the desire and ability to come to consensus. Another statement might be, "We have lots of diversity in our group. We need to be certain we have drawn on all of the perspectives."

The norm of "pursuing a balance between advocacy and inquiry" is drawn from the works of Bohm (1990) and Senge (1990). Group members naturally promote ideas they support. If good decisions are to be made, positions must be explored and deeply understood. Advocacy illuminates a perspective. When balanced with thoughtful inquiry, complexities are revealed. Different perspectives are illuminated and long-range implications can be discovered. The skill of inquiry from Cognitive Coaching^{SM} serves groups moving toward collaboration. As inquiry mediates individual thought processes, so too, it mediates group thinking and learning.

Consciousness plays a major role in the work of groups wanting to utilize the seven norms of collaboration. For behaviors to become habituated they must move from awkward early use, to mechanical use, to automaticity. The Adaptive Schools assists groups in moving along a continuum from little use of the norms to routine use. This is accomplished through conscious monitoring and reflection.

Four Hats of Shared Leadership

The Cognitive Coaching^{SM} capability, "Knowing one's intention and choosing congruent behaviors," (Costa & Garmston, 2002), is applied in Adaptive Schools. Leadership is viewed as a function and not a role. Skills are developed about four hats or choices a leader makes in any interaction—coaching, consulting, facilitating, or presenting. The first two hats, coaching and consulting, parallel two of the four support functions described by Costa and Garmston (2002). Coaching and consulting can be applied in either an individual or group context. In working with groups, leaders might also choose to present or to facilitate the third and fourth hats presented in Adaptive Schools. Although the work of an individual varies depending on the context of the work, the key feature of responding appropriately is deliberation about intention and thoughtfulness about aligning behaviors with intention. Significantly, all players are encouraged to wear all the hats.

• Coaching	• Facilitating
• Consulting	• Presenting

Figure 7-2.   Four Hats of Shared Leadership

Several explicit tools used in Cognitive Coaching^{SM}—pausing, paraphrasing, probing, and inquiring—transfer into each of the four hats of shared leadership in Adaptive Schools. To know one's intentions and select congruent behaviors is a form of executive control—or self-monitoring of one's thinking—used in coaching and also for participation in a collaborative group.

In working through a difficult scheduling decision for her school, we observed a skilled principal make conscious choices about which hat to wear. She began by **presenting** carefully formatted data to her teachers, outlining options available to them that met district guidelines and budget constraints. Her expertise allowed her to then shift to **consultant**, responding to their questions about the options available and the limitations and implications for teachers and students. Over the next weeks, she served as a **coach** to mediate the thinking of individuals who brought concerns to her. In meetings, she coached by paraphrasing and asking questions designed to deepen the thinking of the faculty. Finally, when it came time to make a final decision, she designed and had a staff member **facilitate** a process to reach consensus. Over the course of several months, this principal engaged all four hats. She knew that the best decision on scheduling would result from the informed collaboration of her staff. Her recognition that she could develop that collaboration by using a variety of hats was instrumental in the staff's ability to move together. At the end of the process, the staff celebrated its accomplishments and thanked the leader for providing an environment that empowered them to do what was best for student learning.

Group Member Capabilities

Garmston and Wellman (1999) state that meeting success is influenced more by the collaborative norms of the group than by the knowledge and skill of the group facilitator. Based on this premise, Bill Baker has said that we have been training the wrong people about meeting effectiveness. To be an effective member of a group is more cognitively complex than to be its leader. For these reasons, four group member capabilities are defined in the Adaptive Schools work. Notice their similarities to capabilities learned in Cognitive Coaching[SM].

Some staffs post these capabilities on the walls of their meeting rooms to serve as conscious reminders in their ongoing work. One principal, new to a school, interviewed every staff member at her new school. She then used the data to put notes under each capability to remind her how to interact with the staff in her early months of entering the school. She knew that there were issues and topics that were important to her that were not important to her staff. She gauged her decisions about when to self-assert and when to

Adaptive Schools	Cognitive Coaching[SM]
Know one's intentions and choose congruent behaviors.	Know one's intentions and choose congruent behaviors.
Set aside unproductive patterns of listening, responding, and inquiring.	Set aside unproductive patterns of listening, responding, and inquiring.
Know when to self-assert and when to integrate.	Adjust one's style preferences.
Know and support the group's purposes, topics, processes, and development.	Navigate among and within coaching maps and support functions to guide mediational interactions.

Figure 7-3. Comparing Adaptive Schools and Cognitive Coaching[SM] Capabilities

integrate based on the data she collected. She consciously framed purposes of meetings to be congruent with the language she had heard from staff in the interviews. She carefully monitored when her own needs surfaced and kept the thoughts internal until the group needs were aligned.

Using Data

In the Cognitive Coaching Foundation Seminar®, data is taught as one of five categories of feedback. Cognitive Coaches use data to support an individual in examining perceptions and impressions for accuracy. Data are a neutral means for inviting thoughtful analysis when paired with reflective questions. In the *Adaptive Schools* (Garmston & Wellman, 1999) work, data are a foundation for developing common understanding and shared examination of challenges and opportunities.

Groups who do not use data for decision-making work from impressions that may or may not be accurate. The loudest voice often wins the day. When groups ground their work in data, shared learning is enhanced and decision-making tends to be more thoughtful and long lasting. As districts become clearer in defining what students should know and be able to do, assessment data is becoming more refined. Technology that provides sophisticated means for displaying data in accurate and easily accessible formats is being refined.

The *Adaptive Schools* (Garmston & Wellman, 1999) work, like Cognitive Coaching[SM], provides skills and processes for groups to think together at high levels. As groups learn such norms as advocacy and inquiry, probing for specificity and paraphrasing, they have processes for skillfully using data. Other protocols such as dialogue (conversations that examine assumptions, reveal thinking, and seek meaning) and discussion (conversations that produce decisions) enhance a group's ability to use data in meaningful ways.

The time educators have to spend together is precious, and too often used for unproductive interactions such as sharing information that could be printed or working to solve problems without common maps or tools. As staffs use data to inform their work, shared time uses are changing. We know many staffs that schedule time to examine student work, study parent feedback, analyze standardized test data, or plan responses. In *Collaborative Analysis of Student Learning* (Colton & Goff, 2003 in press) teacher teams are taught to combine the essences of Cognitive Coaching^SM and Adaptive Schools. They learn skills of collaboration, develop data analysis skills, and group coaching skills. They routinely meet to analyze the work of two students in their class, design, and test new teaching approaches. Student achievement gains are posted for entire classes even though the initial focus has been on just two students from each class.

In another example of gathering and using data, one school interviewed students about what they were learning. From those interviews, they discovered students could not articulate the learning goals of instruction they were receiving. Students could only describe activities in which they were engaged. Teachers developed action plans for how to ensure that students were clear about their learning and were able to articulate the purpose of the activities in which they were engaged. Signficantly, Marzano, Pickering and Pollock (2001) found that student's knowledge of learning goals was one of nine categories of instructional strategies that affect student achievement.

The Coaching Questions for Groups

Identity, who we believe ourselves to be, the ongoing narrative that is us, influences and informs our perceptions, values, beliefs, and behaviors. The work in Cognitive Coaching^SM recognizes this and places a premium on coaches developing an identity as mediator. Groups, too, have identity; and this collective sense of who we are informs, not only the hypothetical organizational values, but also the real ones, the ones that shape policies, practices, and daily choices.

In our work with Adaptive Schools, we have found the following three questions to have unusual potency. Principals have told us that these questions have literally transformed their schools. Why? Because the first ques-

---

- Who are we?

- Why are we doing this?

- Why are we doing this, this way?

Figure 7-4. Three Coaching Questions

tion lives at the level of deep structure and identity, and the remaining two are practical ways of testing the first. When the questions are raised, staffs commit to thoughtful interaction about them.

Who Are We?

"Who am I?" In Cognitive Coaching^{SM} seminars, a goal is to develop the identity and skills of a mediator. From a person's identity flow a congruent set of beliefs, values, capabilities, and behaviors.

Likewise for groups, identity drives perceptions and the work of the group. A site council was asked this question, and it became a source of long-term dialogue. When a third-grade team asked the same question, it became clear about what was important in their work with students and what was superfluous. When we know what our purpose for being is, all other decisions become clearer. A middle school could be seen by its staff as a holding tank, a purveyor of basic skills, a place for exploration, or an academic institution. "Who are we, what do we stand for, how much do we care, and how much do we dare?" are deep and directing questions for groups to address. This is fundamentally the most essential inquiry any group makes and is true for site councils, leadership teams, or grade-level groups. Until groups are clear about this question, their work is likely to be scattered and unfocused.

Why Are We Doing This?

Once identity is clear, a group is able to examine each decision and practice through a new lens. Old practices have a way of persisting in schools without question—ability grouping, teaching cursive writing, 45-minute periods, and so forth. As groups become more thoughtful and reflective, they learn a second key question: "Why are we doing this?" This question serves to surface hidden assumptions underlying practice. The *why* question is one we are cautious about in individual coaching as it tends to create defensiveness if asked about behaviors. In a group, the question lies somewhat outside the self and is safer to address. When one group asked itself why they started school at the time they did, they became clear it was because of bus schedules and after school activities. Surfacing that assumption allowed them to examine if that was congruent with their sense of identity and mission. If a school's identity is about teaching academic skills, does it make sense to do something based on convenience to the transportation department or to accommodate a sports practice schedule? The answers are challenging but unless asked, they never get addressed

Why Are We Doing This, This Way?

This final question causes us to examine our decisions about how we do things. Schools live on pressing schedules and calendars with just-in-time thinking. This question, a valuable coaching question with an individual, also adds value to a group's understanding of its thought processes. It promotes flexibility in thinking. A leader who asks this question invites staff to examine other possibilities and to analyze rationale behind decisions.

The administrator who asks questions about scheduling, grouping, student assignments, homework, assessments, and so forth in this manner is inviting. Staffs who become habituated in asking this question start to ask it themselves for themselves in their work with students and to develop students who also ask the question.

In Closing

Our challenge in working with Adaptive Schools is to transfer the skills that mediate thinking of individuals into groups with an intention to promote meditative environments and self-directed learning. Recognition of the complexity of this value-added application is critical. The successful leader of today's schools attends to the development of individuals and the organization. The skills of Cognitive Coaching[SM] ground leaders in mediating individuals in becoming self-directed learners focused on quality. When applied in group settings, the same skills enhance the capacity of groups.

In closing, we offer these questions for your consideration. Who are you? Why are you doing what you are? And why, in that particular way?

Endnotes

[1] States of Mind as hallmarks of Cognitive Coaching[SM] are referred to as energy sources in the Adaptive Schools work (Garmston & Wellman, 1999).

[2] A Team Development survey for self-assessment of group energy sources is available through the Center for Cognitive Coaching, www.cognitivecoaching.com, 303-683-6146.

References

Bohm, D. (1990). *On dialogue.* Ojai, CA: David Bohm Seminars.

Costa, A., & Garmston, R. (2002). *Cognitive Coaching[SM]: A foundation for renaissance schools* (2nd ed.). Norwood, MA: Christopher-Gordon.

Colton, A., & Goff, G. (2003) *Collaborative analysis of student learning.* In press.

Edwards, J. (2001). *Cognitive Coaching[SM]: A synthesis of the research.* Highlands Ranch, CO: Center for Cognitive Coaching.

Elmore, R. (1995). Structural reform and educational practice. *Educational Research, 24* (9), 23–26.

Elmore, R. F. (2002). *Bridging the gap between standards and achievement: The imperative for professional development in education.* Washington, DC: The Albert Shanker Institute.

Garmston, R., & Wellman, B. (1999). *The adaptive school: A sourcebook for developing collaborative groups.* Norwood, MA: Christopher-Gordon.

Hyerle, D. (2000). *A field guide to using visual tools.* Alexandria, VA: Association for Supervision and Curriculum Development, p. 55.

Marzano, R., Pickering, D., & Pollock, J. (2001). *Classroom institution that works.* Alexandria, VA: Association for Supervision and Curriculum Development.

Senge, P. (1990). *The fifth discipline: The art and practice of the learning organization.* New York: Doubleday.

Chapter 8

Designing and Constructing the Holonomous School

By: Arthur L. Costa, Robert J. Garmston,
Joe Saban, Augie Battaglia, and Bill Brubaker

Introduction

The threads and fabric of a culture are reflected in its artifacts as well as in the behaviors of the group members. School buildings represent the beliefs and values of the designers and leaders. It takes little time to walk through any school observing its features to determine what was valued by those who constructed it. The way a building is utilized, down to the displays on the walls, reflect the values of the inhabitants.

The leaders of Crystal Lake High School Community District 155 challenged themselves to envision a high school building reflecting the concepts of holonomy and the Five States of Mind. This chapter describes how the community came together to plan for and to construct a school that fostered efficacy, flexibility, consciousness, craftsmanship, and interdependence among all who entered its walls. The perspectives presented in this chapter include those of the developers of Cognitive Coaching[SM], the district superintendent, and the architects.

David Perkins (1992) asserts that "managing the surround" is tantamount to causing the environment to be a thinking member of the human community, connecting in countless ways to interact with and influence human learning.

What messages lie in the walls, corridors, and the organization of internal and external space of any public school building? Is the building itself not a metaphor for what the architects, educators, and draftsmen envision regarding the purposes, uses, and philosophies of their endeavors? Here in Crystal Lake these questions were directed at the design of Prairie Ridge High School. This is a high school dedicated to developing holonomous individuals capable of living and working successfully in a dynamic and unpredictable future. What possible form might a high school building take if the educational values of holonomy were translated into steel, stone, concrete, and space?

Holonomous persons are simultaneously successful at independent and interdependent tasks. The term *holonomy* is significant in that it describes an increasingly important reality emerging in 21st century America. Educators must work as individually as do skilled professionals. At the same time, they are required to work collaboratively across the system. Without a term, a concept has difficulty existing in a culture. Just as there is no word in Russian for privacy or efficiency, and hence no common realization of those concepts in Russia, there was not any English word for the state of being simultaneously whole and part until the 1970s. Arthur Koestler coined the term *holonomy.* The term *holon* comes from the Greek *holos* which means the whole and the suffix *on* which means part. The concept of holonomy transcends the notion of an autonomous individual organism as it functions as only a subpart of a larger organization. Each individual organism is always in a reciprocal interaction with the larger universe.

In a holonomous educational community, each member—parent, student, administrator, secretary, or teacher—may be thought of as proud autonomous individuals—self asserting, self-assessing, self-modifying, and self-authoring. An important goal of schooling is to develop this practical and hardy self-actualization. However, autonomous individuals are simultaneously part of a larger whole and are influenced by their surroundings. These environmental influences include the attitudes, values, and behaviors of the school culture of which they are members, the buildings in which they learn, the windows through which they observe, and the grounds on which they work. The school, in turn is an autonomous unit, organized around its own unique community, identity, vision, and goals. Yet it maintains an interactive relationship with the larger district and community.

Holonomy means acting autonomously and working interdependently, simultaneously. The twin functions of holonomous environments, therefore, are (a) to support and transform the capacities of individual members of the school community—students, teachers, support staff, and parents—in becoming autonomous and self-actualizing, self-referencing, self-renewing, and self-modifying; and (b) to support and transform the capacities of the organization itself and the larger community as an interdependent culture of continuous learning.

Prairie Ridge High School was designed with holonomy in mind. A conscious effort was made to allow the building facilities to act both autonomously and interdependently with other parts of the building. For example, Prairie Ridge was built to allow the building to operate as an 1800 student high school, but also as two 900 or four 450 student schools if desired. This was accomplished by the thoughtful placement of specialty spaces, such as chemistry labs, vocational areas, and computer labs, so that floors can be isolated into two completely autonomous schools of 900 students. If desired, the floors could be divided in half so that each floor of 900 could be separated into two schools of 450 merely by the addition of partitions. The individual schools would share the various common areas like the gyms, student cafeteria, and the theater. The subdivision of large schools into smaller schools, know as the "house concept," would accommodate the educational trend toward smaller school buildings without compromising the possibility that schools of the future may again go toward larger student programming (New Designs, 1996). In this way, the school may operate both autonomously and interdependently.

The building was conceived to represent Aristotle's conceptualization of the interrelationships between the human mind, body, and spirit. Prairie Ridge was organized around three major separate yet interrelated functional areas: (a) the classroom/academic areas to represent the mind, (b) the physical education/athletic area to represent the body, and (c) the theater/art area to represent the spirit. Each of these areas was zoned to be able to act independently from one another. Yet in the course of the normal school day, the three areas interdependently form a total learning community.

Environmental Factors That Support the Development of Individual Capacities

Good schools have always supported the development of the individual. Schools that combine successful practices from the past with modern research in teaching and learning will support individual development by building four intellectual foundations for high performance (Costa & Garmston, 2002).

Efficacy is the capacity for self-empowerment, an ongoing striving to master and to control one's destiny.

Flexibility is the capacity to change and adapt and to take a perspective other than one's own. The work world of the future means many career changes and working at jobs not yet created.

Consciousness is the capacity to monitor and reflect on ourselves. It is the source of self-improvement and distinguishes us from all other forms of life.

Craftsmanship is the capacity to be clear, elegant, precise, congruent, and integrated along with the unending desire for high standards and peak performance in whatever we do.

Educational environments designed to facilitate each of these capacities would provide space and time for personalized student coaching, assisting each student in setting high goals and standards, monitoring their achievement, and helping students synthesize cumulative learnings regarding the continuing development of their performance capability.

Building Design Manifestations of Four of the States of Mind

Efficacy is enhanced by providing opportunities for students to exceed their limits instead of placing limits and ceilings on their capacities. Facilities would allow students to explore and to make connections among a variety of subjects and topics. The schedule would allow students to work until completion of an activity or project rather than being determined by bells and periods.

At Prairie Ridge High School, a student resource floor was created where students go when not scheduled in class with a teacher. This space has computer rooms, resource rooms, library, communal and/or quiet study areas, the cafeteria, student lounge, and large or small meeting/conferring areas. All faculty offices are on this floor so that students are able to access expertise in any field when not in class. Other resources such as guidance counselors, social workers, deans, and nurses are also housed in this space. Remaining floors or wings of the building have all disciplines or grades intermingled. As an example, chemistry rooms are not isolated in one floor or wing. They reside instead in a space that also has rooms and associated resources for English, math, social sciences, foreign languages, and so forth.

Flexibility at Prairie Ridge means providing walls that are movable, interiors that can be changed, and opportunities for various forms of learnings and styles: artistic, kinesthetic, logical/mathematical, visual/spatial, musical, verbal, interpersonal, and spiritual. Flexibility in learning from multiple perspectives is thereby supported by the building structure.

Exterior walls primarily serve as bearing walls so that the inside of the building can assume virtually any configuration as educational needs evolve over the years. Most walls are not block, but instead thick reinforced drywall over metal studs to facilitate ease of remodeling. Initially room sizes have been varied to provide adequate spaces for a wide variety of programming options. Furnishings include not only traditional desks and chairs, but also tables of various shapes that can easily be moved into a range of physical configurations depending on the instructional technique being used. Whenever practical, furnishings were not fixed in order to support programming flexibility.

The entrances of the building are strategically placed so that Prairie Ridge can serve the community in varying ways. For instance it would be possible on a given evening to be simultaneously hosting the Cub Scouts in the cafeteria, a girl's volleyball match in the gym, a community band concert in the theater, local junior college classes in classrooms, and a travelogue in a conference room while keeping each event segregated and secure in each individual space.

Craftsmanship requires providing opportunities for students to test and refine ideas, to create presentations, and to stage dramatizations and exhibits requiring rehearsing and fine-tuning. Reference materials, visual, audio, computer, and human resources need to be available as data sources from which students verify and research.

The academic areas in the school encompass numerous conference and breakout spaces where students and faculty are able to go privately, in small groups, or in large groups to assemble and/or to rehearse. This calls for a variety of sizes of rooms different from the typical auditorium, cafeteria, gym, study hall, or theatre. A number of these areas are adjacent to vocational, art, music, media, computer-aided drafting, library, or other computer rooms where materials or equipment are typically located to support creativity.

Consciousness is supported when opportunities are provided for students and staff to plan, monitor, execute, and reflect on strategies. This would mean that there would be provisions for private reflection and small and large group discussions and interactions. Aside from the conference and breakout rooms discussed above, meeting rooms are interspersed throughout the building to encourage spontaneous as well as planned encounters between the building inhabitants. Some of these spaces have comfortable lounge-type seating areas and others have movable tables, chairs, and room for audio-visual aids. Every room in the building has been wired for video, sound, and data.

Prairie Ridge designers supported reflective thinking by drawing panoramic views of the site's environment into the building through the incorporation of many windows and glass curtain walls. The hallways and stairwells have views of the external environment, which serve to give the feel of being outside the walls of the building. Care was even given to orienting the academic areas to the path of the sun across the school site so that natural light is maximized in all classrooms. A large courtyard was incorporated also to bring nature and natural light into the interior of the building.

The school was placed on the site not for convenience to roadways, but instead to utilize the pleasing natural terrain and features of the property. The high school is constructed along a ridge that falls off both to the south and the east. Conscious decisions to fit the school to the topography were made in an attempt to give the building a feel of oneness with its physical surroundings. Attention to Prairie Ridge's location allows a wetland and a creek (found on its 140 acres) to be integral learning opportunities for children. A prairie grass area was also preserved as a place for students to learn and to reflect.

Environments That Support and Transform Organizational and Community Capacities

Even the most effective self-modifying, self-authoring autonomous individual is still a member of a larger community. The second facet of holonomy relates to capacitating individuals to work collaboratively in collegial groups engaged in continuous cycles of self-improvement.

Interdependence

Interdependence, the fifth State of Mind, is the capacity to be in reciprocal relationships by contributing to and learning from others. As members of a community, individuals realize that they will benefit from their participating in, contributing to, and receiving from relationships with others. Educational environments designed to facilitate interdependence would provide opportunities for group planning, collaborative projects, small and large group interactions, and reaching out into the community. To reach out to the community might mean that students who attend Prairie Ridge invite members of the community in for recreating, learning opportunities, researching in the library, using computers, viewing performances, or art galleries, and so forth. For these purposes, entry and hallways are configured to allow for ease of access to spaces that support these activities yet maintain a secure environment in other parts of the building. The location of parking and administrative offices is such that directions, safety, and assistance for visitors are facilitated.

The learning spaces have been shaped for sharing—configured to facilitate conversion for multiple purposes and to promote connections between members of the school and the community. Intergrade and department configurations have been designed to maximize learning opportunities for everyone in the organization. Cross-function teams, comprised of members from various departments, engage in collaborative learning, problem-solving, and envisioning potential futures. Having teacher offices not isolated in pods but instead joined in one large area encourages not only planned but spontaneous opportunity for interchange. Open forums and cross-age and intergenerational collaborations foster communication, reinforcing the notion that each member of the community, at all levels, is an integral part of and has a unique contribution to the whole (Learning By Design, 1997). Because many agencies serve the same clients, the school has been linked closely with other community resources such as human resource development agencies, social welfare, housing, child protective agencies, parks and recreations, libraries, and so forth. Site selection was factored so that parks and libraries were accessible.

Architect and contractor selection for Prairie Ridge was determined through a process that audited companies for their states of mind and professional value systems. The selection process ensured that design and construction firms had similar orientations toward teamwork and collaboration. Similar convictions lead to more creative partnerships between design, construction, and school professionals.

Recognizing that the inhabitants of this school are part of a larger environment, care was given to both the internal and external climate of the school (Miller, 1995). Construction materials were selected so that they do not outgas noxious chemicals such as formaldehyde. Ventilation and air filtration received priority status with operable windows in each classroom for fresh air. Carpeting was held to a minimum to reduce odors, mold, dust, and dust mites (Leach, 1997). Natural light found its way to every learning space, and materials indigenous to the given environment were incorporated in the color and construction schema.

Conclusion

Prairie Ridge has become a center of inquiry, where every inhabitant is in a continuous learning mode. The underlying philosophy directing curriculum, instruction, and assessment decisions are learner and learning centered. Cooperatively structured interactions, authentic learning tasks, and performance-based instruction and assessment promote learning for all members of the organization—in classroom settings, faculty meetings, community forums, student/parent/teacher conferences, and so forth. Sensitivity to the internal and external conditions of the system through environmental scanning foster flexible scheduling, diverse role orientations, and close continual involvement with the community and a team-based approach to data-driven decision-making.

Forums for dialogue are vital to the second function of the holonomous environment—supporting and transforming the larger community. Locations are provided in this environment where members of the school community can come to dialogue with the intention of viewing educational and community problems from new perspectives and with new understandings. What transforms communities most is serious, active dialogue where community members wrestle with resolving problems, exploring differences in philosophy, exploring crucial strategic and operational issues, designing experiments, and structuring feedback mechanisms. Even as Prairie Ridge took form, the mental dispositions described here were modeled as parents, students, and faculty assembled to brainstorm and reach consensus on the school colors, mascot, and the school song!

While many educational architects have attended to reflecting the goals and outcomes of education in their building design, the overt expression of a community's value system may be more rare. To achieve a fractal quality, the community's values have been expressed not only in the curriculum, the day-to-day interactions, the district's policies, the culture, and the various forms of instruction, but also in the school building itself. That enduring set of values will be mirrored in the endurance of the edifice: permanent and flexible, subtle and complex, monumental and inviting, grounded and uplifting.

References

Costa, A., & Garmston, R. (2002). *Cognitive Coaching^SM: A foundation for renaissance schools* (2nd ed.). Norwood, MA: Christopher-Gordon.

Leach, K. (1997). In sync with nature. *School Planning and Management, 36* (4), 32–36.

Learning by design. (March 1997). From the publishers of *The American School Board Journal.* Alexandria, VA: National School Boards Association.

Miller, N. (1995). *The healthy school handbook.* Washington, DC: National Education Society Professional Library, National Education Association.

New designs for the comprehensive high school. (Fall 1996). St. Paul, MN: Vocational and Technical Education Department, University of Minnesota.

Perkins, D. (1992). *Smart Schools.* New York: Free Press.

Chapter 9

Cognitive Coaching[SM] With Small Groups

By: Carolee Hayes

Introduction

A common concern expressed by educators relates to time. Time has become a liability rather than a resource. Teachers are also striving to work more collaboratively, yet are often frustrated in their efforts to do so in effective, efficient, and satisfying ways. Roadblocks to collegiality can become excuses when they are not addressed with alternative ways of thinking.

Carolee Hayes presents small group coaching as a means for addressing today's common frustrations. This chapter invites the reader to consider how group coaching differs from facilitation and individual coaching. Core group coaching capabilities are described as a framework for thinking about how small group coaching skills build on individual coaching skills. Applications and possibilities for the impact of group coaching are considered.

Two seemingly discordant conditions are impacting schools in this new century. The first condition is in regard to time. Time is one of the most precious resources in schools today. Teachers spend most of their time with students conducting instructional activities. When not with students, teachers must communicate with parents, complete paperwork, do extra duties, complete assessments of student work, prepare lessons and instructional materials, and attend professional development and staff meetings, in addition to a myriad of other tasks. All of those demands leave little time for in-depth coaching to plan, reflect, and resolve problems. Teacher collaboration is another critical variable. A growing body of research is suggesting that the significant variable in schools that are improving compared to schools that are more stagnant is staff collaboration (Bryk & Schneider, 2002; Louis, Marks, & Kruse, 1996; Newman & Wehlage, 1995; Smith, 2001). It makes intuitive sense that staffs that work together on common goals would achieve more. Given these seemingly paradoxical realities, a key question that must be addressed is "How do schools find time for teachers to examine their practices in meaningful ways that encourage collaboration?"

There are undoubtedly many structures in professional development that can address this need—use of Annenberg Protocols' study groups, peer coaching pairs, traditional staff development in the form of common presentations, and so forth. A recent implementation pattern in many schools is to create full time coaching positions such as resource teachers, mentors, peer assistants, instructional coaches, literacy and math coaches, and teacher specialists. The author and other Cognitive Coaching[SM] Training Associates have had many requests from people in those positions to provide frameworks for coaching small groups. This chapter will explore small group coaching utilizing the maps and tools of Cognitive Coaching[SM]. This type of coaching does not exist in an institutionalized form or as common practice in the lives of many educators. The purpose of this chapter is to explore the premises, possibilities, and promises for small group Cognitive Coaching[SM].

Assumptions of Small Group Coaching

Knowledge is Personally and Socially Constructed

When professional interactions focus on data and shared understanding of that data, individuals learn *and* a group's common understanding is developed. Individual coaching develops one person's internal capacity and self-directedness. Group coaching adds value by maximizing group capacity. As groups increase their efficacy, craftsmanship, interdependence, flexibility, and consciousness, even more students benefit. Schools facilitate enhanced learning when structures are provided for shared growth.

Shared Goals Are the Focus of Group Coaching

When coaching an individual, the coach supports the coachee in moving from where s/he is to where s/he wants to be. The same is true for small group coaching—the goals and intentions of the group are held as primary to the coach's decisions. Clarity about shared goals is critical to the process in order to ensure that individual needs do not dominate over group goals. When a group holds shared goals related to student learning and focuses on those goals there is a strong likelihood that student achievement will be enhanced (Louis, Marks, & Kruse, 1996).

Coaching Is Not Facilitation

While the skills and neutral stances of a coach and facilitator are similar, the intentions are different. A meeting facilitator is charged with designing, managing, and monitoring the process of a group's time together in order to accomplish predetermined outcomes. The coach utilizes a specific process, Cognitive Coaching^SM, to mediate shared cognition of the group to develop self-directed learning among the group and for individuals. While there may be a product or outcome achieved, it is driven by the group's shared thinking and may be unanticipated prior to the meeting. The Cognitive Coach navigates among three maps—planning, reflecting, and problem resolving—as determined by the group's stated needs and outcomes. Facilitators use multiple processes aligned to varied outcomes.

Small group coaching and facilitation in group settings do share some overlapping qualities. Both the coach and the facilitator take a role that is disengaged and neutral in relation to the content. The skills utilized by the facilitator and the coach are similar: acknowledging, pausing, paraphrasing, probing, and inquiring. Coaches and facilitators make in-the-moment decisions based on group responses, requiring careful ongoing assessment.

Goals of Small Group Coaching

How might a person working as a group coach frame his/her goals? The goals of a group coach parallel the goals of a person coaching an individual. Drawing on the mission of Cognitive Coaching^SM, "to produce self-directed persons with the cognitive capacity for high performance both independently and as members of a community" (Costa & Garmston, 2002, p. 16), the group coach works for the same outcomes as the coach of an individual. However, interdependence is even more pronounced as a capacity to be developed in group coaching because of the ever-present paradoxes posed by autonomy and community inherent in a group's dynamics. The coach is developing holonomy in the group and individuals and is required to monitor all of the tensions of holonomy in the coaching process (Costa & Lipton, 1997). The conscious attention to the interaction of individual and group states of mind may be the greatest source of complexity in the goals of a small group coach. Simultaneously, the group and individual dynamics may be the greatest source of influence in the work of the small group coach.

Group Applications

The possibilities for applications of group coaching are unlimited in educational settings as well as other institutions. Observations in schools and district committee work provide a menu of possibilities:

- Vertical, interdisciplinary, and grade level teams
- Discipline-based school departments, e.g., social studies, world language
- Administrative departments, e.g., staff development, curriculum
- Task forces
- School or district leadership teams
- School or district improvement teams focusing on using data for continuous improvement
- Community groups
- School boards

A consideration in using small group Cognitive Coaching[SM] is the group's understanding of the concepts and the purposes of group Cognitive Coaching[SM]. A history of Cognitive Coaching[SM] as a valued process in the culture is helpful prior to including coaching in work of a group. Most often, the group is self-determining in selecting Cognitive Coaching[SM] as a process for its own development.

Role of The Coach

Groups vary in membership and composition. Similarly the role of the small group will vary accordingly. A continuum of choices for the role of the small group coach varies from low, indirect levels of intervention to more direct coaching interventions.

- Level One—The simplest and most minimalist small group coach operates as a member of the group who possesses Cognitive Coaching^{SM} skills and expertise, utilizing them to mediate thinking of the group. The group member uses coaching skills in his/her normal group member interactions, but doesn't formally identify him/herself as the group's coach. The coaching behaviors occur with intention to mediate the group's thinking and build its resourcefulness as a group, but may or may not be at a level of full understanding for every member of the group.

- Level Two—A second level is when an individual informally coaches the group. It may be a group member who informally serves as the person who initiates or is invited by the group to lead such things as planning conversations or reflections at the ends of meetings. It can also happen because an outsider to the group enters periodically and takes a mediative stance. An example is a principal who drops in on grade-level meetings or an instructional coach in a building who serves as an ex officio member of a team and utilizes coaching behaviors.

- Level Three—Another option is a more formalized coaching role where a person is designated by the group to be a coach. It may be an outside consultant who has provided training expertise to the group and then shifts to a coaching role for follow-up. Another example is a formal designation as a person to coach the group around important content, such as analyzing student work through a reflecting conversation map. Another example might be a person who works regularly with a team to collect the data they request during their meeting times followed by supporting the group in making meaning of the data. An example is coaching a school board seeking to become more collaborative in their interactions.

- Level Four—A final option is a person whose Cognitive Coaching^{SM} skills are at a level of expertise where the small group coaching role is to develop coaching skills within the group in addition to coaching the group. The intention of the coach is to develop internal capacity within the group so that the formal coaching by an outsider is no longer needed; the group becomes self-directed in using the skills of coaching. This may be officially designated after some training such as Adaptive Schools (Garmston & Wellman, 1999); or it may be more informal where the coach provides data to the team about its interaction patterns and mediates thinking about which behaviors were most productive in expanding and elevating the group's common planning, reflecting, and problem-resolving.

Although the most desirable level of small group Cognitive Coaching^{SM} is certainly to develop mediative skills within a group (Level Four), it is unlikely to be the level where most groups start. The thoughtful practitioner of Cognitive Coaching^{SM} will assess the group's level of knowledge and skill, analyze the context and the culture of the organization, negotiate with the group, and make informed decisions about what role best supports the unique needs of a group.

Coach's Capabilities

Costa and Garmston (2002) have explicated overarching capabilities a coach develops and consciously applies to maximize the impact and integrity of coaching:

- Knowing one's intentions and choosing congruent behaviors
- Setting aside unproductive patterns of listening, responding, and inquiring
- Adjusting one's style preferences
- Navigating within and among coaching maps and support functions

Drawing on individual coaching capabilities, the four group coaching capabilities listed in Figure 9-1 support effectiveness and thoughtful application of Cognitive Coaching^SM with groups.

- Knowing the group's goals and choosing coaching behaviors that mediate group and individual thinking in relation to those goals

- Monitoring and mediating the states of mind of the group and of individuals

- Monitoring and managing one's internal and external responses

- Navigating within and among maps and support functions

Figure 9-1. Group Coaching Capabilities

Mediating Group and Individual Thinking in Relation to Group Goals

Like a coach of an individual, the group coach draws on stated goals of the individual as a source for decision-making. The group coach is conscious that individual needs may not always be congruent with the greater purpose of the group. The coach elicits and acknowledges individual needs through questioning and paraphrasing, while simultaneously supporting the group in developing clarity about its shared goals. The summarize and organize paraphrase is a critical skill in synthesizing multiple perspectives. The coach checks for understanding, clarity, and agreement by posing a paraphrase such as, "There seem to be three key intentions here: to support the diversity in students, to honor developing the group, and to support individual decision-making by teachers." The coach carefully monitors the group's nonverbal and verbal responses. The coach continues to paraphrase individuals until a group "summarize and organize" or "shift focus" paraphrase receives sign-off from the group as a whole.

Attention to clarity about group goals is a dynamic process requiring constant attention and refocusing by the coach. As a group develops, its common goals are reformulated. Shared insights and analysis of data cause a group to refine and redirect its energy and intention. The group coach is monitoring for shifts in thinking and reclarifying goals on an ongoing basis to ensure group consciousness and energy focus on common goals rather than individual goals. The group coach questions and paraphrases to assist groups in differentiating individual goals from group goals, while simultaneously supporting the group and individuals in accessing the interfaces between the two.

An operating principle for the group coach is that group goals are primary and individual goals are secondary. Individual goals may drain energy from the group if they receive too much time and attention without connection to the greater purposes of the group. Some examples of mediative questions to consider when individual goals emerge and shift the focus of the group include:

- Sharon has raised an issue from her own work. How does the group see us proceeding with that issue in relation to our stated goals?

- What are some connections you see to that topic and to the goals of this group?

- How does that issue relate to and support the goals of this group?

- How can this group support you in exploring that issue for yourself?

- What might be some other venues where your concern could be explored?

The coach is challenged to honor the individual need while still mediating the group's thinking. It is a delicate balance that requires the full attention of the coach. The skilled coach mediates group consciousness to assist the group in becoming self-monitoring, self-managing, and self-modifying in relation to the need to balance individual and group goals.

Monitoring and Mediating the States of Mind of the Group and of Individuals

Cognitive Coaching^{SM} requires complex thinking on the part of the coach to attend to verbal and nonverbal feedback while simultaneously monitoring one's own metacognition. The internal thoughts of the coach require decision making about his/her response behaviors using feedback provided by the person being coached. When coaching moves from an individual to group context, the process becomes even more complicated. Assessing States of Mind of an individual requires attentive listening, sorting and categorizing, and drawing inferences about what the coachee's words reveal about deep structures. Again, taking that sophisticated listening from an individual level to a group application is cognitively challenging and complex for even the master coach.

Like the first group coaching capability related to goals, the group coach must subjugate the States of Mind of the individual to the states of mind of the group. A group may consist of 6 to 7 efficacious individuals but lack efficacy as a group. The same is true for each of the other four States of Mind. For example, a team may look at data on student performance and note individual successes in classrooms. They may simultaneously respond to the individual successes with resentment around issues related to the group's ability to have common success. Low efficacy might be manifested with statements like, "We don't all have the bilingual knowledge that teacher X has, so how can we all achieve the same results," or "You've been on the standards committee and have materials and knowledge we don't have." The coach is challenged to move the group to higher efficacy in spite of low individual efficacy and even jealousy and blame. Mediative questions might include:

- What might be some other factors that account for our differences? (flexibility, craftsmanship, consciousness)

- How could we examine the data in more depth to determine areas of concern which are common in our classrooms? (craftsmanship, interdependence)

- What characteristics of Teacher X's classroom are congruent with your classrooms? What are some areas of focus that we have control of in making modifications? (efficacy, interdependence, consciousness)

- What key questions does the group want to consider in comparing the varied data? (interdependence, consciousness, craftsmanship)

- How can we learn from the data from Teacher X and still keep our common focus? (consciousness, interdependence)

The skilled group coach will draw on the group's strengths and trust in selecting questions which support ongoing shared study and dialogue to enhance capacity in each of the states of mind.

Two tools for assessing States of Mind of groups are currently available. Garmston and Wellman (1999) explicate critical aspects of States of Mind in groups as group energy sources.

State of Mind	Manifestations in Groups
Efficacy	• Learns from its experiences and shapes itself accordingly • Productively manages the tension between the vision of the desired state and the realities of the existing state • Knows what it doesn't know, needs to know or do, and develops strategies for attainment • Focuses it resources where it can make the biggest difference • Is motivated by and committed to achieving shared goals
Flexibility	• Collectively shifts perspectives • Accesses a wide repertoire of thinking and process skills • Attends to rational and intuitive ways of working • When stuck, generates and uses multiple options for moving ahead • Navigates internal tensions related to confusion and ambiguity • Honors and utilizes diversity within the group
Consciousness	• Is aware of how its own assumptions and knowledge interfere with its learning • Is aware of its core values, norms, and group identity • Monitors congruence with its meeting standards • Is explicit and aware of its criteria for decision making • Is aware of and stands outside itself to reflect on its processes and products
Craftsmanship	• Creates, holds, calibrates, and refines performance and product standards • Envisions and manages multiple time orientations • Invests energy in honing and inventing process tools • Honors the pathway from novice to expert performance • Continuously refines inter- and intra-group communications
Interdependence	• Values its interactions and trusts the processes of dialogue • Is aware of its relationships and how its webs of interconnections are sources of mutual influence • Regards knowledge and knowing as fluid, provisional and subject to improvement from information outside itself • Regards disagreement and conflict as a source of learning and transformation for the group • Envisions the potential of the group

Figure 9-2. Group Manifestations of States of Mind

These energy source characteristics serve as a framework for the group coach for determining States of Mind of the group. The challenge for the coach is to sort group themes from individual themes. Marker words assist in doing that sort. These are words in the speaker's/group's language that provide insight into key themes and concerns. The coach asks him/herself, "What are the recurring key words, phrases, and themes being expressed over and over? How do those connect to states of mind?" "What are the differences in individual themes and group themes?" A second source for group analysis is a Team Development Survey developed by Ellison and Hayes (1998). It consists of a series of 60 questions, 12 per State of Mind. Individual and group scores are totaled and utilized as data for a group to examine its States of Mind. It is nonevaluative and serves as baseline data for the group and the coach. The scoring allows a group to develop shared consciousness and goals about its work, often moving them to become more self-directed.

Monitoring and Managing One's Internal and External Responses

The effective Cognitive Coach is highly conscious, attending to his/her own listening set asides, decision-making, judgments, personal States of Mind, and internal responses. Small group Cognitive Coaching^SM requires the same consciousness and craftsmanship at heightened levels because of the increased amounts of data coming from a group as compared to an individual.

Humans are a judgment-making species and as such internal responses are natural and common. The challenge for the coach is to monitor and manage how those internal responses are manifested in behavior. A natural tension exists between internal thoughts and external behavioral responses (Costa & Lipton, 1997). If individual makes a statement that the coach finds offensive, a choice point emerges in determining how to respond. The coach might respond with a nonverbal such as a scrunched face, with responsive words, or by doing nothing. The group coach is using enhanced consciousness to decide when to respond and how to respond. Group coaching requires intentionality in choosing the most effective verbal and nonverbal responses. Choices are based on what best serves the thinking of the group. The coach constantly attends with thoughtfulness to complex data and makes rapid-fire decisions focused on the perceived needs of the group.

A group coach is bombarded with data from the group. The group coach is unable to ignore internal thought processes that include connecting the data with prior knowledge and experiences, categorizing the information, and looking for patterns while making judgments about the meaning of the data. But s/he can manage how s/he externalizes interpretations. Humans feel what they feel and think what they think. Executive control means humans choose how to react and behave in relation to feelings and cognition. The conscious group coach carefully monitors internal reactions to each member and to the group. It is natural to be attracted by certain personalities and propensities and to be averse to others. However, the group coach maintains a stance that does not project those inner responses. The effective group coach attends to them metacognitively and plans to focus on decisions that support individuals and the group.

This capability connects directly to the third Cognitive Coaching[SM] capability of adjusting one's style preferences. To coach a group, the coach must attend to self-knowledge regarding personal style preferences, as well as individual style preferences and group style. Some individuals in the group are visual and others are auditory and kinesthetic. Using diverse language patterns serves the group. Some are task-focused and others are process-focused. The coach's questions assist the group in honoring and managing diversity.

Navigating Within and Among Maps and Support Functions

This group coaching capability parallels the individual coaching capability described by Costa and Garmston (2002). The small group coach uses the same maps as the individual Cognitive Coach—planning, reflecting, and problem-resolving. Awareness is also present about making choices among the support functions of coaching, collaborating, consulting, and evaluating.

In working with groups, the need for flexibility is enhanced. More than one train of thought is occurring simultaneously and the dynamics of the group's needs and thinking can shift rapidly. The group coach must move among the elements of the map in a fashion that follows the group's shifts and changes in direction. Similarly, what begins as a planning conversation can rapidly shift to another map such as problem-resolving based on new data introduced to the conversation. Exquisite listening and monitoring is required. Paraphrases become even more critical to ensure that both the coach and the group are understanding the developing thought processes of both individuals and the group. Metaphorically, the coach is watching the movements of the herd while monitoring the movements of each individual within the herd. The border collie never loses sight of the flock, moves it strategically, while simultaneously being conscious of, attentive to, and quick to intervene with an individual.

The group Cognitive Coach is also attending to the effects of mediation on the group's thinking, task accomplishment, and processes. Occasionally the group coach will assess that coaching may not best serve the group at that moment and will step out of coaching in order to serve the greater purposes of the group. However, a group coach would rarely become an evaluator of the group's work. The navigation between evaluation and coaching is delicate and the trust that might be compromised by such a move is hardly worth the risk. More likely, the group coach might move from Cognitive Coaching^{SM} to an intention to collaborate or to consult. The decision to do so would probably depend on how the coach was working with the group. As a group member, the shift from simply serving as a skillful mediator of thinking to collaboration or to consultation would be far more subtle and appropriate than such a shift made by a person designated with the role of group coach.

Under what circumstances might a person make a shift to collaboration or to consulting? The decision is highly contextual. Some possible conditions might be:

- The group makes a request for the shift
- An individual makes a request for the shift
- The coach senses some expertise is lacking in the group, that if added to the interaction would build the group's capacity
- The group is losing resourcefulness and a collaborative or consultative intervention will allow the group to shift back to a more capable stance

If the coach makes a decision to shift, it should be clearly communicated both verbally and nonverbally. The coach makes a shift in body position and states the intention to take a different role in the group. An example of the verbal statement is, "I have some information that would be helpful to your group's thought processes that doesn't seem to be forthcoming from any group members. I am going to share that information and my knowledge about it from a stance that is consultative. Is that acceptable to the group?" Or the coach might say, "The group appears to be uncertain about strategies to address this issue. Is that accurate? In the spirit of collaboration, I'm going to ask permission to share some thinking for your consideration. Is this acceptable to the group?" Both shifts give rationale for the coach's decision to shift and ask for permission to do so.

After making a shift to another support function, the small group coach quickly and intentionally moves back as rapidly as possible to a coaching function, knowing it best serves the group and preserves the coaching relationship. Again, the coach signals verbally and nonverbally that a change in relationship is occurring. With a shift in posture, the coach states, "I have shared some thinking and now would like to mediate your thinking." A question follows such as, "How does that information connect to your thinking? or "What thoughts does that evoke for this group?"

Possibilities and Promises
of Small Group Cognitive Coaching^{SM}

In imagining an ideal environment for developing thoughtful reflective practitioners, a vision surely includes each professional being invited to think at high levels with support for doing so. Every teacher deserves the opportunity to engage in meaningful conversations about the important work s/he does. Yet those opportunities elude most educators. It is not the fault of any individual. It is merely a lack of structure and resources dedicated to providing structures for such a way of working. Small group Cognitive Coaching^{SM} is a structure that is economical, practical, and efficient. It increases the resources in schools dedicated to reflective practice. Simultaneously, it enhances the collaborative work of teachers. The possibilities for employing small group coaching groups are endless.

A second promise of small group Cognitive Coaching^{SM} is its inherent focus on student learning. The conversations that occur among professionals are the most important medium for shared learning. Many of the conversations occurring in schools are random or unfocused. By structuring for small group conversations with shared goals and focused mediation, the emphasis on examining data and practices related to student learning is heightened. The professional conversations in schools shape and become the culture of the school. Conscious attention to those conversations is a critical strategy for reshaping school cultures.

When every staff member becomes a part of a mediated learning group with common goals, individual thought processes are reshaped. Simultaneously, groups develop shared insights that would not be accessed without small group planning, reflecting, and problem-resolving. Private practice is a norm for teachers. Collaborative practice is the norm of the future required to move classrooms from isolated entities to places of shared inquiry.

A professional is differentiated from a layperson by his/her body of knowledge specific to a discipline. Teachers have been challenged in defining themselves as professionals. Unless teachers work in a common manner like other professionals to develop a common knowledge base with shared understandings, they will continue to be questioned for their expertise. Small group Cognitive Coaching^{SM} is a means to produce shared planning, reflecting, and problem-resolving in a manner that develops common understandings and common language. When these ways of thinking and talking are habituated, a culture of professional practice is created and sustained. The habituation of thoughtful practice is essential to developing genuine professionals. The same mental dispositions developed in Cognitive Coaching^SM become models for students emulating their teachers. When students internalize those habits, they become learners. Being collaborative thinkers is among the most important work teachers can do.

References

Annenberg Protocols. (1997). Looking at student work. Available at http://www.lasw.org/protocols.html.

Bryk, A., & Schneider, B. (2002). *Trust in schools: A core resource for improvement.* New York: Russell Sage Foundation.

Costa, A., & Garmston, R. (2002). *Cognitive Coaching*^SM*: A foundation for renaissance schools* (2nd ed.). Norwood, MA: Christopher-Gordon.

Costa, A., & Lipton, L. (1997). *Holonomy: Paradox and promise.* Available at www.cognitivecoaching.com.

Ellison, J., & Hayes, C. (1998). *Team Development Survey.* Highlands Ranch, CO: Center for Cognitive Coaching.

Garmston, R., & Wellman, B. (1999). *The adaptive school: A sourcebook for developing collaborative groups.* Norwood, MA: Christopher-Gordon.

Louis, K. S., Marks, H. M., & Kruse, S. (1996). *Teacher's professional community in restructuring schools.* American Educational Research Journal, *33* (4), 757–798.

Newman, F., & Wehlage, G. (1995). *Successful school restructuring: A report to the public and education by the Center on Organization and Restructuring of Schools.* Madison, WI: Wisconsin Center for Education Research.

Smith, L. (February 7, 2001). Can schools really change? *Education Week.* Vol. 20, No. 21, pp. 30, 32, 33.

Chapter 10

Integrating Cognitive Coaching[SM] With a Framework for Teaching

By: Lynn Sawyer

Introduction

The mission of Cognitive Coaching[SM] features three important concepts: developing the cognitive capacities for self-directedness, achieving intentional holonomy, and achieving excellence. The Cognitive Coaching Foundation Seminar® focuses on understanding self-directedness and holonomy, leaving the definition of excellence to those who engage in the coaching process. One definition of excellence is provided by Charlotte Danielson (1996) in *Enhancing Professional Practice: A Framework for Teaching.* In districts where *A Framework for Teaching* is adopted, staff can use the tools of Cognitive Coaching[SM] to support the pursuit of excellence in teaching.

Lynn Sawyer, Staff Development Director in Washoe County, Nevada, was a Cognitive Coach when she became an authorized *Frameworks* trainer. From the beginning, she saw connections between Cognitive Coaching[SM] and *A Framework for Teaching* and has experienced the positive impact of coaching on the *Frameworks'* conversations in her district.

Cognitive Coaching[SM], a model that enhances professional performance by developing self-directedness, is unique in that it targets another person's thought processes as the focus of behavioral change. In and of itself, it has had a profound effect on the capacity of thousands of educators to be self-monitoring, self-managing and self-modifying. Charlotte Danielson's (1996) *Enhancing Professional Practice: A Framework for Teaching* provides a scaffolding upon which educators can build common understanding of high performance and excellence in the art and craft of teaching. Many educators are finding that professional conversations based upon issues and questions raised by the collegial examination of standards of professional practice, such as the *Framework,* to be particularly useful. This chapter explores the outcomes that resulted when Cognitive Coaching[SM] was applied to *A Framework for Teaching.*

A Foundation for Collegial Conversations

Many educators, including novice and experienced teachers, as well as their administrators, have embraced Charlotte Danielson's (1996) *Enhancing Professional Practice: A Framework for Teaching* with great enthusiasm. Put simply, it provides a structure for what teachers should know and be able to do in order to support student achievement. Danielson presents a highly accessible, concise definition and interpretation of the knowledge base on teaching. The definition of exemplary practice, or the *what* of teaching, together with the explanation of the process used to derive that definition, enable educators to advance professional learning. As they debate the levels of performance, discuss how good teaching is manifested in a variety of settings, and discuss whether or not the skills of teaching apply equally in all contexts, educators engage in professional conversation in collaboration with colleagues, and also reflect on their own practice (Danielson & McGreal, 2000, p. 26).

As Carl Glickman (2002) describes it, the *Framework* offers a comprehensive definition or classification system of the domains, components, tasks, and subtasks of the art and science of teaching. *A Framework for Teaching,* as a set of standards of professional practice for teachers, conveys to educational practitioners and to the larger community that educators hold themselves to the highest standards by establishing definitions of expertise in the field. This parallels the way that sets of standards define professions such as architecture, medicine, and accounting (Danielson, 1996).

In my work with teachers, I pose two questions to groups of teachers: "How, in the beginning of your teaching career, did you know what you were supposed to know and be able to do?" and "How did you continue to find the answers?" Some answers are predictable; a few teachers say they had a wonderful cooperating teacher during their student teaching experience who unlocked the secrets of teaching. Others cite the teacher preparation courses provided by their colleges of education. Many educators relate how they were lucky enough to have a generous mentor who thought aloud about teaching decisions and strategies—someone who was actively practicing metacognition for the benefit of the novice. Many talk about how tough it was in the beginning to realize that they didn't know everything they needed to know to teach well and how difficult it was to admit to the daunting nature of the myriad tasks of day-to-day teaching. Teachers with many years of experience relate that the complex and ever-expanding sets of skills that they are expected to possess still seem elusive to them. They actively want to know what strategies really result in learning for students, and they feel uncomfortable if they believe that there are aspects or nuances of teaching that they are unsure of or that are known by others but not themselves (Danielson, 1996).

It should be said that *any* set of teacher performance standards, either *A Framework for Teaching*, The California Standards for the Teaching Profession, to which it is related, or many others that have been formulated by school districts or educational organizations, could be the foundation for increased professional dialogue among and between teachers and school administrators. Many districts chose *A Framework* above others because it is widely known as a summary of extensive research. *A Framework*, easily generalized, can be applied to a range of individual teaching assignments including the second-grade reading specialist as well as the tenth-grade mathematics teacher.

The nearly 4000 teachers and the administrative staff in Washoe County School District, Reno, Nevada, have appreciated the value of *A Framework* as a foundation for dialogue about what constitutes adequacy or excellence in teaching (Sawyer, 2000). For them, having clearly stated teacher performance standards provides an external instrument with which to calibrate their own perceptions, thought processes, and teaching decisions. Critical dialogues based on *A Framework* helped teachers expand their own professional knowledge base for self-improvement and led us to choose it as the basis for mentor/novice interactions, teacher learning teams, and evaluation of teacher performance.

Standards of Performance
and Teaching Behavior

Many of the efforts we expend in education outside the realm of actual student interactions, such as professional development, grade-level or department meetings, teacher evaluation processes, mentoring, and professional learning teams, aim toward a common goal—the continuous improvement of professional teaching practice leading to an outcome of increased student achievement. The mission of Cognitive Coaching^{SM}, self-directedness, helps to sustain the growth in professional practice and student achievement.

Glickman (2002) asserts that educators cannot improve their craft in isolation from others and that they must have formats, structures, and plans for reflecting on, changing, and assessing their practice. Simultaneously, genuine and lasting improvement in practice comes only when the individual is self-directed, that is self-managing, self-monitoring, and self-modifying. In fact, the more external feedback such as advice or value judgments from others, the more the capacity for accurate self-assessment diminishes. As Carol Sanford (1995) states,

> The foundational element in effective work systems is self-correcting, self-managing, self-accountable, self-governing behavior. Energy spent on monitoring and attempting to affect the behavior of team members or other entities from the outside is energy wasted and energy that could be better expended on improving the business and capability of people. The critical element is to increasingly create self-governing capability.

The tension that exists when using external performance criteria while working toward the over-arching goal of self-directedness can be reconciled by committing to the practice of Cognitive Coaching^{SM}. Simply identifying standards of performance will not change teacher behavior. Coaching enhances the *what* of teaching as described in *A Framework* by providing a model for examining the *how* of teaching through professional dialogue. The Cognitive Coaching^{SM} conversations for planning, reflecting, and problem-resolving increase the likelihood that effective processes of teacher cognition will become habituated, which translates to changed practice. The value of standards of professional practice, such as *A Framework*, is increased when colleagues engage in Cognitive Coaching^{SM} because coaching enhances the intellectual capacities of teachers by mediating their thinking. *A Framework* without coaching could put the cognitively complex craft of teaching into an archaic, behavioristic model. With coaching, teaching becomes artifacts of internal mental processes, rather than a set of behaviors or skills.

Self-Directedness as the Common Outcome

Practitioners ask whether or not a particular interaction would be better served by coaching or evaluation, acknowledging specific differences between the two. Garmston and Costa (2002) identify four support functions that either peers or supervisors might engage in with a colleague: coaching, collaborating, consulting, and evaluation. When Cognitive Coaches move to the support function called *evaluation*, they are fulfilling their professional responsibility for evaluating teacher performance. School principals, assistant principals, and, in some cases, supervising teachers are required to make a summative evaluation. In those cases, evaluators find that using clearly defined external performance criteria such as *A Framework*, is a useful basis for talking about discreet teaching behaviors. Although the evaluation function is remarkably different from the coaching function in which the performance criteria is internally determined by the coachee, Cognitive Coaches rely on their skills in rapport, pausing, paraphrasing, probing, and inquiring and other tools of coaching during evaluation. It is the constant intention of the coach to mediate the internal thought process of the person being supported, believing that the individual can continue toward higher states of resourcefulness. Indeed, summative evaluation can influence a teacher's self-directedness if done in combination with structured professional coaching conversations. The practiced coach does not discard the tools of coaching during any type of professional dialogue.

With self-directedness as a primary goal, a mentor/coach may begin in the coaching model during a conversation with a novice teacher. By employing the maps and tools of coaching, for example, paraphrasing the novice's frustrations with her student's lack of attention at crucial points in the lesson may illuminate some insight about her direction-giving. If that teacher asks for hints about giving directions, the coach can move to the consulting function, offering to describe some possibilities from which the teacher might choose. Expertly moving back to coaching, the mentor assists the novice in a planning conversation about the use of direction-giving strategies.

In the basic application of Cognitive Coaching^SM, the *coachee* identifies the focus of the planning, reflecting, or problem-resolving conversations usually based on current concerns or events related to his or her teaching. One difference in applying Cognitive Coaching^SM to *A Framework* lies with how the topic for conversation is chosen from the domains, components, or elements of *A Framework*. In some cases, the particular domain may be specified by the district's evaluation schedule. For example, novice teachers may concentrate on Domain One (Planning and Preparation) and Domain Two (Classroom Environment) during the period of time before their first written evaluation is due. The person coaching, whether a mentor or supervisor, conducts a planning conversation with the novice, during which the novice is able to clarify specific outcomes, identify indicators of success, and anticipate approaches. Without the coaching process, some important cognitive processes might not occur during this crucial stage of the teacher's development in which his or her mental models are being created.

We know, through research on teacher cognition (Dahllof & Lundgren, 1970), that all behavior is based on rather simple cognitive maps of reality, that teachers talking aloud about their thinking and their decisions about teaching energizes them and causes them to refine their cognitive maps, and that invisible cognitive skills drive teaching performance. These invisible cognitive skills occur in four domains: preactive, interactive, reflective, and projective. Thinking takes place at the intersection of three ways of knowing: linguistic, nonlinguistic, and affective. Coaches take these ways of knowing into account and attend to the teacher's language, sensory memories, and feelings, which can raise these forms of knowing to a more conscious level so that the teacher can elaborate, clarify, evaluate, and alter them (Costa & Garmston, 2002).

A Coaching Conversation

By applying Cognitive Coaching^{SM} to *A Framework for Teaching*, a safe environment for exploring, connecting, experimenting, and constructing meaning of new ideas and concepts is created. Figure 10-1 provides an example of a conversation between a coach and a teacher, showing how Cognitive Coaching^{SM} and *A Framework* combine to facilitate a structured professional conversation.

Teacher's Comments	Coach's Comments	Coach's Strategy	Correlation to the Framework
I'm trying to get better control of my students. No matter what I do, they don't listen to me and they're always off task. All I seem to do is yell at them.		Listen and think about teacher's states of mind. Notices that teacher expresses low efficacy.	
	You are frustrated because you've tried several ways to get students' attention, and they aren't getting on task the way you'd like them to.	Coach paraphrases, acknowledges and labels the content and emotion.	
Yes, and I don't like the way I sound when I can't think of what to do.			
Teacher nods.	Listening to yourself, you're not satisfied with the results you're getting. Since we're working in the Domains of Teaching, let's refer to A Framework. Which of the domains seem to fit this situation?	Paraphrases, then asks question to focus teacher.	
Well, let's see. It certainly is part of classroom management. I don't seem to be making progress there, especially Component II, Managing Classroom Procedures.	So as we read the elements of that component, what hunches do you have?	Coach allows the teacher to compare what's happening to what she's reading.	Domain 2: Classroom Environment, Components 2a, and 2b: Managing Instructional Groups and Managing Transitions.

Figure 10-1. A Conversation Combining Cognitive Coaching^SM and *A Framework*

(Continued on next page)

Teacher's Comments	Coach's Comments	Coach's Strategy	Correlation to the Framework
Ugh! This is me! When I'm working with one group, the others are off task, and it's taking too long to go from one activity to another.			
	You're identifying two areas of concern: keeping students engaged and not losing instructional time during transitions.	Coach's paraphrase offers categories that help organize the topics.	Component 2c, Elements: Managing Instructional Groups and Managing Transitions.
Yes, that's exactly it! I really want to get this handled. I guess I need some new ideas.			
Absolutely!	It's important to you that your students are actively involved in what they're learning and taking responsibility for themselves in the classroom. As you think about how you'd like it to be, what kind of things will you see and hear from the students when they are as involved as you'd like?	Coach's paraphrase names the teacher's overarching goals and values. Coach assumes teacher's internal resourcefulness, and intends to assist teacher in accessing.	

Figure 10-1. A Conversation Combining Cognitive Coaching℠ and *A Framework (Continued)*

(Continued on next page)

Teacher's Comments	Coach's Comments	Coach's Strategy	Correlation to the Framework
Students would get started on their small group work without asking so many questions about what I just said. They would find their materials and begin their projects. I would be roving from group to group, checking progress. Others would stay on task. Just like it says here in A Framework, *"students productively engaged and assuming responsibility . . . maintaining momentum without need for continuous monitoring,"* that's just what I'm working towards.		Coach helps teacher to clarify student goals and identify indicators of success.	Domain 2c: Classroom Environment Components 2c, 2d, and Managing Classroom Procedures and Managing Student Behavior. Domain 3: Instruction Components 3a and 3c, Communicating Clearly and Accurately, and Engaging Students in Learning.
Nods.	So, students would be listening more carefully at the beginning and working as independent groups, knowing you'll be coming by to assist if needed. As you look ahead, what are some of the strategies you are planning?	Coach paraphrases success indicators and then asks teacher to think about action plan.	Domain 1: Planning and Preparation

Figure 10-1. A Conversation Combining Cognitive Coaching^{SM} and *A Framework (Continued)*

(Continued on next page)

Teacher's Comments	Coach's Comments	Coach's Strategy	Correlation to the Framework
Well, first I'd think about my instructions before I give them, so I won't have to repeat myself. Maybe I will have to write them on the board so students can refer to them. Also, I'll have the materials more organized so students can move right into the activity.			
	One thing you're planning is to think out your verbal instructions ahead of time, and possibly to support students by giving written hints on the board, and changing how you provide the materials. What else is occurring to you?	Coach uses presupposition question to further extend thinking.	Domain 1: Planning and Preparation Domain 2: Classroom Environment Domain 3: Instruction
At this point, I think this is going to make a big difference. I'm realizing that the chaos was caused by my lack of clarity in what I expected students to do.			
	As you make these changes in your classroom, what things will you be focusing upon for your own learning?	Coach asks teacher to consider a personal learning focus, toward the goal of self-direct-ness for the teacher.	Domain 4: Professional Responsibilities (Growing and Developing Professionally)

(Continued on next page)

Figure 10-1. A Conversation Combining Cognitive Coaching[SM] and *A Framework (Continued)*

Teacher's Comments	Coach's Comments	Coach's Strategy	Correlation to the Framework
I'm looking forward to finding out if I can get more done in the time frame if students are more on task.			Domain 4: Professional Responsibilities (Growing and Developing Professionally)

Figure 10-1. A Conversation Combining Cognitive Coaching^{SM} and *A Framework (Continued)*

In the preceding example, the teacher was able to refer to *A Framework* to narrow down the source of her frustration about classroom management issues. She used the rubric description of excellent teaching performance to clarify the goals she had for herself and her students. The coach supported the teacher's thinking by using the tools of Cognitive Coaching^{SM} to mediate her thinking, thereby developing self-directedness.

The Power of a Structured Professional Conversation

As a young teacher in the mid-1970s, I personally experienced the positive effect of structured professional conversations. Dr. Art Costa helped me to make quantum leaps in my everyday teaching practice by mediating my thinking, or cognitive processes. During a workshop he was teaching for a group of high school teachers, we learned teaching strategies for higher level thinking. It surprised me to be asked to do metacognition, to think about my own thinking, to think about what I know and how I know it. In my experience no previous teacher or class ever focused on the internal thought processes of the teacher. Dr. Costa's questions that triggered metacognition, and many other support strategies, which later came to be called Cognitive Coaching^{SM}, had a profound and continuous effect on the teaching decisions I made for my classroom teaching and, subsequently, on the way I think about the professional development activities I design for educators. It is because of the lasting effect coaching had on my capacity to be self-directed that I consider Cognitive Coaching^{SM} to be the essential model for mediating teachers' thinking about all aspects of their professional practice.

References

Costa, A., & Garmston, R. (2002). *Cognitive Coaching[SM]: A foundation for renaissance schools* (2nd ed.). Norwood, MA: Christopher-Gordon.

Dahllof, U., & Lundgren, U. P. (1970). *Macro- and micro-approaches combined for curriculum process analysis: A Swedish educational field project.* Goteborg, Sweden: University of Education.

Danielson, C. (1996). *Enhancing professional practice: A framework for teaching.* Alexandria, VA: Association for Supervision and Curriculum Development.

Danielson, C., & McGreal, T. (2000). *Teacher evaluation to enhance professional practice.* Alexandria, VA: Association for Supervision and Curriculum Development.

Glickman, C. (2002). *Leadership for learning: How to help teachers succeed.* Alexandria, VA: Association for Supervision and Curriculum Development.

Sanford, C. (1995). *Myths of organizational effectiveness at work.* Battle Ground, WA: Springhill.

Sawyer, L. (February 2001). Revamping a teacher evaluation system. *Educational Leadership.* Vol. 58, No. 5, pp. 44–47.

Chapter 11

Opening a School
With Five States in Mind

By: Sandy Ripplinger

Introduction

Most principals implement Cognitive Coaching^{SM} with an existing staff, some of whom have more of a disposition for coaching than others. What if a principal were able to select a staff, using the Five States of Mind as a filter through which interview data was passed before making hiring decisions? Chapters 11 and 12 offer glimpses into what a school might be like if a principal were able to do just that.

Chapter 11 was written by Sandy Ripplinger, a principal in Boulder, Colorado, who, when given the opportunity to open a new school, used the Five States of Mind as the organizer for each interview and themes for professional development. This chapter includes the list of qualities sought with each State of Mind, as well as the chart she used to record notes during interviews.

The States of Mind took on new meaning as sources of energy when used as a framework for hiring staff for a new school. As an experienced principal selected to open a new K–8 school in Boulder Valley School District, the questions uppermost in my mind were, "What kind of school do we want to create?" and "What kind of people do we need to hire to make it a success?"

Fortunately, during the year of construction on the school, I was released to take care of the myriad details involved in opening a new school. Most importantly, I was given the freedom to select a qualified staff. With a strong belief that all stakeholders in the school should be part of the visioning process and knowing that the time line for that visioning would extend beyond the initial hiring period, I was aware that my focus should be on hiring a staff that would be adaptable and successful in any school.

A deepened understanding of the States of Mind came with the idea of using them to hire staff members. If my ultimate goal was to bring together a high-performing group of people who could work both independently and as members of a professional learning community, it made sense that hiring people who exhibited these energy sources would start us in the right direction. An interview committee was formed to select the Initial Planning Group for the new school. Recruited to serve on the committee were in-district teachers known for their instructional expertise and parents from the school community. In a training session prior to the interviews, all committee members met and brainstormed the characteristics necessary for teachers who would open the school. Following the brainstorming session, I gave them an introductory lesson on the States of Mind. The group then melded the characteristics brainstormed with the States of Mind and developed an overall "look for/listen for" list shown in Figure 11-1.

CONSCIOUSNESS

* Problem-solver
  Reflects on implementation of standards/strategies
  Assessments—how they inform instruction
  Middle level philosophy—interdisciplinary teaching, teaching in the block
* Sense of humor
* Child advocate
  Energetic
* Leader
  Believes all kids can learn *(Continued on next page)*

Figure 11-1. Characteristics of the Five States of Mind

INTERDEPENDENCE
Team player; openness and willingness to share * Committed * Dependable * Sense of humor Communicator with all * Leader * Problem-solver Commitment to vertical learning
FLEXIBILITY
Ability to work in K–8 Creative Culturally aware (representative materials) Knowledge of developmental levels—ability to adapt Diverse thinking; conscious of differentiation * Child Advocate
EFFICACY
* Committed * Problem-solver Confident * Child advocate * Sense of humor * Leader * Dependable
CRAFTSMANSHIP
Experience (in and out of Boulder Valley School District) and initiative Detail-oriented; organized Knowledgeable in assessment, standards/strategies, curriculum, developmen- tal levels, and middle-level philosophy Expertise in technology Willingness to be a coach/club sponsor Commitment to personal professional development
Denotes qualities that apply to more than one State of Mind.

Figure 11-1. Characteristics of the Five States of Mind *(Continued)*

The next step was to develop the questions to be used for the teacher interviews. We intentionally chose questions that did not focus directly on the States of Mind; rather, we wanted to listen for words and phrases embedded in the responses given us by the candidates that would show

evidence that the States of Mind were present. Some of the words we antici-
pated listening for and that were consistently used by all candidates chosen
were: teamwork, creative, intuitive, heart, sharing, reflection, make a difference for children, problem-solvers, and learners.

Once the interview committee made its recommendations, I followed up
with reference checks and classroom visits for all finalists. The Initial Planning Group was selected following completion of all of the interviews. The
Initial Planning Group was comprised of six classroom teachers, a PE specialist, a Library Media Specialist, a counselor, and the principal's secretary.
They represented a balance of experience, diversity, and the States of Mind.
At no time was there the expectation that every staff member would have
every state of mind present and fully developed. Instead, we looked for evidence of potential in developing the energy sources. I created a chart (see
Figure 11-2) that allowed me to consider all the candidates and their strengths
in relationship to the group. The decisions were not easy ones; but after a
month of interviews, visits, and phone calls, the Initial Planning Group was
selected. My excitement was hard to contain as I counted the days until this
group of professionals, hired using the States of Mind, would meet for the
first time.

Teacher	Content Area	Interdependence	Flexibility	Craftmanship	Consciousness	Efficacy
A	PE	Has teamed w/ PE		Admin degree—strong knowledge of standards		Concrete examples of student success in class
B	PE	Experience w/teaming w/other PE, art, music, classroom	Good examples of cooperative learning	Has designed curriculum; award winning fitness program	Uses reflective language, learns from experience	Has been mentor, evidence of strong leadership
C	Special Ed.			10 years in BVSD, knows assessments, strong professional development		
D	Special Ed.	Family advocate, ARC leadership, "What do you need from me?"	Strong focus on diversity, not disability "Mostly, he's Larry." It's OK to be different.	Solid literacy technology, invites risk-taking high expectations	Uses assessment to identify breakdowns in learning	Kids are kids, teaches self-advocacy skills to students

Figure 11-2. Teacher Candidates and States of Mind Characteristics

That meeting occurred at my home on a snowy day in December. Few of the staff members knew each other, so the first order of the day involved introductions. One of our teachers was living in New York City at the time, so she joined us for part of the morning via telephone. I decided to introduce them to each other and to the States of Mind simultaneously. Using an historical perspective, I explained the States of Mind framework and showed how their selection to be part of the Initial Planning Group for this school had been intentional and made with great care. Using statements from the teachers' interviews, I explained the States of Mind one at a time, using the teachers' words as evidence that these energy sources were present to some degree in each of them. To further their understanding of the energy sources, I provided each of them with a "States of Mind Toolkit." The toolkit consisted of five items, each representing one of the energy sources: a puzzle represented interdependence, consciousness was represented by a journal, the book *The Hero's Journey* (Brown & Moffett, 1999), was the symbol of craftsmanship, a slinky represented flexibility, and a quote by Nelson Mandela ("Our deepest fear is not that we are inadequate; our deepest fear is that we are powerful beyond measure.") was framed for placing in their classroom as a reminder of efficacy. The toolkit was wrapped in a purple bag tied with a gold ribbon, our school colors. The journal was used that day for reflection and continues to be used as part of each meeting. *The Hero's Journey* has served as our metaphor for the joys and struggles of opening a new school and was the focus of our first study group.

Following that important meeting, the Initial Planning Group continued to study and internalize the States of Mind. We have revisited and deepened our understanding at each meeting and taught the framework to each interview committee. The States of Mind have clarified our recommendations and have solidified our choices. We usually waited until the end of the debrief for each candidate and then asked for each State of Mind, "What evidence do we have that this State of Mind is present in this candidate?" We then referenced the candidate's remarks (or omissions) in the interview to support our claims. On more than one occasion, teachers verbalized amazement at the power of the States of Mind. They have become part of our culture and are evidenced in all the work we do together. For example, at a recent staff meeting we were examining our current behaviors as a staff and focusing on our relative areas of strength and weakness. A discussion ensued as to whether it was all right to be satisfied with our work or whether it was important to maintain an atmosphere of dissatisfaction as we strive to improve. Using what we had learned about craftsmanship, our teachers soon realized that only by challenging our progress on a regular basis would we get better at what we're doing. Satisfaction could signal the beginning of stagnation! These types of discussions keep the States of Mind alive and deepen individual teachers' understandings.

Upon completion of the work of the interviewing and hiring, the word "Initial" was dropped; and we all became part of the "Planning Group." Teachers from the initial group took on the responsibility of welcoming new staff members by presenting them with the "States of Mind Toolkit." I have continued to make my introductions with references to States of Mind from each teacher's interview. It has become a powerful means of validation for each member of our staff and immediately extends our connections with each other. As group members leave the interviews, having made their recommendations filtered by the States of Mind, they believe that they have chosen teammates and colleagues who will help them to achieve our vision of a high performing group. They confidently take new teachers under their wing and assume personal responsibility for modeling collaboration as they participate in meaningful professional development. The excitement of our newest staff members, upon learning of the criteria upon which they were hired, strengthens and motivates those who may be "settling in." An example of this happened a few weeks ago, as a new round of interviewing was about to start. One of our recently hired teachers expressed interest in being on the interview committee. As the group shared their interest in being on the "other side of the table," this individual shared that our school's way of interviewing appeared to be unique and different from experiences he had had at other schools—he felt this was an opportunity to be part of a dynamic process that was important in helping us to achieve our vision.

Several months after our school opened, I came across the chart I had developed while hiring the Initial Planning Group. As those first teachers were hired, I had to depend more on my own thoughts and insights into the States of Mind than those of the interview committee. Although I introduced the States of Mind to the teachers and parents who worked with me in hiring the first group of teachers, I felt I was asking too much to expect them to internalize something so complex in a half-hour training. The notes I originally took were based on an intuitive response, from one interview and, in some cases, a visit to the teacher's classroom. In revisiting the chart, I was fascinated to compare those initial notes with the first-hand knowledge of the individuals after working with them for almost a year. I reflected on some of the events of the year as I reviewed the chart.

The opening of our school did not exactly proceed as planned. Our building was far from complete as the other schools in our district began the school year. A decision was made to open two weeks late; in the meantime, the teachers and I were to work off campus, planning and preparing for a school many had only seen once or twice. The building was still a "hard hat" area, and we were told we would be able to set up classrooms the day before school started. The experience was "wearing" on even the most experienced teachers. While we were preparing for the unknown, we continued to hire teachers, even after the school year "officially" began. All of us, with the additional support of approximately 100 administrators and central office staff spent a long holiday weekend unpacking two gymnasiums full of textbooks, supplies, equipment, and everything else needed to run a school. In the early evening of the night before school started, with minutes to spare and the water on site just having been approved, we hosted an open house and opened our doors for the first time.

The teachers hired for the Initial Planning Group had lived and breathed the opening of this school for almost a year by the time it finally occurred. They rose to the occasion as leaders during this stressful period, providing the energy and enthusiasm necessary to propel the staff and each other through some tumultuous times. Their collective sense of efficacy roared as they accessed resourcefulness to solve problems never experienced before. With the exception of one or two people, none of us had ever opened a school before and the questions became just as important as the answers. Flexibility was a key—we were constantly seeking alternatives and adjusting to the ambiguity of our situation. Interdependence was evident over and over again—teachers formed an assembly line to move furniture to an upper floor when the elevator broke down, they set up their own classrooms quickly and then offered to help in other ways to assure that everyone would be ready for students. We were tired but happy when that day finally came.

Although our opening days provided some data as to the future success of this group, I knew that the real challenges were ahead of us. Once the adrenaline wore off and reality set in, how would the staff respond? One of my biggest challenges was helping the group maintain balance and a sense of being grounded during those opening months. The staff worked hard and overcame incredible obstacles—missing materials important to classroom instruction, no gymnasium, classrooms that were freezing one day and over 100 degrees the next.

When it came time for a retreat in January, it should not have been a surprise to me that there was some resistance. The retreat had been planned and placed on the calendar by the Initial Planning Group in the Spring before we opened. At that time, it was seen as an opportunity to refocus on what was important to us as a staff, following the opening of school. We didn't anticipate the anxiety that accompanied that event, however, and never considered that there would be any who would not support a day devoted to our own learning. It became evident that it was difficult for some teachers to give up time that could be spent in the classroom (needs of self) to talk about our history, our culture, and our purpose (needs of the group). This was to be a day of increased consciousness for all of us; their resistance made it even clearer to me that we needed a day to refocus.

To perpetuate our purpose, we spent the morning of our retreat bringing our newest teachers "onboard." We introduced the states of mind, and I gave them each their "Toolkit." Members of the Initial Planning Group were introduced for the last time and thanked for their hard work in opening the school. They each took a few minutes to share their memories and reflections of the past year and, in doing so, built the history for the rest of the group. We briefly revisited the questions asked in an Adaptive School (Garmston & Wellman, 1999): "Who are we? Why are we doing this?" and "Why are we doing this, this way?" Then a group of teachers used a chapter from *The Hero's Journey* (Brown & Moffett, 1999) to model a Socratic Seminar. It was a powerful learning experience for all of us, both in the connectedness of our work as a heroic journey and in the effectiveness of the Socratic Seminar as a comprehension strategy. Following the session, a poll was taken as to the number of teachers who would be interested in participating in the optional 24-hour training in Socratics. The majority of the staff raised their hands, evidence of this group's efficacy, craftsmanship and their commitment to their own professional growth.

The afternoon was spent acknowledging our accomplishments and looking toward the future. As part of our culture, we reflected at the end of the day and shared our new learnings. Some of the teachers' reactions were: "As much as I didn't want to go, I can see now how valuable the day was." "I'm looking at every person I see today in a new way." It was an incredible day and provided the balance necessary to reenergize us for the remainder of the school year.

Recently, as we were participating in K–8 staff development focused on literacy, the facilitator asked our staff to journal. Within a minute, the teachers were all engaged in writing about the experience and the room was silent. The facilitator came to me later and expressed her amazement. She said, "I've never seen a staff quiet down so quickly and start journaling. Most of groups talk and never get to it." I see it as evidence of States of Mind—a group committed to its own craftsmanship, and consciousness.

So, how did my notes validate my thinking on the first teachers hired? Did my chart show me that I could trust my insights? Absolutely!! I never set out to hire people who had all of the States of Mind developed to their fullest capacity. I was looking for those who had the potential for growth in these areas. In almost every case, I can look at the notes I took identifying the person's stronger resources and see evidence in their behavior and work that support my initial thinking. Two questions that I asked myself when I decided to use this filter were, "Would we hire a group that lacked diversity?" "Would everyone be the same?" I'm happy to say that we have a staff of very diverse thinkers. It's a strong group of educator, each coming from different backgrounds with different ideas of how to do things. That is one of our greatest strengths and one of our greatest challenges. We recently began learning the skills of collaboration, and I look forward to watching the group grow as they learn more about how to collaborate.

Another powerful lesson for me has been that of watching the culture develop. We used the States of Mind as a filter in hiring 95% of the teaching staff—how are the other teachers adapting? As we revisited the states of mind with staff, it has been important to stress that we are looking toward the development of all of these energy sources within all of us. We are also shifting the focus from what these energy sources look like in individuals to what how they emerge and develop in groups. It's a natural shift to take when teaching the skills of collaboration. Meanwhile, I think we have validated everyone's strengths and created a cohesive, inclusive staff.

I recently received an e-mail from a teacher that began, "My sense of efficacy is being challenged, and I'd like to talk with you about it." As we begin to use the language and internalize the States of Mind by making connections with what happens in our school on a regular basis, I expected to see even more evidence of our success. The more we work with it, the clearer it becomes. Several weeks ago a teacher who was part of the Initial Planning Group approached me and said, "We're going to use the States of Mind as we hire our new teachers this year, aren't we?" She breathed a sigh of relief when I assured her that we would not give up a successful strategy. An added bonus has been the validation and empowerment given the teachers hired through this purposeful process.

Time will tell if using the States of Mind to select individual staff members will help us develop into a high performing group of professionals. Already I know that this is an efficacious group, one that truly believes they have the ability to create something special at our school. They are also interdependent and believe in working together. The States of Mind used as sources of energy for hiring individuals will continue as the sources of energy we draw on as we strive for excellence as a professional learning community.

References

Brown, J. L., & Moffett, C. A. (1999). *The hero's journey.* Alexandria, VA: Association for Supervision and Curriculum Development.

Garmston, R., & Wellman, B. (1999). *The adaptive school: A Sourcebook for developing collaborative groups.* Norwood, MA: Christopher-Gordon.

Chapter 12

Teacher Recruitment
in an International Setting

By: William Powell

Introduction

Chapter 12 was written by Bill Powell, an international schools educator, who values the States of Mind as resources which support the spirit of inclusion that is so critical in an international school setting. This chapter includes questions and scenarios used to hire teachers.

One of the most profound challenges that face school leadership is the identification and recruitment of outstanding educators. High quality schools, particularly those that welcome exceptional students, do not just happen. They cannot be mandated by a central office, and they do not seem to result from formulaic reform and restructuring recipes. High quality schools do not just spring forth like blossoming flora following a desert cloudburst. Such schools are created—dare we say manufactured—usually slowly and quietly, through the skilled and caring craftsmanship of master teachers and administrators. The process begins with recruiting, interviewing, and hiring prospective teachers.

For international schools[1], often located in remote areas of the world, there is an even greater challenge—to identify those individuals who have inclusive values and teaching strategies and to ascertain that there is a match between the prospective teacher and the country and culture. The principles of Cognitive Coaching[SM] have provided a valuable framework for this process, producing outstanding results at the International School of Tanganyika, Ltd. (IST), Dar es Salaam, where I served as an administrator.

A Philosophy of Inclusion

Inclusion, as the term is being used in this chapter, is an attitude and not a dogma. It is a frame of mind that presumes a sense of belonging and membership. An inclusive school begins with the assumption that every child is a member in good standing and has a right to be welcomed into a safe, secure, and personally meaningful school community. Not every school can provide for the needs of every child, but every school can *start* from a presumption of membership and belonging. Such a safe, secure, and meaningful school community is created by individuals who share common values and attitudes about education and about children. The States of Mind of Cognitive Coaching[SM] (Costa & Garmston, 2002) have served as a common set of values and attitudes around which to recruit, interview, and hire teachers.

The school philosophy can be the single most important document in the recruitment of an outstanding teaching staff. It makes explicit the values and practices, the traditions and shared attitudes of the school community. A carefully crafted school philosophy will include statements about:

- Why we educate children
- What we hope that education will achieve
- What that education will include
- How that education will be planned and structured
- Who will be invited to participate in that education
- What we will strive for in our relationships

More than all the glossy photographs and impressive "league-table" test scores, a well thought out, articulate school philosophy will attract the kind of teachers for which high quality, inclusive schools are searching.

Assumptions

A school philosophy contains assumptions about children, about teachers, and about learning. This chapter also contains assumptions about inclusive education. They are

- All children can, do, and will learn.
- Effective teachers can teach most children.
- Diversity enriches children's and adults' learning.
- Strategies that define and comprise good teaching are applicable to all children (and adults).
- A professional partnership is exponentially more effective (and more satisfying) than the sum of its parts.

Inclusive Teachers and the Five States of Mind

The five assumptions were integrated into a recruitment strategy at IST that has as its overarching goal the continuous process of moving the school towards becoming a genuine community of learners. The work of Costa and Garmston (2002), especially the Five States of Mind, was particularly useful in developing a recruiting profile for IST. They constitute the attributes of vital, effective members of a learning organization. As "a force directing one towards increasingly authentic, congruent, ethical behavior, the touchstones of integrity" (Costa and Garmston, 1994, p. 134), the States of Mind were most useful in constructing our profile of an outstanding, inclusive educator.

Efficacy

Why would an inclusive school want to recruit efficacious teachers? Research has shown direct correlations between: (a) individual efficacy and teacher effectiveness and (b) organizational efficacy and school success. Teacher efficacy has been shown to have a profound effect upon improved student learning particularly in the area of basic skill mastery (Rosenholtz, 1989) and has been identified as a vital factor in the successful implementation of educational change (Fullan, 1982). The Rand Corporation found that teacher efficacy was the single most consistent variable related to school success (Berman & McLaughlin, 1977).

Efficacious teachers are resourceful. When I first arrived in Tanzania in the early 1980s, the government followed a policy of radical socialism and food and consumer goods were very scarce. Rationing was in effect for even basic commodities such as rice, flour, and cooking oil. A colleague of ours came to the conclusion that, "If we can't buy sugar and soap in the shops, we simply need to open our own store." Charlye's logic was that we were more likely to procure basic staples if we bought in bulk directly from the wholesaler. Charlye was an efficacious individual who, recognizing a need, had the confidence in himself to bring change to a situation. It was not long afterwards that the teachers at The International School Of Tanganyika opened their own cooperative shop (G.R.A.B.—Group Resource Acquisition Bureau) where members were able to obtain basic commodities on a regular basis.

Flexibility

Flexibility of mind is crucial for the truly inclusive teacher, and it may be one of the highest states of intelligent pedagogical behavior. Flexibility requires a person to step beyond and outside of the shell of self. It requires the individual to view a situation from a multitude of different perspectives. In the wake of *El Nino's* visit to Africa in 1997, there was severe drought in the south of Tanzania. A geographer colleague in the social studies department wanted 10th-grade students to develop a meaningful, personal project that would bring home to them what it meant for people to live at the mercy of unpredictable weather patterns. Together with his students, he planned a pilot, small-scale, perma-culture farm project in a leprosy village 6 hours south of Dar es Salaam. Students were involved in every stage of the project— in discussions with village elders, in clearing land, planting drought resistant crops, and thinking of ingenious ways to defend the crops against bands of marauding wild bush pigs. This colleague had found a way to combine the curriculum with existing weather conditions and make the program personally meaningful to the students. He had been flexible in his thinking by implementing a project that required the students to view a situation from a different perspective.

Craftsmanship

The pursuit of craft perfection is as old as our species and our myths are replete with stories that praise the skill and the wisdom of our master craftsmen. In ancient Greece, the master artificer was represented in the Icarus and Daedalus story. The lure and the danger of the pursuit of craft perfection were poignantly displayed in Icarus's fatal plunge into the Ionian Sea and in the ancient Persian custom in which the master carpet maker would deliberately include one mistaken knot into an otherwise flawless creation. Whether in art, music, sports, or business, the master craftsman in his or her pursuit of perfection continues to feature among our most popular hero figures.

When recruiting inclusive teachers, it is vital to remember that the most successful teachers may be those who are also the most dissatisfied with their own work. Appropriate self-criticism can be a valuable attribute. One fourth-grade teacher, already considered a master teacher, attended a series of workshops in which she learned new strategies for grouping students. "In the past I always let the students choose their own groups," she said towards the end of the workshop, "but I have a feeling that varying the groupings would be good for them." Although not confident how her efforts would turn out, she attempted the strategies for mixed grouping that she had learned at the workshop and then reflected on her efforts—what had worked, what hadn't worked, and what she needed to try the next time.

Consciousness

Examining the critical role of consciousness within the framework of inclusive teaching and learning, its complexity becomes self-evident. Consciousness is the construction of meaningful knowledge about the world around us, our immediate environment, our workplace, and our family. It is also the interior knowledge of thoughts, our feelings, hidden anxieties, fleeting impressions, and ourselves. In short, consciousness is deliberate attention to events that are both internal and external.

A mathematics teacher, coming from a strict, traditional, and authoritarian society, began to be troubled by his relationships with his students. He recognized that there was a distance in those relationships that he wished to overcome. He was puzzled that students sometimes misread him, taking him seriously when he was joking and thinking that he was joking when he was actually serious. He began to observe other teachers' relationships with students, sitting in on their classes and watching their interactions. At the beginning of the next year, he resolved to make developing positive relationships with his students one of his professional goals. He asked colleagues to help him reflect on his interactions so that he might learn how to modify his own behavior in order to develop more positive relationships with his students.

Reflective consciousness is vitally important in teaching and learning, especially in an international setting where cultural awareness of self and others is critical to success. One way to gain a window into the reflective consciousness of a prospective teacher is to end a formal interview five or ten minutes before the appointed time, announce that the interview is over, and suggest taking a few minutes to reflect upon how the interview itself has gone. Was it what the candidate had expected? Were there any questions that had not been asked of the candidate that should have been?

Interdependence

The traditional isolation of teachers is legendary and has contributed significantly to a lack of individual efficacy, low staff morale, widespread teacher burnout, the absence of a sense of professional belonging, and the resistance of schools to positive change (Kusuma-Powell & Powell, 2000; Lortie, 1975; Sarason, Levine, Godenberg, Cherlin, & Bennet, 1966).

Fortunately, what we now know about collaboration between teachers suggests a way forward, an opportunity to harness the immense energy that is released when dedicated and skilled craftsmen come together to creatively plan and to teach. The foundation of this recently emerging collegiality is interdependence, the understanding that within an inclusive school it is natural that one should give and receive help (Kusuma-Powell & Powell, 2000).

Interdependence is the profound understanding that human beings need each other. "A Field Trip to South Africa" describes a time when a learning situation was punctuated by the giving and the receiving of help.

A Field Trip to South Africa

The interdisciplinary field trip had been organized by 3 teachers and had involved almost 30 international school students. They would spend a week in the Johannesburg/Pretoria area, combining the study of history, psychology, and biology. The trip was carefully planned and included visits to historical sites, research at the University of Pretoria, lectures, a tour of Soweto, meetings with political leaders, and even a first-hand observation of a radical prostatectomy at Pretoria Urology Hospital.

Everyone was troubled at the end of the second day, students and teachers alike, probably the most distressed were Annelise and Stephanie, two White South African 12th graders who had just walked out of the evening's class meeting. The second day had been taken up mostly by an historical tour of Pretoria. The tour had focused exclusively on White South African history and had culminated at the Voertrekker Monument, in front of which is a large statue of a White woman standing with her two children.

The White South African guide explained that the woman symbolized "the bringing of light to the Dark Continent." The international school students, many of whom were African, Asian, or mixed race, listened in stony silence.

Before the class that evening, the 3 teachers met in closed session. They recognized that they had to address the racism that the students had encountered during the day. While nothing had been said so far, the teachers agreed that a number of the students showed signs of hurt, outrage, and even anger at what they had experienced. The teachers planned how they would handle the class. It was agreed that the social studies teacher would introduce the topic by attempting to create an historical context for apartheid. The psychology teacher would then pose a series of critical thinking questions that related to what they had seen and heard (and what they had failed to see) and their perceptions of it. The biology teacher was to monitor the emotional climate of the class, particularly the two White South African girls who were clearly proud of their country and pleased to show it off to their foreign classmates.

As was predicted by the teachers, many of the students were upset and hurt by the tour. Once the subject had been introduced, a number of the students spoke passionately of the one-sidedness and bias that the tour represented and the deep resentment that they felt

Annelise and Stephanie were silent and withdrawn until just before the end of the class meeting, when both rose and walked out of the conference room. The biology teacher waited a few minutes before following them to their hotel room to help them process the hurt and disappointment that they were feeling.

At the same time, the social studies and psychology teachers asked the remainder of the students why they thought Annelise and Stephanie had walked out. A discussion ensued which ended with several of the non-White students planning to deliberately to include Annelise and Stephanie in the class's activities the following day.

Two weeks later, after the students had returned home to Dar es Salaam, Annelise confided to her biology teacher that she had seen South Africa for the first time through non-White eyes, and she had learned a lot about her country and about herself.

Meeting the educational needs of diverse learners (for example, children with learning problems or with English as a Second Language) is a challenge; and when it fails, it often does so because individuals have tried to go it alone, having assumed a heroic but foolishly solitary responsibility for each and every child. It is not only children who belong in inclusive schools, teachers do so as well; and that sense of belonging comes from a shared mission and collaboration with teaching colleagues. Interdependence is not a naturally occurring state but a series of sophisticated and complex learned behaviors. It is nothing less than an explicit statement about how we choose to perceive, value, and interact with the rest of our species and, in doing so, how we choose to define ourselves.

Interviewing for Inclusion

When recruiting teachers for an inclusive school (particularly an inclusive international school), there is no substitute for a face-to-face interview. Too much of what is "said" is spoken silently through body language. Researchers suggest that more than 65% of our communication may be conducted through nonverbal behaviors (Burgoon, Buller, & Woodall, 1989). The face-to-face interview provides an opportunity to assess the candidate against an inclusive profile such as that provided in Costa and Garmston's (2002) five states of mind.

In recruiting for an inclusive school, content and pedagogical knowledge are important to balance and strengthen the collaborative work of grade-level teams. But, although specialization and content area expertise are important, they are not sufficient in and of themselves. Equally important are the five states of mind, for it is these energy sources that will ensure the work of a cohesive and productive team, able to capitalize on the strengths of all its members.

The purpose of such a selection interview is for two people in a relatively short period of time to gather as much information as possible about each other. As such, interview questions should provide the candidates with an opportunity to open a window into who they are—how their mind works, what their values are, their degree of subject area mastery, why they entered education, and why they like working with children. The interviewer also needs to be sensitive to cultural considerations, which cause certain questions to be inappropriately personal in specific contexts.

Interview questions should probe and challenge, and the interviewer's body language and tone of voice should reassure and establish a climate of rapport and trust. In this regard, the Cognitive Coaching^SM verbal and nonverbal strategies for enhancing rapport can be most valuable. If the interview questions are sufficiently challenging, the interviewer will also need to be encouraging. The purpose of the interview is not to trick the candidate; on the contrary, the purpose is to create an atmosphere of relaxed alertness in which the candidate will do his or her very best. The staff at IST has become particularly partial to questions that are based upon brief scenarios. This type of question demands on-the-spot thinking and judgment and provides an excellent window for coming to know the candidate and what he or she stands for. We have included several such scenarios in the sample interview question section at the end of this chapter.

How do our five assumptions about inclusive schools help to integrate and frame an effective interview?

1. All children can, do, and will learn (focus is on learning).
   - Optimism
   - Efficacy
   - Value placed upon democracy
   - Sense of belonging and membership
   - Secure and trusting class climate
   - Flexibility
   - Teacher relationship with students—partnership
   - Fairness—how does it "work" in an inclusive classroom?
   - Thorough practical knowledge of learning theory.

2. Effective teachers can teach most children (focus is on teaching).
   - Self-confidence, efficacy
   - Internalized locus of control and self-motivation
   - Expertise in or previous experience with exceptional children
   - Flexibility of approach
   - Subject area mastery
   - Wide repertoire of creative, engaging teaching strategies
   - Passion/enthusiasm for learning
   - Teacher knows his/her own preferred learning styles and how they effect his/her teaching
   - Empathy

- Reflectiveness and self-renewal
- Consciousness of self and others

3. Diversity enriches (focus is on consciousness).
   - Cultural sensitivity
   - Empathy that extends across linguistic and cultural barriers
   - An openness and appreciation of differences
   - A tolerance of frustration
   - The ability to delay gratification
   - Self-confidence
   - Flexibility of perspectives

4. Strategies that define and comprise good teaching are applicable to all children and adults (focus is on craftsmanship).
   - Mastery of subject/content area
   - Thorough knowledge of the variety of ways in which children learn
   - Knowledge of constructivism and brain based teaching
   - Creating relevance and connectedness
   - Flexibility
   - Awareness of multiple intelligences
   - Appreciation of different learning styles
   - Ability to identify and start with the large concepts

5. A professional partnership is exponentially more effective and satisfying than the sum of its parts (focus is interdependence).
   - Interpersonal skills and sense of collegiality
   - Collaboration and teamwork
   - Flexibility
   - Consciousness of self and others

- Idealism and optimism
- Shared values and vision
- Common goals
- Tendency towards presuming positive intentions in others
- Trust and mutual support
- Self-confidence and humility

Sample Interview Questions

What follows are some sample interview questions which we have used with some success in the past.

1. If I were to visit your classroom next week, what would I see? (flexibility, craftsmanship, consciousness)

2. Tell me about a mistake you have made recently in your teaching and what you have done about it. (efficacy, flexibility, consciousness)

3. Describe to me how you would teach the concept of _____ (e.g., the seasons, absolute zero, the Third World, the beauty of mathematics, tragedy, the interdependence of global supply and demand). (craftsmanship, consciousness, flexibility)

4. How would you respond to the following student question: "Why are we studying _____ (e.g., quadratic equations, *Romeo and Juliet*, entropy)." Is the student's question fair? (flexibility, consciousness, interdependence)

5. What are the most influential factors in the success or failure of a lesson? (craftsmanship, consciousness, interdependence, flexibility)

6. What specific strategies do you use to ensure that your students are engaged in active learning? (craftsmanship, flexibility)

7. If I were the parent of a child who learns differently, why would I want my child in your class? (consciousness, flexibility, efficacy)

8. What specific aspects of your teaching are you currently working to improve? (efficacy, craftsmanship, consciousness)

9. How has recent educational research affected your teaching? (craftsmanship, consciousness)

10. Sentence completion questions:
    - When I am criticized . . . (efficacy, consciousness)
    - When I am not sure about something . . . (interdependence, efficacy, consciousness)
    - When I am told what to do . . . (consciousness, interdependence)
    - When someone doesn't agree with me . . . (flexibility, efficacy)

11. What are your preferred learning styles? (consciousness, craftsmanship, flexibility)

12. How do you know that you are continuing to learn how to learn? (consciousness)

13. What is the most significant learning experience of your life? (efficacy, flexibility, craftsmanship, consciousness, interdependence)

14. What do your students learn from you that you do not explicitly teach? (consciousness)

15. All egos require gratification. What satisfies yours? (consciousness, efficacy, flexibility)

16. Give me a metaphor for a _____ (e.g., pre-school child, middle school student, high school student.) (flexibility, consciousness)

17. What is the most important outcome for a parent conference? What strategies do you use to accomplish this outcome? (efficacy, interdependence, flexibility, craftsmanship)

18. Develop a higher level critical thinking question that is related to _____ (e.g., the AIDs epidemic, human rights, ocean tides, Romantic poetry). (craftsmanship)

19. What is the most difficult aspect of co-planning and co-teaching? How have you addressed this issue? (craftsmanship, interdependence, flexibility)

20. What does differentiated instruction mean? Can you give me a recent example of how you have provided individual accommodation to make a lesson more accessible for an exceptional student? (flexibility, craftsmanship, consciousness)

Sample Interview Scenarios

Some of the longer scenarios can be given to candidates in advance of the interview so they have a chance to prepare.

1. You have prepared a brilliant lesson plan, but when you reach the classroom (candidate's choice of subject and age level) you find your briefcase empty except for a large potato. How do you use the potato to teach _____ (mathematics, reading, music, etc.)? (flexibility, craftsmanship, efficacy)

2. It is seven weeks after the start of the school year and your class has just begun to bond nicely. A group identity is emerging. The principal informs you that a monolingual Japanese child will be joining your class next week. How do you respond? What preparations might you make? (flexibility, interdependence, craftsmanship)

3. As you know, professional development is very important at our school. Let's imagine that you have been appointed as a teacher and have enrolled in a graduate level course entitled "Recent Developments in Neuro-Psychology." The course is taught by a professor from a leading U.S. university and 30 other teachers are in the class. Twenty-five minutes into the first lecture you find yourself completely lost. What do you do? (efficacy, consciousness)

4. Reflect back on a recent field trip you have organized. What large concepts were you attempting to teach? How did you make the trip relevant for the students? What other implicit learning objectives did the trip include? What learning took place on the trip that surprised you? (craftsmanship, consciousness, flexibility)

5. Nishad's mother is waiting to see you for a parent conference. Nishad is in the fifth grade and is struggling in

virtually all his subjects. His frustration threshold is low, and you have noticed an increasing number of temper outbursts. Nishad has not been formally assessed for a learning disability. Informal observation suggests he is reading on a first- or second-grade level. He steadfastly refuses to write but loves to draw pictures in art. He is constantly losing his books and papers. Nishad's mother is a single parent. She is aggressive and domineering and blames the school for Nishad's difficulties. She has her heart set on Nishad becoming a medical doctor. What specific objectives would you have for the parent conference? What specific strategies might you use? (consciousness, craftsmanship, interdependence)

6. Shamneez is a hardworking, although somewhat withdrawn, 12-year-old student in your class. At the end of today's lesson she tells you that she will be absent from school tomorrow because her god is arriving on the KLM flight tomorrow morning. She has to be at the airport to meet him. How do you respond, and what do you do next? (flexibility, consciousness)

7. Marina poses a problem in terms of admission and placement, and your advice has been sought. Originally, Marina comes from a primitive hunter-gatherer tribe in the remote southern islands in the Philippines. Her first language was her tribal mother tongue. Following the death of her parents, Marina at age 7 was moved to an orphanage in Manila where she was spoken to exclusively in Tagalog. Two years later, she was adopted by German missionaries and began to learn German. Marina is age appropriate for the 7th grade, but there are serious questions whether or not she can cope with the level of work. Physically mature, Marina is socially quite shy and withdrawn. What advice would you give about her admission? About her placement? (flexibility, interdependence, craftsmanship)

8. Matthias is a learning-disabled child in the third grade. He was evaluated and diagnosed some 12 months ago and since that time has been making excellent progress in your class. This has been due in large part to the partnership you have formed with Matthias's mother. You

have worked closely with her and a trusting friendship has resulted. Matthias understands that he learns differently than other children in the class. However, he also believes that he is a capable student who can succeed in school. The school year is coming to an end and Matthias's mother requests that he be retained in the third grade next year. You are puzzled by the request and telephone her about it. When questioned further, Matthias's mother bursts into tears and admits that her concern centers on the personality of the one fourth-grade teacher who has a reputation for no nonsense discipline and sarcasm. What do you say to Matthias's mother? What do you do next? (consciousness, interdependence, flexibility)

9. Carmen is in your ninth-grade homeroom. Her last report card was mixed but the comment of her music teacher has stayed with you: "Carmen continues to function adequately in music, but I sense there is a wealth of untapped talent—not just musical talent, intellectual talent—which we, as her teachers are missing. I have watched Carmen take a back seat to her peers in class discussions and projects. It is almost as though if she showed herself to be gifted, this would in some way ostracize her from her peers." Her English teacher was more prosaic: "Carmen is an above average student who is going through all the usual ninth grade girl-boy stuff which is, of course, interfering with her school work." Last year, Carmen won a prize for writing an operetta entitled "Codex 1181," a work inspired by the 1633 trial of Galileo Galilei. Last month, Carmen's father wrote to the school complaining that his daughter was not being assigned homework. Last week, Carmen was found smoking in the girl's toilet. Yesterday she cut school and was suspended by the principal. As her homeroom teacher, what might you do? (consciousness, flexibility, interdependence)

10. Stefano joined the school earlier this year as an ESL student in your 6th-grade class. Before entering the school, Stefano spoke almost no English. His previous schooling was in Italian, and his reports indicate that he had been an

above average student. The transfer to the present school has been a difficult one for Stefano. He left a close circle of friends in Italy and for the first few weeks appeared insecure and reticent. In addition to his regular schooling, Stefano attends Italian language classes twice a week and on Saturday mornings goes to catechism class. At the present time, Stefano's English is insufficient for him to deal with the abstract concepts that he will have to encounter in the 7th grade. The question you have been asked to address is whether Stefano should begin the study of a foreign language in the 7th grade. His father wants him to study French. The guidance counselor believes that an additional language will simply serve to confuse him and that Stefano should use the time for additional English. (consciousness, flexibility, interdependence)

Conclusion

Given the importance of what is at stake—children's learning—it makes no sense that teacher recruitment should be left to unexamined practice. From anecdotal evidence gathered from teacher candidates at international recruitment centers, the quality of much interviewing and candidate evaluation appears to be superficial. Furthermore, from discussions with the recruiters themselves there appears to be a level of insecurity and discomfort about the entire recruitment process. One headmaster of a large international school summed up his annual recruiting foray as "avoiding the turkeys and nailing the stars."

Masterful teaching in a diverse setting is one of the most complex and demanding professional activities that an individual can be called upon to perform. Recent research into constructivist learning theory—the role of emotions in learning, critical thinking, and the biology of the brain—confirm how enormously complex learning and teaching actually are (Caine & Caine, 1991, 1997). To find individuals who will combine innate talents and intelligences, cherished values and humane dispositions, content area expertise with empathetic and reflective pedagogical practice is a challenge of the highest order.

For years the challenge of quality teacher recruitment has been taken up without much critical examination. The assumption was that experienced school administrators would intuitively know a quality practitioner when they saw one—and this may be what in some cases actually happened. However, with so much at stake, we suggest that it is time for teacher recruitment to undergo a rigorous explication and that the principles of Cognitive Coaching[SM] offer an excellent starting point for this important work.

Endnote

[1] The examples cited in this chapter are taken from The International School of Tanganyika Ltd. (IST), Dar es Salaam, Tanzania, in which the author served as an administrator.

References

Berman, P., & McLaughlin, M. W. (1977). *Federal program supporting educational change: Factors affecting implementation and continuation.* Santa Monica, CA: Rand.

Bargoon, J. K., Buller, D. B., & Woodall, W. G. (1989). *Nonverbal communications: The unspoken dialogue.* New York: Harper & Row.

Caine, R. N., & Caine, G. (1991). *Making connections: Teaching and the human brain.* Alexandria, VA: Association for Supervision and Curriculum Development.

Caine, R. N., & Caine, G. (1997). *Education on the edge of possibility.* Alexandria, VA: Association for Supervision and Curriculum Development.

Costa, A., & Garmston, R. (1994). *Cognitive Coaching[SM]: A foundation for renaissance schools.* Norwood, MA: Christopher-Gordon.

Fullan, M. (1982). *The meaning of educational change.* New York: Teachers College Press.

Kusuma-Powell, O., & Powell, W. (2000). *Count me in! Developing inclusive international schools.* Washington, DC: Office of Overseas Schools, U. S. Department of State.

Lortie, D. (1975). *School teacher: A sociological study.* Chicago: University of Chicago.

Rosenholtz, S. (1989). *Teachers' workplace: The social organization of schools.* New York: Longman.

Sarason, S., Levine, M., Godenberg, I., Cherlin, D., & Bennet E. (1966). *Psychology in community settings: Clinical, educational, vocational and social aspects.* New York: John Wiley & Sons.

Part 3

Classroom Applications

A culture is strongest when the values and beliefs are aligned throughout all facets of the organizational environment. A culture sustains its values and beliefs by passing them on to its children. Without applying Cognitive Coaching[SM] in the classroom, there is a flaw in the fabric of the organization. The values and beliefs of Cognitive Coaching[SM] will live and die with the adults in the system.

This section represents a challenge for the coaching community in that few practitioners have translated the adult coaching work into their interactions with students in a formal way. Many teachers use the principles of Cognitive Coaching[SM] intuitively or informally with their students. The practitioners featured in this section, however, have applied Cognitive Coaching[SM] in a deliberate, intentional way to determine how it might affect student learning. One chapter extends this work into interactions with parents; the other two chapters focus on adapting the maps and tools of Cognitive Coaching[SM] for use with students.

Chapter 13

Using Cognitive Coaching^{SM} in Parent-Teacher Conferences

By: Jane Ellison and Carolee Hayes

Introduction

As Cognitive Coaching^{SM} permeates the culture of a school and becomes a part of the way staff interacts with each other, that way of communicating is also extended to parents and community members as they interact with school staff. When applied to communication with parents, the community at large as well as the school staff experiences the benefits of coaching. Perhaps the most basic unit in any school's communication with those outside the school is the parent-teacher conference. Applying Cognitive Coaching^{SM} to this key form of communication enhances parents' understanding of their child's learning, their teacher's interpersonal communication skills, and the school's norms of thinking and collaboration.

While working in Douglas County Schools in Castle Rock, Colorado, Jane Ellison and Carolee Hayes developed a map teachers could use to integrate the principles and practices of Cognitive Coaching^{SM} into their parent conferences. The map merges the elements of the three Cognitive Coaching^{SM} maps with the concept of shared understanding and agreement on the meaning of data. The tools used to navigate the map are those familiar to a cognitive coach, with special emphasis on when and how to use them. The authors are interested in further anecdotal evidence of use of this map; please contact us at ccsjane@aol.com or ccscarolee@aol.com.

When Cognitive Coaching℠ is woven into a school's culture, it not only changes the way teachers and administrators interact but also the way school staff and parents interact. One application of the maps and tools of Cognitive Coaching℠ is in parent-teacher conferences. All the tools and many of the elements of the Cognitive Coaching℠ maps can be used to support the relationship and thinking of the most important individuals in a child's education.

The Parent-Teacher Conference Map is designed explicitly to embed the core values and principles of Cognitive Coaching℠ into a common practice in schools. It provides a structure for working more effectively with parents in partnership to support student learning at high levels of achievement. The Parent-Teacher Conference Map is a tool for working holonomously, serving the student from one's best professional practices while simultaneously serving the student as part of a larger system including family and home.

Assumptions of the Map

The first of four Cognitive Coaching℠ capabilities is to "know one's intentions and choose congruent behaviors" (Costa & Garmston, 2002). In developing a map for parent-teacher conversations, a key step was to address intentions. In thinking about working with parents, one cannot assume the specific needs or intentions until entering into the territory of the conversation. This map assumes flexibility in assessing intentions before and during the conference. The teacher enters the conversation with neutrality, with an intention to hear the needs and wants of the parent(s) in serving the child's learning. In addition, this map also assumes that teachers have professional expertise that will be shared in the conversation. There is equal value placed on the knowledge of the parent and the teacher in understanding the child's progress in learning.

Thus an overarching assumption of this map is that parents and teachers work as partners in supporting a child's learning. The Parent-Teacher Conference Map provides a pathway to a collegial dialogue where different perspectives are heard and a process of mutual meaning making occurs. Another key assumption in using the parent-teacher conference map is the fourth Cognitive Coaching^SM capability, "navigating between and among maps and support functions to guide mediational interactions" (Costa & Garmston, 2002). While the map is a powerful tool in working with parents, it is only one choice in a teacher's repertoire. The elements of the parent-teacher conference map represent an integration of the planning, reflecting, and problem-resolving conversations. During the conference, the teacher may choose to switch from Cognitive Coaching^SM to collaborating (e.g., brainstorming with the parent) or consulting (e.g., providing suggestions at the parent's request). The teacher must be comfortable with all maps and support functions in order for the conversation to flow smoothly.

Elements of the Parent-Teacher Conference Map

In the parent-teacher conference map, the teacher confers with the parent to:

- Agree upon purpose/goal
- Share data (to support evidence of claims about student progress and areas of concern or about interests, needs, strengths)
- Develop agreements on meaning of data
- Summarize content of conference
- Clarify future goals and objectives
- Reflect on conference process and content and explore refinements

Agree Upon Purpose/Goal

The map begins by clarifying and developing shared intentions between the parent and teacher. It is the clear, shared purpose that forms the foundation for a partnership. The teacher is drawing on the states of mind of craftsmanship, consciousness, flexibility, and interdependence in navigating this first element. The teacher listens carefully and paraphrases until the parent signs off on the purpose of the conversation. The teacher is careful and conscious to balance his or her talk with that of the parent, attending carefully to elements of rapport. The teacher keeps the focus of the conversation on the purpose, not allowing the conversation to stray. Attention is given to hearing differences in perspective and integrating those differences into shared purposes and common ground.

When intentions are shared, the coach (teacher) makes decisions based on the shared purposes for the conversation. As the coach works with parents, there are choices that require conscious attention. Some of those choices are

- Am I planning, reflecting or problem-resolving?
- What student learning goals are informing our interactions?
- What assumptions inform my decision-making?
- What assumptions inform the parents' thinking?
- How do these assumptions align with the assumptions on which the student is operating?
- What states of mind impact my thinking about this student?
- What states of mind exist in this student's performance that influence his or her work?
- How do the parents' states of mind impact our collaboration?

In the first element the teacher and parent agree upon the purpose or goal of the conference. The purpose may be predetermined (for example, the parent or teacher requested a conference to talk about a specific topic) or it may be a regularly scheduled conference (for example, twice a year) or it may be a spontaneous conversation initiated by either the teacher or parent. In each situation, it is critical that the teacher and parent both know and agree on the purpose.

This element might be addressed through a paraphrase by the teacher (for example, "Our purpose today is to review the progress report."). It might also be initiated with a question (for example, "What would you like to accomplish during meeting?"). What's most important is that there is agreement on the purpose. If the parent has a different purpose from the teacher, a decision needs to be made about how both the parent's and teacher's purposes might be accomplished (perhaps through scheduling another conference).

Share Data (to support evidence of claims about student progress and areas of concern or about interests, needs, strengths)

A challenge for teachers is to listen to parent perceptions and share professional perceptions in a manner that allows for each individual to understand the mental model of the other and to find mutual ways to serve the student. When perceptions are different, this is especially challenging. Speaking from data, allows the teacher to be neutral and nonjudgmental. Data enhances the likelihood that the parent will see the teacher as honest and trustworthy, rather than as a person who is an adversary. This element is the gateway to shared meaning-making and deliberate partnership.

The second element of the Parent-Teacher Conference Map is to share data to support evidence of claims. A claim is "to say, without proof or evidence, that something is true." Both the teacher and parent are likely to make claims during the conference. It is the data about a student's progress, areas of concern or interests, needs, and strengths that are central to this element. The data the teacher shares should support his or her claims. The teacher also wants to elicit data from the parent (including parents' perceptions) to support the parent's claims. When both parties can reference data, the conference stays focused and purposeful.

This element can be addressed by asking for supporting information each time a claim is made. When the teacher says, "Caitlin's lack of attention in class is becoming a problem," the teacher needs to explain her concern by describing specific behaviors of Caitlin's that are of concern. In providing data, it is important to use nonjudgmental language and avoid labels to describe the student. Instead of saying, "Mario is unmotivated," The teacher would say, "Mario comes to class after the bell has rung and has not turned in his last 3 homework assignments." The data to support this claim would come from the teacher's record-keeping system that can be shared with the parent.

The teacher can also elicit data from the parent through probing and inquiry. For example, when a parent says, "Jose is not feeling like he has friends at school," the teacher can paraphrase and probe. The response might be, "You're concerned about the social aspects of your child's education. What specific things are telling you that friends are an issue for Jose?"

Develop Agreements on the Meaning of the Data

Developing agreements on the meaning of the data is the third element and the core of the conversation. If the data means different things to the teacher and the parent or if the meaning of the data is not addressed, the conversation will have little impact on the student. The significance of the data needs to be understood by both the parent and the teacher, not just the teacher. For the parent and teacher to truly be partners in supporting student learning, they must have shared understanding of the needs and achievements of the child. This element facilitates that shared understanding.

The key skill of the coach in this element is to invite shared analysis. This is done through questioning and paraphrasing. The teacher ensures that both parties understand the meaning of the data by saying, "So you feel that Elliott has not been turning in his work because he is confused when he takes it home." (pause) "What are some things that he does to deal with his confusion?" "So we both think that assisting Elliott with some strategies to deal with not understanding would be helpful."

Summarize Content of the Conference

After the data have been shared and meaning established, the next step is to summarize the content of the conference. Although it might seem redundant to repeat what's been said with all parties present, this is a critical element for clear communication. It is not unusual that different people in the same meeting come to different conclusions about what's been decided. Either the parent or the teacher can summarize; what's key is that both parties agree on the summary.

A paraphrase usually begins the element to check for congruence with all parties. The teacher might say, "So we've agreed that I [teacher] will check with Nathan to be sure he has his assignment notebook before he leaves school and you [parents], will be sure Nathan has a set time and place to do his homework each night." If agreement is reached, the element may be short. If there is not agreement, further inquiry and probing will be required.

Clarify Future Goals and Objectives

This element flows directly out of the summary and provides connection between this and future conferences. It lets the parent know that this conference is but one event on a shared journey to support the student's learning. It sets the tone for future conversations and provides focus as to further intentions of the partnership. Clarifying future goals and objectives heightens consciousness and craftsmanship of the parent and teacher for the work ahead.

The teacher paraphrases to summarize and organize next steps, as discussed in the conference. The paraphrase helps everyone understand next steps. For example: "So just before Spring Break, we will meet again to determine Carla's progress in math. By that time we will have results from both the standardized achievement test and the district criterion-referenced test."

Reflect on Conference Process and Content and Explore Refinements

Reflecting on the process and content of the conference and exploring refinements is the last element of the map. The intention of this element is to provide feedback to the teacher about the nature of the parent's thinking and to give data to the teacher regarding decisions made in the conversation. It provides closure and allows both the parent and teacher to be aware of what was effective about the conference and what adjustments might need to be made in future conferences. Again, shared consciousness is developed between the parent and teacher. This element, like the last element of all three Cognitive Coaching^{SM} maps is initiated with a question, such as, "How has our conference been helpful to you?" or "How has this conference supported you?"

Tools Used to Navigate the Map

The Cognitive Coaching^{SM} tools used to navigate the parent-teacher conference map are the same tools used to navigate the other Cognitive Coaching^{SM} maps. Key tools in navigating this map are:

- Rapport
- Nonjudgmental response behaviors—acknowledging, pausing, paraphrasing, probing, providing data
- Inquiring
- Pacing and leading

Nonjudgmental Response Behaviors

First, the teacher establishes rapport in the following ways:

- Position the parties around a round table or near the corner of a table. Be sure all parties are included in the same physical space.
- Match posture, gesture, intonation, and language.

Throughout the conference, the teacher uses the nonjudgmental response behaviors of acknowledging, pausing, paraphrasing, probing, and providing data. Acknowledging includes head nodding, saying "uh-huh," and facial expressions that reflect what the parent is saying. The essential coaching pattern of pausing, paraphrasing, and probing should be used throughout the conversation. Pausing is essential to provide time for thinking and responding. Paraphrasing is especially important to let the parent know that the teacher understands (even if the teacher disagrees) with the parent. Understanding is the connection that allows the conversation to continue to deeper levels. Probing for specificity ensures that there is clarity in the communication. Providing data can be used throughout the conference, but especially in the second element.

Inquiring

The tool of inquiring (with the pattern of pausing and paraphrasing) will allow the teacher to explore the parent's thinking and understanding. When the teacher asks reflective/mediational questions, it signals to the parent that his or her thinking is important and also brings insight and understanding to the conference.

Examples of reflective/mediational questions that might be asked are:

- What might be going on for Jeremy that is interfering with his paying attention in class?

- What are some resources outside of school you have tapped for support?

- What are some of the things you've tried with Will?

Pacing and Leading

The most sophisticated tools the teacher uses in the parent conference are actually two tool clusters: pacing and leading. Taught in the Cognitive Coaching Foundation Seminar® as the tools used to navigate the problem-resolving map, pacing and leading can be used at any time "stuckness" is experienced during the parent-teacher conference. For example, if the parent disagrees with something the teacher says, the teacher would pace with something like, "So you're unsure that what I'm saying is true, [pause] and what you want is to feel confident that I have Josh's best interest at heart." Leading would consist of asking mediational questions to help the parents feel more resourceful, such as, "So how might you know that I have Josh's best interests at heart?")

Other examples of pacing and leading are:

- So you're concerned about Maria passing this class. And what you want is to be certain that she will graduate.

- So you're upset because you didn't know Michael was cutting class. And what you want is to be aware of your son's progress and problems.

A Parent-Teacher Conversation

So how might a parent-teacher conference play out when the teacher is using this map? Following is an example of how a parent-conference might flow, using the map and tools of Cognitive Coaching^(SM).

T: Thank you for coming tonight. I wanted to have some time to go over Jenny's report card.	**Agree on purpose/goal**
P: We're anxious to talk to you about her math grade.	
T: So, after reviewing her report card, it's just math that concerns you.	
P: Yes	
T: So you would like this conference to focus on how Jenny can improve in math.	
P: Well, we're interested in what else you have to say about Jenny's work, but mostly math.	
T: OK, so we'll start with math; then if there's time, we'll look at other areas.	
T: Jenny did not do well in math this semester. Her *D* grade is an average of her test scores, homework, and her participation in class. Here are all her grades	**Share data to support evidence of claims**
P: She turned in all homework assignments.	
T: Yes, she turned in her homework and seemed to understand it, as you can see from the grades I gave her on her homework. She does not participate in class and her test scores are up and down—from an *F* to a *B*. It's only her homework that allowed her to pass this class.	

Figure 13-1. Parent-Teacher Conference Map and Cognitive Coaching^(SM) Tools

P: Well, a *D* is passing **T:** Yes, it's a passing grade, but what is she learning about math? I don't think she's very confident in math. **P:** How can she do her homework and get such low grades on tests?	**Share data to support evidence of claims (continued)**
T: Well, what do you think? **P:** Well, when I ask her if she has done her homework, she says she did it on the bus. **T:** So you thought everything was OK because she was doing her homework and turning it in. **P:** Yes, exactly **T:** What does Jenny say about math class? **P:** Nothing, she never talks about school. **T:** So, what's your hunch about how much she understands math? **P:** I don't know—I'm not good at math, so maybe she's not either. **T:** Well, we're trying hard to help all students understand math and not leave school with an attitude that they're not good at math. Jenny doesn't ask questions in class, and she has never come in for help. **P:** Maybe she's getting help with her homework on the bus and not really understanding what she's doing. Her boyfriend is good at math—maybe he's doing it for her. **T:** That would explain why she does well on her homework and not well on the tests. How does she do on tests in other subjects? **P:** She does OK when she studies. Things don't come easy to Jenny like they do to her older sister. Jenny has to study. She is shy, and I don't think she will say anything in front of the	**Agreements on meaning of the data**

Figure 13-1. Parent-Teacher Conference Map and Cognitive Coaching^{SM} Tools

class. She probably thinks that because I'm not good in math, it's OK for her not to be good. **T:** So you think maybe you haven't shown her that you expect her to be good in math. **P:** Probably not. **T:** I know there are a lot of people who think they're not good in math—that they just learned enough to get by in school, but they don't like math and avoid doing anything that involves math. I want all my students to really understand math, so it won't keep them from doing something in life they might want to later. So when I teach math, I emphasize understand-ing, not just memorizing answers. **P:** Isn't the answer what's most impor-tant. **T:** Well, yes and no. The answer is one part of understanding math, but the processes of math are what's key to understanding. I want Jenny to know WHY she's doing what she's doing in math—not just to memorize. **P:** That sounds different from how I learned math. **T:** It probably is different. How does it sound? **P:** Well, I guess I would like her to do more than memorize math—I want her to understand too.	**Agreements on meaning of the data (Continued)**
T: So let's go over what we've talked about. First, Jenny is shy and prob-ably doesn't think she can achieve in math. She's been getting help with her homework; and when it comes to tests, she often doesn't understand enough to do well. We both agree that Jenny can do better and we want to support her in that.	**Summarize content of the conference**

Figure 13-1.   Parent-Teacher Conference Map and Cognitive Coaching^SM Tools

T: Let's talk about next steps. I would like for us a talk with Jenny to let her know that we've talked and are in agreement on two things: We both want her to be successful in math and that we think it's important for her to do her homework by herself, participate in class and study for tests.	**Clarify future goals and objectives**
P: I will be sure she has a time and place to do her homework each night. What should I do if she doesn't understand something and I don't understand it either.	
T: I give homework so students can practice what they learned in class. If Jenny doesn't understand something, I would like you to write me a note saying that. That way I will know that Jenny tried to do her homework but was not clear enough on what we did in class to understand it.	
P: And what about class participation?	
T: I will help her participate in class by encouraging her to respond to questions and making sure that I call on her whenever she raises her hand. When she answers, if it's not exactly correct, I will not embarrass her but will help her get the correct answer by prompting her.	
P: That sounds good—I don't want her to be embarrassed in front of her friends. That would discourage her from ever saying anything.	
T: I agree—that's why I always help students get the right answer if they don't give it to me the first time. Also, another thing I will do is ask Jenny to explain how she got her answer—that will help her understand that the process is as important as the answer.	

Figure 13-1. Parent-Teacher Conference Map and Cognitive Coaching[SM] Tools

T: So how are you feeling about our conversation today?	**Reflect on the process and content**
P: I feel I understand a lot more about what Jenny should be doing in math and how I can help her. I didn't think Jenny could really understand math, but now I know that she can be good in math and that the way you teach will help her in the future.	
T: Our time is up—do you want to schedule another conference to talk about anything else?	
P: No, I think now that we've talked about math, that's what I was most concerned about.	
T: Thanks for coming in. I'm looking forward to talking with your about Jenny's math work again after we've had a chance to help her. How about if we set up an meeting for a month from now.	
P: That will be good. Thank you.	

Figure 13-1. Parent-Teacher Conference Map and Cognitive Coaching^SM Tools

What Makes This Conference Unique?

When Cognitive Coaching^SM becomes institutionalized in a system, it is common for ways of talking and working to change. In the past, many parent-teacher conferences have been monologues by the teacher with parents sitting passively listening. Others have been largely a simple report of information recorded in a grade book. Sometimes they have become adversarial, with parents lodging complaints about the classroom followed by defensiveness on the part of the teacher. When this map is utilized along with coaching skills and attention to the five states of mind, a different experience can be created. Teachers using this map tell us they have had rich dialogues where honest collaborative examination of data has led to new insights about students and classroom practices. We believe it is the mutuality and reciprocity developed in this map that leads to richer, more productive conversations. Value is given to both perspectives—that of the professional and the parent. Reflection is encouraged in a shared manner. Caring for the learning of the student becomes elevated over egos and personal agendas.

Other Applications

This map is intended to support one-on-one parent conversations, and it may be useful as well in special education staffings. We believe using this map will empower parents of special needs students in situations where they often feel victimized or confused. Another possible application might be in team meetings where specific students are being discussed among teachers. For instance, one teacher in a middle school team might bring a concern about a student to the team. In might also be useful in bringing a concern about student work to a team, such as, "I am concerned that our students are not using the conventions of language." The team would probe the intention of the person bringing the concern and proceed to mediate the thinking of the group, using the map.

Summary

The Parent-Teacher Conference Map provides a template for working with parents in a manner that supports collaboration and interdependence around student achievement. Use of this map assumes the foundational skills of coaching are already in place. When this map becomes part of normal practice in working with parents, trust within the community will increase and a broader perspective in addressing the learning needs of today's students will develop.

Reference

Costa, A., & Garmston R. (2002). *Cognitive Coaching*[SM]: *A foundation for renaissance schools* (2nd ed.). Norwood, MA: Christopher-Gordon.

Chapter 14

Coaching Students: Promoting Self-Directed Learning in the Classroom

By: Bill Baker, Pat Forte,
and Peg Luidens

Introduction

Ultimately, the application of Cognitive Coaching[SM] impacts the learning of students as several studies document (Edwards, 2000). Previous chapters in this book describe applications that directly affect the adults and indirectly affect students. Chapters 14 and 15 describe ways Cognitive Coaching[SM] is being used in classrooms.

Chapter 14 was written by Bill Baker, Pat Forte, and Peg Luidens who have adapted the maps and tools and applied them in many classrooms. An exciting outcome of the work of using coaching skills with students was the unanticipated changes in the culture of the classroom. The threads woven in the classroom enhanced the students' learning, metacognition, and achievement on state assessments.

Imagine the following conversation between a teacher and a 7th grader who has read a book and now must do a project to demonstrate his understanding of the book.

Teacher: So how is your book project going?

Student: Well, I finished the book, and now I have to pick a project to go along with it.

Teacher: So you need to decide on a project before you can begin. What might be some of your ideas for a project?

Student: I'm glad I get to choose my own project, because I can do something I like. I liked the book a lot because my character visited so many places, so I think I might do a travel brochure because I really like to draw and I could summarize all the places he visited with pictures. Then I need write some things to explain the rest of it.

Teacher: So you're thinking a travel brochure will let you use your artistic skills and still accomplish the goal.

Student: Yeah, it's a fun way to bring the things I learn in art class into this class.

Teacher: So how will you know you've done a good job on the brochure?

Student: Well, I have the rubric you developed with the class. And I think that I have to make sure the pictures are accurate and I clearly summarized all the places. It should be neat, no misspelled words, and make sure I hand it in on time.

Teacher: So you've got a pretty good idea of what the project should look like. What other skills do you need to work on to finish this project?

Student: Well, you know my spelling's not very good, so maybe I could go to my language arts teacher and have her help me proofread my writing.

Teacher: So you have a strategy to help you with spelling. What steps might you need to take to make sure you finish your travel brochure on time?

Student: Well, I need to draw my pictures and go back to the book to make sure that my sketches are right.

Teacher: So that's the drawing part—what else?

Student: I have to write a rough draft summarizing my pictures, rewrite the summary after you look at it, put it all together, and maybe have someone check over the whole report when I'm done.

Teacher: So you've thought of five steps. When do you think you will finish each step?

Student: Well, I should try to get my pictures done by Friday, maybe write my summary over the weekend, have my teacher read it on Tuesday, put it together Wednesday, and have it totally done by Friday.

Teacher: So you could be done in a week. What might be some things you need to think about in order to do a good job on this project?

Student: Well, you know I'm not very organized. You've helped me get a good plan, so I want to be sure and follow the plan, so I won't have to do anything at the last minute.

Teacher: So you need to focus on organization, content, and sticking to your schedule.

Student: Yeah, I guess that's it.

Teacher: How has our conversation helped you?

Student: Well, now I have a time line, and I know all the things I have to do to do a good job. I think I can get an *A* on this project!

The above conversation is an example of a teacher using the Cognitive Coaching^SM planning conversation map to talk with a student about a project. Research on Cognitive Coaching^SM indicates that students achieve at higher levels when their teachers are coached (Edwards, 2001). It makes sense then, to assume that if teachers coach their students, they would not only see further increases in achievement but also support students in becoming reflective, self-directive, life-long learners. This chapter outlines how teachers can use the maps and tools of Cognitive Coaching^SM to promote self-directed learning in classrooms at all levels.

Self-directedness can be defined as a person's ability to take charge of, take control of, and be responsible for one's self. Self-directed learning involves students in taking control of and being responsible for their learning. Teachers can enhance student's capacities to develop the characteristics of self-directedness by consciously applying the maps, tools, and states of mind of Cognitive Coaching^SM in their daily interactions with students. With a few changes in language, students can learn and apply the planning map, reflecting map, and the energy sources of holonomy.

The Reflective Cycle

Simply stated, the reflective cycle can be perceived as a cycle that can move in either direction, forward or backward. One has a task to accomplish. One thinks about the task looking into the future, thinking ahead, trying to figure out how one will go about accomplishing the task: What resources one needs? What steps to take? What will success look or sound like? One accomplishes the task! Then, one thinks about it, looking back, trying to figure out how and why things went well or did not go well, what one learned out of the process, and what might be a next step for follow-up. The same holds for learning. Students can be involved at varying levels of complexity and difficulty in making decisions about and reflecting on their learning: What they will learn? How they will learn it? How they will know they've learned it well? They can assess their learning by reviewing or reflecting on it: How did it go? What was easy? What was not so easy? How come? What are they learning? What do they need or want to learn next?

Jane Hansen (1998) in her book *When Learners Evaluate* combines the processes of thinking ahead and thinking back when she describes the questions that she asks students about their reading or writing experiences. She asks the following set of questions and inquires for clarification, elaboration, amplification, and personalization along the way:

- What do you do well (in your reading or writing)?
- What is the most recent thing you've learned to do?
- What do you want to learn next in order to grow as a (reader or a writer)?
- What will you do to accomplish this?
- What might you use to document your learning?

This set of questions invites the learner to think back and assess oneself and then to think ahead to continue on a path of growth and improvement. Cognitive coaches recognize these ideas of thinking ahead and thinking back as being the coaching maps for planning and reflecting. These two maps help students in the same way that they help teachers to think ahead about their work, to reflect back on their work, and to learn.

Thinking Ahead

As teachers we can help our students be more self-directive by engaging them in planning conversations or processes before they carry out a task, start a project, or embark on a learning experience. When thinking ahead, we think about some or all of the following:

- What we want to do, what we want to learn, what we want to make, or what we want to accomplish? We call the results of this thinking goals, aims, directions, or outcomes.

- How we will go about doing, learning, making, or accomplishing what we are setting out to do, learn, make, or accomplish? We call the results of this thinking strategies, steps, activities, or means to employ to accomplish our goals, aims, or outcomes.

- How we will know we've done it, learned it, made it, or accomplished it well? We call the results of this thinking criteria, indicators, or evidence for determining success or achievement.

- What information or data we might gather to assess our learning, doing, or accomplishments? Or, how we will document our growth? We can call the results of this thinking data or information to gather for assessment.

A shortened version of the thinking ahead mental map can be described as follows:

- What will I do or learn?
- How will I do or learn it?
- What will success look or sound like?
- What data will be useful to assess my progress?

The following are some examples of ways teachers can support students in thinking ahead:

Planning a Project

- What do you want to accomplish?
  – What do you want to learn?

>   – What interests you about this project?
>   – How have you made the decision to do this project?

- What will you need to consider in carrying out this project?
    - What resources or information will you need?
    - What steps will you take to carry out the project? What's first? Second? Etc.
    - When will you start? How long might it take? When will you anticipate finishing?
    - Who might you include in working with you on the project?

- How will you know that you've done the project well?
    - What will you use to judge the quality of your project?
    - What success indicators will you use to assess your project?

- What information will you gather to assess your work?
    - What data or information will you use to help you judge the quality of your project?
    - How will you document your efforts?

Hold a Conversation With a Person or a Group.   Raise the kinds of questions listed in the above map with an individual or a small group of students. Encourage students to form their own responses. Respond to the students' answers by paraphrasing to make sure their thinking is understood. Craft questions so that they invite students' best thinking. After holding the conversation for a while, ask the students to make some choices regarding each of the major elements of the Think Ahead Map. Invite them to record a summary of their decisions on a Think Ahead Map form that includes the four major divisions of the map.

Provide the Map to Students as a Structure for Their Conversations With Each Other.   Give students an expanded version of the Think Ahead Map. Invite them to talk with a partner or in a small group about their project. Have them discuss and then record their responses on a form that has enough space for them to summarize their thinking and decisions regarding their goals, actions, assessments, and data gathering.

Planning to Do Homework

- What's my homework this evening or week?
    - What do I have to do?
    - What do I need to do to make sure I get it done?
- How will I do my homework?
    - When? Where?
    - How much time will it take?
    - Do I want to do it with a classmate? Who?
    - How might I make it a fun thing to do?
- What will I do to make sure I've done my homework well?
    - How will I check it?
    - What will be some signs of success?
- How will I make sure I get it in on time?
    - How will I remember to bring my homework to school?

The Think Ahead Map applied to homework was designed for students to ask themselves these questions. Teachers could also give students a worksheet asking them to take a few minutes to think about their homework for the evening or the week and to respond alone or with a partner to the questions before leaving school. Or the teacher could raise these questions with the students orally, just before they leave for the day, asking partners to respond to the questions about their homework.

Thinking Back

Teachers can help students be more self-directive by engaging them in reviewing conversations or processes after they have completed a task, project, assignment, or learning experience. When thinking back, we think about some or all of the following:

- What did I do? What took place? What did I learn? We recall what took place, form impressions about our involvement, and recall data that supports our feelings.

- How did it go? What went well? What didn't go so well? How come? We wonder why things went that way? We analyze and look for reasons to explain how come things went the way that they did. We compare what we wanted to happen with what happened and try to find out the reason for the differences.

- What am I learning from the experience? What might I apply from this experience to a similar experience in the future? We construct new learning and make applications for use now or in the future.

- What's next? We think about next steps that lead into planning or looking ahead, thus completing the cycle.

A shortened version of this mental map can be described as follows:

- What happened? How are you feeling about it?
- How did it go? What went well? What didn't go so well?
- How come things went that way?
- What are you learning?
- What's next?

The following are two examples of the Thinking Back Map applied to the same situations as when students were thinking ahead.

Reviewing a Project

- What did you do to complete the project?
    - What steps did you take?
    - How do you feel about it?
    - What data supports these feelings?

- How did the project go?
    - As you did the project, what worked best for you? Why do you think so?
    - As you did the project, what didn't work so well for you? Why do you think so?
    - How do you know the project was done well? List at least three reasons.

- What are you learning?
    - In doing this project, what did you learn?
    - In doing this project what did you learn that you might apply when doing another project?
    - If you were to do this project again, what might you do differently?

The Thinking Back Map can be used to review a project in a couple of ways. Teachers could hold a conversation with the individual or group about the project and raise some of the questions articulated in the above map. They could also give the map to an individual or a group with space for responses and invite the person or group to think about their project and respond in writing to the questions raised.

Reflecting on Homework

- What did I do to complete my homework?
  - What steps did I follow?
  - Where did I do it?
  - When did I do it?
  - How am I feeling about it?

- How did it go?
  - How did doing my homework go as I had planned? How did it work?
  - What caused it to go well or not so well?
  - How do I know that I did a good job?

- What am I learning?
  - What am I learning about getting my homework done?
  - What changes might I want to consider in doing my homework in the future?

The following is an example of how a 10th-grade math teacher might support a student in thinking back about a Problem of the Week (POW) on probability.

Teacher: So how are you feeling about the Problem of the Week that you've been working on?

Student: Well, it was about probability and I got an answer, but I'm not sure if I did it right.

Teacher: So you're not confident about your answer.

Student: No, not really.

Teacher: So what makes you not sure?

Student: Well, I did it by myself because I wanted to see if I could, but now I think I should have talked to some other people to see if I was on the right track.

Teacher: So you think others might know more than you?

Student: Well, they seem to be more sure of themselves than I am.

Teacher: One of your strategies from the Think Ahead Conversation was to test your strategy to see if your answer worked. What happened when you tested it?

Student: Well, it worked, but I'm not sure of how I got the answer. You're always telling us the right answer is not the only important thing in math; understanding how you got the answer is important, too.

Teacher: Yeah, I guess I do say that a lot. So what are some strategies you've used in the past to find out if you used the right process.

Student: Hmmm. Well, one thing I've done before is look back at some of my other POW's and see what I did. And sometimes you look over it to see if I'm on the right track. And one time I had someone else read it to see if they understood my write-up.

Teacher: So you have three strategies to help you. Which of those did you use this time?

Student: Uh, well, none of them. I totally forgot about them.

Teacher: So what are you learning about yourself.

Student: Well, for one thing, I should remember what's worked for me in the past.

Teacher: Why do you think you forgot them.

Student: Well, I guess I was trying to prove that I could do it by myself. And now I know what's more important is that I'm learning, even if it means I ask for help

Teacher: So how has this conversation supported you?

Student: It makes me feel like I'm smarter than I thought I was. And even when I don't know something for sure, I have ways of finding out how I'm doing. I know what to do when I don't know!

Promoting Self-Evaluation in Students

An approach to consider while exploring ways to enhance students' self-directedness is to involve them in reflective activities that actually support them in gathering their own data to make judgments about how well they are or are not doing in a given area. Carol Sanford (1995) makes the case that feedback can be counter productive to an individual's becoming self-governing (self-managing in Cognitive Coaching[SM] terms). She maintains that if any collective group is to be viable, vital, and growing appropriate to the changing world around them, the individual members of the group must be self-governing, self-accountable, and have a commitment to the welfare of the whole of which they are a part. She argues that for an individual to become self-governing (self-managing) of his/her own behavior, he or she must be aware of his/her own behavior and its impact on self and others. She suggests that enabling individuals to be self-reflective is a more productive way to enhance individual's capacity to be self-managing. She defines self-reflection as: "Able, on demand, by oneself, to see one's self in the moment of action and to regulate and adjust one's own behavior while in motion." She maintains that this is not an easy thing to do and that the culture in which we live tends to promote just the opposite. The traditional ways in which parents parent, teachers teach, and bosses boss, emphasize external feedback. Sanford believes that feedback from others is often counter-productive and develops dependency upon others for determining one's worth. Individuals can have difficulty becoming self-governing or self-accountable when not given opportunities to generate their own feedback.

If adults are always telling students how they are doing in their schoolwork then they are not drawing on the internal resources of the student to support them in their efforts towards self-directedness. One could argue that in most schooling experiences students are told what they will learn, how to go about learning it, and then whether or not they have learned it. Involving students in thinking ahead and thinking back, invites them to make decisions regarding what and how they will learn. It invites them to develop some criteria that they can use to judge their work. And, it suggests that they identify data to gather to use to reflect on their work. This process can be carried out in both assigned as well as self-initiated projects. Inherent in these two maps is the implication that learners need to be involved in gathering their own feedback about how they are doing and how it's going. They will not become more self-directed if teachers and/or parents are the ones who provide them with the majority of the feedback they receive about their work.

One example we have of engaging students in generating their own feedback is Karen and her fourth-grade class. Karen was a very experienced teacher in a school in Washington State. Bill had raised this issue of getting students to develop, over time, their own sense of quality and in some way creating their own feedback. He invited the teachers to select an activity that they had students do on an on-going basis through the year and agree not to give the students any kind of external feedback, positive or negative, about the activity. Instead the teachers would involve the students in reflecting on the activity in order to develop their own feedback, assessment, and evaluation of their work. Karen chose to use oral book reports as the activity. Students had the on-going assignment of presenting an oral book report to the class every month. Karen chose to video each student's oral book report. In the weeks following, Karen sat down with each student and had the student view the video. She then invited the student's reflection by asking: How do you feel about your report? What did you like/not like about your report? What are you learning that you want to be sure and do next time? Of course, these questions were followed up with additional questions and responses for clarification and amplification of the student's thinking. Karen video-taped the students' book reports eight times throughout the year. In reporting out to the faculty, Karen said she had never seen such growth made by students in her 20 plus years of teaching. And, she added, "I didn't tell them what to do to make things better. The students did that."

Five States of Mind as Habits of Thought

In Cognitive Coaching^SM the internal resources that one draws on to become holonomous, and thereby self-directed, are the Five States of Mind. The same resources exist in students. The term *Habits of Thought* has been selected to make the ideas a little more friendly for students and parents. Three of the States of Mind (craftsmanship, flexibility, and interdependence) are appropriate language for students. Two, however, were changed to more student-focused language: awareness is used instead of consciousness and resourcefulness instead of efficacy.

Supporting Habits of Thought in Self-Directed Learners

There are many ways that teachers can interact with students that invite them to develop the habits of thought. The descriptions of these ways are divided into two major categories: the first category describes how teachers use the habits of thought to inform their listening, observation, thinking about, and teaching of students; the second category describes ways to have the students develop their understanding and use of the habits of thought as a guide for their own learning.

In using Habits of Thought to inform their teaching, first teachers can use the habits of thought as an assessment tool to make judgments about which ones students are or are not demonstrating. Teachers do this primarily through listening and observing their students. This assessment is then used to decide which habits of thought to focus on and how. Second, teachers can use the Habits of Thought as a framework to guide their daily interactions with students. Third, teachers can review their curriculum units to determine how best to promote particular habits of thought with their students.

In helping students develop their understanding and use of the framework as a guide for their learning, teachers can introduce the habits of thought to students as resources to think about as they do their work. We suggest a couple of ways to do this: (a) Teachers can use characters from literature who demonstrate significant aspects of the habits of thought. (b) Teachers can introduce these habits of thought to students in a brainstorming session. Second, teachers can invite students to use the habits of thought as an assessment tool to review their learning.

Category 1—Teachers Using the Framework to Inform Their Teaching

1. Listen and observe students to discover which habits of thought students are and are not demonstrating.

   Listen to their language. Watch what they do. Which habits of thought are or are not being displayed? When you hear a student say something like, "Well, I've got to get working on this assignment. It's due next week, and I still have work to do. So, I better get at it!" You recognize that s/he is taking responsibility for and initiating working on it. Conversely, you hear a student say, "I don't know what to do!" or "What assignment!" when responding to a question about her/his assignment. You know that s/he is either not feeling very resourceful, s/he may not know what to do, or s/he was not paying attention when the assignment was given; therefore s/he was not very aware at the time or the assignment was not very interesting to her/him. Use the framework on the previous page to help you form your listening patterns.

2. Use the Habits of Thought to guide your interaction (questioning and responding) with students.

   After you've taken some time to assess how students are performing these thinking habits, you decide which ones you want to focus on. Choose to focus on one or two at a time. You decide that it will be productive to focus on the Habit of Thought of *awareness*. You want your students to become more aware of themselves and what's taking place in the classroom. They need to pay attention to themselves and others. Anticipate scenarios in class or on the school grounds that are likely to take place in which you will be interacting with students and in which you can raise questions that will enhance their paying attention to themselves and others. Some likely scenarios might be: reviewing the assigned homework at the end of the day, getting ready to perform a task, altercations taking place on the playground/school grounds. There are many possibilities. Then, construct a number of questions that you might use that will invite students' increased awareness. Some examples are

- At the end of the school day:
  - What are some things that you might do to help you remember to do your homework tonight? (awareness & resourcefulness)

- After you get home from school today, how might you make sure to get in your free time with friends as well as getting your homework done? (awareness, resourcefulness, and interdependence)

- On the Playground or in class:
  - You and Nancy have been having some difficulties in getting along with each other. How might you anticipate an argument taking place between the two of you, and what might you do to keep it from happening? (combines awareness and resourcefulness)

- Getting ready to perform a task:
  - As you are preparing to complete _____, what things do you want to pay close attention to so that you will do the _____ well? (awareness and craftsmanship)

- Having completed a piece of written work:
  - What kinds of thinking and actions were you carrying out that helped you complete the work well? (awareness & craftsmanship)

A Question Bank for Inviting Students to Access Habits of Thought

Asking questions that will invite students to manifest some of the behaviors and thinking that demonstrate these attributes is an art form. One needs to embed this framework in your mind and then have a number of questions in your question bank that you can access on the spot in order to use this framework well. We suggest that you add your own questions to this question bank.

Resourcefulness (Efficacy)

- Assume responsibility
    - How will you make sure that your task is carried out?
    - When you decide on a direction or course of action to take, what do you do to make sure that you carry it out?

- Taking initiative
    - How might you begin?
    - Of the steps you've been thinking about, which steps are most inviting to you?
    - Of the resources that you've identified, which will you use?
    - How do you decide on a direction to take?
    - What invites you to get involved?

- Being resourceful
    - What might you do about _____?
    - What resources will you need to accomplish _____?
    - Where might you get the help you need to _____?
    - When you are getting ready to do a project, how do you get your ideas?
    - How do you decide what you will need in order to carry out _____?

- Taking action, making choices/decisions
    - What will you do about _____?
    - What helped you to choose this_____?
    - How did you decide on _____?
    - What's your next step?

Awareness (Consciousness)

- Being aware of self and others
    - When you did _____ to Joan, what were you thinking or feeling?
    - As you were _____, what were you noticing?
    - What kinds of things do you think about before you begin _____?
- Being aware of one's own thinking and feelings
    - When you were working on the problem, what kinds of thinking was going on for you?
    - Before you and John got into the fight, what were you feeling?
    - As you were giving your book report, what were you noticing about the audience?
- Monitoring their actions and the resulting effects
    - What might you pay attention to and check on as you carry out this project?
    - When you said _____, what are you recalling about _____'s reactions?
- Gathering information about one's self, others, and the setting
    - As the three of you make this presentation, what might you look for in the audience that will let you know that your presentation is being heard?

Craftsmanship

- Assessing for excellence
    - How will you know that you've done a good job?
    - How did you know that you did a good job?
- Striving to improve and refine
    - If you were doing this project again, what refinements would you want to consider making?
- Seeking clarity and precision
    - How is this paper communicating what you want to say?
- Taking pride in one's work
    - How are feeling about the work that you are doing?
    - What do you like about _____?

Flexibility

- Seeking alternative ways of learning or accomplishing tasks
    - You've tried working on _____ in this way and it seems to not be working as well as you'd like. How might you approach it differently?
- Viewing circumstances, situation, or ideas from different perspectives
    - How do you think Alice is feeling about _____?
- Adjusting to others' ways of thinking and their preferences
    - Thinking about Amy's feelings, how might you change what you're doing to take into account how Amy is feeling about _____?
    - We've heard some different ways of thinking about _____. How might we incorporate these views into a bigger picture?
- Living with the unknown
    - What might you do if you find that you are having a lot of difficulty in coming up with an answer to the problem?
    - We don't seem to have an answer to _____. How are you thinking of handling that as you continue to _____?

Interdependence

- Learning with and from others
    - How might you get help from someone in the class to assist you with _____?
    - Who do you know that knows a lot about _____?
    - How might you tap their knowledge to help you with _____?
- Developing capabilities to interact with others productively
    - What might you need to do to be able to work better with _____ & _____?
- Learning to balance self-needs and group needs
    - How will you make sure that your desires are met as you and _____ do this project?

- Contributing to the common good
  - What will you do to assist the group in accomplishing _____?

3. Examine the curriculum, your daily lessons, or units of work to ensure inclusion of specific habits of thought.

   Review the goals, activities, and assessment procedures to determine how they support the development of one more of the habits of thought that you want to encourage with your students. Review the curriculum, your daily lessons, or weekly units to ask the following questions from one or more of the habits of thought. Make a choice. It is too cumbersome to attend to all five of the habits of thought in a single lesson or unit of work. Review your lesson or unit and determine which one or two habits of thought would be most appropriate to focus on. After choosing one or two habits of thought, choose two or three questions to apply to the lesson or unit. Decide what you need to do with the lesson or unit to include anything that might be missing.

Resourcefulness

- How have I embedded in this unit or lesson activities and resources that will ensure that students have the necessary internal and external resources to complete the lesson or unit successfully and with confidence?
- How have I included opportunities for students to take the initiative or to self-initiate activities?
- What kinds of responsibilities am I asking students to take on? To what extent am I extending opportunities for students to initiate or to determine their own responsibilities? How do I best invite students to assume responsibilities?
- What opportunities are there for students to take action?

Awareness

- How does the unit or lesson engage students in becoming more aware of self, others, and/or the larger context?
- What have I included that helps the student to become more aware of her/his thinking and feelings as s/he is learning?

- What kind of self-monitoring suggestions have I included?

- How am I having students gather and record information or data about themselves, others, and/or the setting? What kinds of self-observations am I suggesting?

Craftsmanship

- How does the lesson or unit have the students set criteria for excellence or quality? How do I invite students to self-assess their work?

- What kinds of invitations do I create that help students construct an attitude of refining and honing their work?

- What suggestions or activities do I build into the unit/ lesson that involves the students in producing greater clarity and precision in their thinking?

- How do the students and I support each other to take pride in their work?

Flexibility

- What alternatives are included in the lesson or unit for students to gain knowledge, accomplish tasks, and/or demonstrate their learning?

- Where am I inviting students to view ideas, concepts, or skills from different perspectives?

- How am I involving students with others so that each can learn from and with each other, understand each others' ways of thinking, and adjust to each other accordingly?

- Where is it appropriate to involve students in "living-with" unanswered problems or questions? Given the nature of the content and skills being learned, are there appropriate times and places to raise the hard and seemingly unanswerable questions?

Interdependence

- How does the lesson or unit include students in working cooperatively to learn with and from each other?

- How am I inviting each student to take into account the needs of the whole class and to make contributions to others' learning?

- How am I assisting students to gain the necessary knowledge, capabilities, and skills to work productively with classmates?

- How am I helping students to contribute to the welfare of the group?

- How am I inviting students to know when it's best for them to work alone and when it's more appropriate to work with others?

Category 2—Students Develop Their Understanding and Use of the Framework as a Guide for Their Learning

1. Use characters in literature and stories that exemplify specific attributes of habits of thought.

    Identify examples in literature and stories where individuals exhibit specific and concrete attributes of the habits of thought. Develop posters for each habit of thought with the essential characteristics of the habit of thought and illustrative examples showing concrete behaviors of the habit of thought in action. As students read, invite them to identify specific behaviors that demonstrate one or more of the habits of thought.

Applying Habits of Thought to the Characters in Literature.   Listed below are questions for inviting students to describe habits of thought exhibited by different characters in literature. Each of the questions can be asked from either a positive or negative perspective. How does (a character) show or not show a particular habit of thought? How does (a character) demonstrate or not demonstrate a particular habit of thought?

Resourcefulness

- How does _____ show that s/he is a resourceful and responsible person?

- How does _____ reveal that s/he believes that her/his action can produce results?

- How does _____ exhibit that s/he is aware of the positive and negative aspects of her/his personality?
- How does _____ change the way s/he works or interacts in different situations and settings?
- How does _____ work with other characters in the story to achieve her/his goals?

Awareness

- How does _____ show that s/he is aware of other people's feelings, thinking, or desires?
- How does _____ reveal that s/he thinks about things before carrying out an action or making a decision?
- How does _____ demonstrate that s/he has developed ways of making thoughtful decisions?
- How does _____ show that s/he pays attention to other people's desires and adapts her/his thinking and behavior to meet these desires?
- How does _____ show that s/he checks out how others think about things?

Craftsmanship

- How does _____ show that s/he has high standards for her/his and others behavior?
- How does _____ demonstrate that her/his standards or values guide his/her behavior?
- How does _____ reveal that s/he is striving to achieve her/his ideals, high standards, or values?
- How does _____ exhibit that s/he can accomplish something well in more than one way?
- How does _____ work with others to achieve his/her goals or values?

Flexibility

- How does _____ reveal that s/he is open to pursuing different ways of doing things?

- How does _____ show that s/he seeks information from different sources?

- How does _____ demonstrate that s/he has different ways of making decisions or determining courses of action?

- How does _____ indicate that s/he seeks to understand others by finding out how others think about things?

Interdependence

- How does _____ demonstrate that s/he wants others to accomplish their desires and wishes?

- How does _____ show that s/he is aware of other people's desires and wishes?

- How does _____ indicate that s/he is growing from or through the conflicts that occur in his/her life?

- How does _____ reveal that s/he takes a situation and reconstructs it to the advantage of everyone?

- How does _____ display that s/he values others and draws on them as resources?

2. Introduce the Habits of Thought (or parts of it) to students through a teaching strategy of your own choosing.

   For example, Pat had decided that Awareness and Resourcefulness were two habits of thought that she wanted to focus on with her students. The following descriptions of awareness and craftsmanship were developed with her fourth- and fifth-grade students. They were asked to come up with phrases or words that captured some of the meaning of the habits of thought of being aware or being craftsman-like. The students referred to a thesaurus and after some discussion and exchange of ideas and words, the statements below were developed. As they worked on projects, carried out assignments, read books, and engaged in group work, Pat invited the students to make comparisons with the descriptions of craftsmanship and awareness to assess their behavior in light of these descriptions.

Awareness (Consciousness)

- Awareness of self and others
  - Think about what you're doing while you're doing it.
  - Be aware of what others are saying or doing.
- Listen to others
  - Pay attention to what others say and how they say it.
- Notice posture and body language
  - Look at others' faces and body posture.
- Anticipate results or outcomes
  - Imagine what you want to take place.

Craftsmanship

- Plan ahead
  - Think about what you will do.
- Stick with the task
  - Don't give up.
- Pay attention in class
  - Listen to self and others.
- Compare your work
  - How is your work changing for the better?
- Ask why?
  - Learn reasons for your work.
- Ask for help
  - Check with others if you need to.
- Develop an I-can-do-it attitude

3. Ask students to reflect on their work and identify specific examples when particular attributes of the habits of thought have been demonstrated.

   As students carry out their study and activities in the classroom, from time to time engage them in identifying aspects of the Habits of Thought that they are demonstrating. Ask questions like: "How did your group show resourcefulness?" "In what ways were you taking responsibility for accomplishing your tasks?" Invite the students to identify specific behaviors that illustrate one or more of the habits of thought.

Conclusion

Educators and parents want students to be successful learners in and out of school. We want them to take advantage of learning opportunities so that they can become caring and successful life-long learners, able to perform well the roles and tasks they take on in life. Life-long learners have learned to be self-directive, and they reflect on their experiences. They have learned to forge their own paths in life. They carve out niches that they want to pursue, things they want to learn. They take on tasks that interest them. They reflect on their experiences in order to learn from them. We believe that by applying the principles and practices of Cognitive Coaching[SM] to working with students that we can invite students to become the responsible, reflective, resourceful, and responsive learners that we desire. As teachers, we can enhance students' capacities to develop these characteristics by consciously interacting with them to be more self-reflective, self-managing, self assessing, and self-improving.

References

Edwards, J. (2001). Cognitive Coaching[SM]: A synthesis of the research. Highlands Ranch, CO: Center for Cognitive Coaching[SM].

Hansen, J. (1998). *When learners evaluate.* Portsmouth, NH: Heinemann.

Sanford, C. (1995). *Myths of organizational effectiveness at work.* Battle Ground, WA: Springhill.

Chapter 15

Thinking Ahead:
Applying the Planning Conversation
Map in a Third-Grade Classroom

By: Julia Versaw

Introduction

In chapter 15, third-grade teacher Julia Versaw, uses the planning and reflecting map with her students. Julie's use of the maps are a refreshing celebration of their power to impact thinking. This chapter describes how she translated the maps into "kid language," specific lessons where she applied the maps, and the results she got.

Third grade had been my niche as a classroom teacher for several years. I recently had an exciting professional growth opportunity as a mentor to first- and second-year teachers in Jefferson County Schools in Golden, Colorado. As a result of the program, I was involved in special training several times throughout the year. Cognitive Coaching^{SM} was my most valuable training because it provided a framework and skill base for my work. I had been exposed to it in the past, but this time it "took." Having decided to return to the classroom at Shelton Elementary School, I began to consider my re-entry into teaching third grade. An important question I was asking myself was, "How can we teach kids to use Cognitive Coaching^{SM} skills to help each other learn?" My coaching trainers, Carolee Hayes and Jane Ellison, shared some ideas and supported me with great coaching around my question. I went home to plan. I had a captive research group and couldn't wait to begin.

Getting Started

School began and, as usual, we were swept away in the tides of curriculum and the tyranny of the urgent. October arrived and I still didn't have a specific plan for beginning to use Cognitive Coaching^{SM} in the classroom. I got the start I needed when my instructional coach, Maggie Clark, came to visit me. When Maggie asked if she could spend some time planning and reflecting about a classroom need and, at the same time, invite Chrysann McBride, her supervisor, to observe in my classroom, I jumped at the opportunity. That was exactly what I needed to get going. In math, we had covered several very fundamental topics, and we needed to review them before going on. As Maggie and I conducted a planning conversation, a week-long lesson emerged that would simultaneously serve multiple purposes:

- Students would develop a math game to integrate and demonstrate their knowledge of the math concepts we had studied.

- Students would learn the planning and reflecting conversation and apply it to an authentic task.

- I would gather useful data on student learning to plan for future instruction.

In considering how to make the Planning and Reflecting Conversations Maps from Cognitive Coaching^{SM} user-friendly to third graders, I decided to use the terms "Thinking Ahead" and "Thinking Back" as concrete representations of the intentions of the maps. The titles were inspired by *Promoting Reflection & Self-Directed Learning With Students* by Bill Baker and Pat Forte (1999).

Initial Efforts

Experience has shown me that students remember most easily with a visual "hook." A like-minded friend and I brainstormed ideas for visual cues for each question we wished students to use in a planning map. We each came up with a set. Mine were geared to primary students. I chose

- A basketball hoop: What is your goal?
- Reading glasses (to look closely): How will you know you have done a good job?
- A wagon (transporter of people and tools): How will you get there? What tools will you use?
- A thought bubble over a smiling face: What are some things you will learn?
- A cheering student: What does your coach need to know?

I printed out the graphics and the questions and enlarged them to poster size. The poster also contained a set of reflecting questions or "Think Back" to go with each graphic.

- The basketball hoop: What did you accomplish?
- The reading glasses: How do you feel about what you did?
- The wagon: What things show you met or didn't meet your goal?
- The thought bubble and smiling face: What are some things you learned?
- The cheering student: What does your coach need to know?

Next, I made small cards with the questions and laminated them so students could use them as they met with a partner. I determined that I would use a high interest task, where planning was essential, to initially teach the concept. That later proved to be a very important part of the process.

After the Think Ahead, I asked the students to each fill out a planning sheet. The planning sheet had three purposes:

- It provided me with a list of materials to have on hand for students the following day.
- It reinforced the answers the students gave for each question in the planning conversation.
- It gave me a chance to look over student responses to the questions.

Following this first session, we brought the class back together and asked for feedback. The students were positive about the process helping them think about a good plan for their project. In the past, I have asked students to create games and usually third graders have had difficulty creating something that could actually be played. This time, the games were well planned, were completed quickly, and could actually be played.

Specific Applications and Results in the Early Stage

I wrote up the lesson very formally and revised it each day following each session. I worked alone on the initial discussion for Day One—Getting Started. Maggie joined me for Day Two—Think Ahead, so that we could model a Think Ahead session for the students. We carefully explained each question and each graphic, asking questions and including the students in the discussion. Then we modeled a Think Ahead taking turns coaching. We both coached because third-grade students will do *exactly* what they see. I wanted them to realize that they needed to each plan and to each coach. Following the model, "coaches" were given a Think Ahead prompt card and students began to plan. One Think Ahead took only about five minutes. Then the partners switched cards and the other partner planned. Maggie and Chrysann took notes from a few conversations while I supported those having difficulty getting started.

Initial Impact

After much preparation, my students were conducting Think Ahead conversations to plan math review games. The initial impact of the lesson amazed and excited us. First of all, students took the conversation very seriously. Secondly, many of them were able to articulate a goal and some specific answers to the other questions. The part that excited us the most though was the fact that some students paraphrased their partner's responses until their partner gave an answer that would clearly support the project. I had not formally taught paraphrasing to students. In reflecting, I realized all of the modeling I had done in my teaching and interactions with students had influenced their patterns of communication. At that point, I knew that Cognitive Coaching[SM] was a learning tool that could be utilized effectively by 8-year olds.

Refinements and Focus Throughout the Year

Soon after the initial math lesson, I expanded the focus of the Think Ahead to prewriting. Again, Maggie came in and modeled an entire planning conversation with me. We chose a high interest writing prompt and let the students help ask the questions as we conferred about our own writing. The students then held Think Ahead conversations. The results were equally impressive as our first efforts. All the students began to write as soon as they completed the planning conversation without any down time. The writing was higher quality than it had been a week before using a prompt but no Think Ahead conversation.

Soon we began using a Think Ahead for most writing projects. A conversation took only five minutes. Then students went to their seats and began to write. Some still used another prewriting tool, such as a web, and some just began writing. Occasionally, a student still couldn't get started so I would confer with him again. Usually, his or her goal was unclear. When we clarified the goal, the other aspects of the story fell into place. At times I paraphrased an answer and helped expand it. After a second Think Ahead, I never heard, "I don't know what to write about." More and more students began stating goals relating to their writing, like "I want my reader to imagine . . ." instead of one relating to assessment, such as "I want to get a good grade."

Later in the year, I changed the focus and even the format of the Think Ahead Map. Besides being a tool for planning student work, it also became a comprehension tool for reading. I created a large visual with only pictures, no questions. The basketball hoop still represented a goal, but the new question was "What is the *author's* goal?" The students then helped create questions for each picture that focused on main points and details throughout the passage. Every time we prepared to read a piece of literature, we'd begin with "What is the author's goal?" By the time we were close to taking the state reading and writing test, the question "What is the goal?" became such a staple, that some students actually drew a basketball hoop on their prewriting pages on the standardized writing test and wrote their goal beside it.

Impact on Thinking of Students

By January, I was pleased that the students had learned to easily use the planning map. They could readily repeat the questions and could easily ask the questions of each other. It appeared, however, that they hadn't really internalized them because many still didn't explain their goals or process when I conferred with them about their writing.

With continued practice and effort, a change occurred by April. I knew the students were beginning to rely on a Think Ahead when a student asked for time for a Think Ahead when I assigned a very short writing task and didn't plan to have the students use the map. Also, by this point, many easily stated a goal for their writing and stuck to that goal throughout the entire piece.

Finally, I knew that many students had internalized the Think Ahead when we were in the middle of preparing for Business Day. One young lady raised her hand and stated, "I think I know the goal of Business Day. It is to help us learn to count money and make change and help us understand buying and selling." She and others were approaching everything we did with the question, "What is your goal?" Also, by that time, I could ask any student "What is the purpose of what you are doing?" and they would quickly state a learning goal.

Impact on Student Collaboration

An unanticipated outcome of the focus on expecting students to support each other in planning was a change in the culture of the classroom, specifically how students worked with one another. In the spring, in an e-mail to Carolee Hayes, I wrote, "At this point we do much in our class in partners or small groups. I am very excited about their ability to work together, to coach each other through problems, and to articulate their thinking. I have never had a class work as well in groups. Everyone participates." By this time, students were coaching each other in all subjects when they had the chance to work together. Math was particularly interesting. I had adopted the mini-lesson format. After a brief lesson, students worked on practice activities, and I assisted individuals and small groups. I gave most of them the choice of working alone, in pairs, or in triads. Most chose their own partners, but I regularly assigned a certain three students to various groups because they all struggled with the concepts and always chose to work together. When I assigned them to other groups, they and others worked willingly and productively. The groups changed regularly, without any teacher direction to do so.

When I asked what had helped them learn to work in groups so well, they said, "We've had lots of practice." "We are all friends now." "You have pushed us to be friends." "Learning to do Think Aheads helps us help each other." Interestingly, they agreed that, "It is easier for us to understand kid language so we like working together." As I observed the groups, I heard a great deal of questioning and clarifying. Most students supported each other very reciprocally. When I assessed their progress using independent activities, the concept attainment was greater than it had been before we started working in pairs and groups.

Impact on Standardized Testing

In May we received the results of the third-grade reading scores on the Colorado Student Assessment. This is the note I sent to Carolee at that point:

> I just got the CSAP scores back and have a bit of reflection to share. Two years ago, the scores for my class were disturbing. I was devastated actually. My class was between 50 and 60% proficient and advanced, the lowest class in our grade at our school. This year, we used the Terra Nova to predict scores and 29% of those who took the test this spring were projected to be proficient or advanced in reading. I was worried. The results in the spring showed that 82% were on target when we took the test. At this point, I attribute the increase to several things. First, I have tried to be very diligent about making the goal of each lesson clear to students. Secondly, two years ago, I was often unclear in my goals for a lesson. Now, thanks to Cognitive Coaching[SM], the first thing I ask myself as I plan is, "What is my goal?" Thirdly, students use the Think Ahead map when reading a passage. They begin with, "What is the author's goal?"

Student Feedback

At the very end of the year, as we were writing poetry, I had the students return to a very formal Think Ahead format. They were to write blank verse on any topic. Generally this type assignment has led to several saying, "I don't know what to write." Following the Think Ahead, only one student failed to go right to a desk and begin a poem. He and I conferred again, and he had a poem right away. After the activity, I asked students to give me feedback about how the Think Ahead helped this time. Their responses were exactly what I expected to hear.

- I didn't just think on my own, I could think with someone else.

- I didn't have to waste time. I wasn't in a rush. When I got to my seat I was able to write.

- It helped me plan before I did something.

- It makes me focus on the goal. I have an idea and know how I am going to get there. It helps me feel like I did a good job.

- It got me started thinking. When I got back to my seat, I just whipped it down in five minutes.

- When I thought ahead, it helped me write something no one else would write about.

- It helped me think about questions I wouldn't normally think about.

- If you don't do a Think Ahead, you think you are ready to write; but when you do a Think Ahead, you find out you had all these problems and you figure them out.

- It helped me find descriptive words and helps the reader see the picture.

A Final Reflection and a New Focus

This brief reflection has focused only on the Think Ahead. We also used the Think Back, but to a lesser extent. I used it to help students focus on what they accomplished and help them take responsibility for their own learning. After starting out with both, I chose to focus on the Think Ahead most often. Just as our students need to take small steps, we as teachers need to take small steps when we implement new tools. As teaching the Think Ahead process becomes more automatic, teaching the reflective Think Back will become a conscious effort as well.

In April, I sent Carolee a note that said, "I am doing a better job of teaching because kids are thinking about their thinking and their learning." One of my goals for the year was to meticulously think about the goal of every lesson and to articulate that to students. Using the Think Ahead map took that goal one step higher. It helped students begin to ask "What is the goal?" in everything they did.

Next year I will be teaching first grade for the first time in many years. I fully intend to use the Think Ahead and Think Back with these young students. We will take it slowly. I will not teach the entire map in one lesson. We'll begin with the basketball hoop and talk about what a goal is. We'll brainstorm goals in many aspects of our lives. Then, each day as students begin to write, they will take a minute to ask each other "What is your goal?" A couple of weeks later, we'll look at the glasses and talk about inspecting our work carefully and ask "How will you know you have done a good job." We'll add the rest of the steps slowly, but surely. First-grade students, like third-grade students, will think seriously about their thinking in all aspects of their learning.

Advice to Colleagues

Think Ahead and Think Back Maps are tools like a graphic organizer. If you choose to use the maps with students, make sure that you first think through your reasons for teaching them. Be careful to make them your own, so that they make perfect sense to you. Reword the questions to make sense for your students. Choose a high interest activity that requires some creativity and planning for their initial use. Be sure to give yourself and your students plenty of time to explain, to model, and to practice the conversations the first time. The extra time you initially spend will be returned over and over as students plan their work well. Relax, listen, and enjoy as students use "kid language" to help each other plan their very important work.

References

Baker, B., & Forte, P. (1999). *Promoting reflection & self-directed learning with students.* Unpublished manuscript.

Appendix A

Kids Coaching Kids
With a Math Project

Objectives

1. Students will clarify and share their understanding of four broad concepts already studied in class.

    *   Graphing
    *   Addition and Subtraction Facts
    *   Place Value
    *   Telling Time
    *   Assess student knowledge of the four topics

2. Students will use a Cognitive Coaching[SM] format to plan and reflect on their work on their projects.

Product

1. Students will create a math game or math puzzle that they can use with one or more other students to review and practice one of the four concepts studied this year.

Materials

1. Whiteboard or chart paper
2. Think Ahead and Think Back posters
   - Think Ahead with graphics
   - Think Back with graphics
   - Full poster
3. Copies of Think Ahead and Think Back (for each pair)
   - Think Ahead with graphics
   - Think Back with graphics
4. Copies of game parts
5. Construction paper
6. Paper clips
7. Brass fastener
8. Tape
9. Student supplies—glue, scissors, pencils, crayons

Day One—Getting Started

Gather students in the story corner where they will be close together and close to the posters.

1. Explain that the next few days will be spent making games that review the concepts we have covered in class this year. Have students help list those concepts.

2. State goals.

3. "If you were to create a game for others to play, how would you know that you have a good product that you can be proud of?" List student responses. Hopefully they include things such as fun to play, use the skill, neat work, colorful, correct spelling, accurate.

4. "We will use these things as our grading rubric. Which are important for meeting the standards for third-grade work? What might we do to exceed the standard?" Write "Meet" beside characteristics that meet standards.

5. "What are some ideas you have right away for creating a math game?"

Day Two—Think Ahead

1. An important thing that we are going to learn as we create these games will be a way to help each other before and after we do our work. We are going to Think Ahead and Think Back with a partner.

2. There are five steps to a Think Ahead session. (Discuss each step on the poster.)

3. Model coaching session (with an adult partner if possible).

4. You will Think Ahead about making your game, then each of you will fill out a plan sheet on your own. This will be your map, and it will help me have materials available for you tomorrow. I will assign partners, and I will give each of you a reminder sheet about steps to cover in thinking ahead. You will have about 5 minutes each to plan. I will let you know when it is time to change jobs.

5. Assign partners. Designate first and second planners. Distribute Think Ahead cards.

6. After 5 minutes change partners.

7. Give each student a plan sheet to complete. (This step allows the teacher to know what materials to gather—if you don't need that, you may not want the sheet.)

8. Collect sheets as they finish.

Day Three—Making Games

1. Review student plan sheets.

2. Arrange requested material on a materials table.

3. Return plan sheets to students.

4. Review the overall goal and the rubric created by the students.

5. Discuss guidelines for working. Write the ones that seem most necessary at the time.
    *   Take only the materials you need.
    *   Use materials carefully.
    *   Work quietly (independent work).
    *   Stay on task.

6. Criteria for grade based on rubric. Explain the weight of the grade.

7. Games will need to be completed today. We will play them tomorrow.

8. Allow most of the hour for work.

9. Monitor progress and behavior as students work.

10. Signal 5 minutes before time to clean up.

11. Allow 2 minutes clean up time.

12. Allow 3 minutes to reflect on today's work.

13. Make arrangements for students with incomplete work to finish it before math tomorrow.

Day Four—Playing Games

1. What is our goal again?

2. In a few minutes you will meet with a partner to play your game. You will play one game for 10 minutes. Then I will signal you to switch and play the other one. I'll visit each pair to see your game and assess it.

3. What questions do you have?

4. Choose a partner and decide who is blue and who is orange. You may find your partner.

5. Blues, will you share your game first?

6. At the half way point, congratulate the makers of the games you have seen. Ask them to put those away and get out the others.

7. Stop the group and ask them to clean up.

8. Take a very brief time to hear their feelings about the process so far. Try not to go into Think Back questions!

Day Five—Think Back

Gather students together in the corner for discussion.

1. What amazing wonderful work you have done on your games using a Think Ahead conference, a planning sheet, and very hard work.

2. One of the most important parts of a project is thinking back about it—and that is one thing that is often left out.

3. Why might a time to think back be important?

4. Explain each part of the poster.
   - Goal—how did your game score?
   - Glasses—these help me look at the very fine points. Also, they may be magic glasses that help me look inside to how I really feel about what I did. Ask more questions here to help your partner really get to the details.
   - Wagon—Ask for detail that can be loaded up to prove why the thinker thinks he met or didn't meet the goal.
   - Thinker—probe on this one. Help them think of what they really learned while they were thinking, making, and playing.
   - WOW! As a coach, you are a super help to your partner. Let them tell you what you did that was most helpful.

5. Model (kids might help coach).

6. Assign partners for reflecting. Give prompt cards to askers.

7. Each pair will have about 5 minute to think back. I'll signal when it is time to change.

8. After both have shared, bring the group together.

9. This has been a tremendous process. I am so impressed with your skills. What else uses Think Ahead and Think Back?

Appendix B

Student Planning Sheet

Name: _____

1. What is your goal?

   _____

   _____

   _____

2. How will you know you have done a good job?

   _____

   _____

   _____

3. How will you get there? (What steps will you take?)

   _____

   _____

   _____

4. What tools (materials) might you use?

   _____

   _____

   _____

5. What are some things you will learn?

   _____

   _____

   _____

Editors

Jane Ellison and Carolee Hayes are Co-directors of the Center for Cognitive Coaching^{SM}. They provide consultation to school districts and other organizations in the areas of change and transition, Cognitive Coaching^{SM}, The Adaptive School: Developing Collaborative Groups, quality professional and organizational development, curriculum development, effective instruction, supervision, facilitation, and group development.

Jane Ellison

Jane was the Director of Elementary Education for Douglas County School District Re. 1, Colorado, the fastest growing county in the nation, from 1992–1998. In that position, Jane was responsible for the development of elementary standards and curriculum, the monitoring of instruction, and the supervision of principals. She also facilitated 17 elementary principal search committees. Jane was a principal for 15 years—4 in Douglas County, Colorado, and 11 in Tinley Park, Illinois. Her teaching experience is in the primary grades and at the graduate college level. She holds a B.A. in Elementary Education and Social Sciences from SMU, an M.Ed. in Elementary Supervision from the University of North Texas, and an Ed.D. in Administration from VPI&SU, Blacksburg, Virginia. She is licensed as an administrator in Colorado and Illinois and as a supervisor in Texas.

Jane lives in Englewood, Colorado. Her career has been devoted to improving the quality of public education for all students.

Carolee Hayes

Carolee was the Director of Professional Development for Douglas County School District Re.1, Colorado, from 1989–1998 She developed and directed the nationally recognized Building Resource Teacher program which places a staff developer in every school to support building level staff development, new teacher induction, implementation of innovation in curriculum, instruction, and assessment work. Ongoing staff and organization development to provide for quality implementation of standards-based education in Douglas County, the fastest growing county in the nation, was a priority for Carolee. Prior to working for Douglas County, Carolee was a staff developer and middle school teacher in Jefferson County, Colorado. She holds a B.A. in Family Studies from Colorado Women's College and an M.A. in Curriculum and Instruction from the University of Denver. She is licensed as a secondary teacher and administrator by the State of Colorado.

Carolee lives in Highlands Ranch, Colorado. She is a grandparent who believes deeply in the future potential of public schools to create the futures we want for our children.

Contributors

William Baker

William (Bill) Baker is Director of Group Dynamics Associates, Berkeley, California, and a Training Associate with the Center for Cognitive Coaching. He has been an educator for over 50 years—working at all levels and in many different roles. Bill works with school faculties to promote collaborative behavior, group problem solving, and the taking on of the norms of collaboration. He has been engaged in the Cognitive Coaching[SM] work from its beginnings and conducts coaching training from time to time. Bill has been interested in applying the principles and practices of coaching for reflection and self-directedness with students since the early days of cognitive coaching. He works with educators who are working to promote student self-directedness and reflective behavior in the classroom.

Augie Battaglia

August F. Battaglia, AIA, is currently the Design Director for FGM Architects Engineers in Oakbrook, Illinois. He also serves on the Board of Directors for FGM. Mr. Battaglia's work in Educational Architecture has included programming, planning, designing, and managing more than 800 million dollars of school construction. During his 25-year career, Mr. Battaglia has received the prestigious Francis J. Plym Traveling Fellowship in Architecture from the University of Illinois (1988) and the Young Architect Award from the American Institute of Architects, Chicago Chapter (1991). Additionally, his school projects have received many awards from the American Institute of Architects and school organizations throughout the country.

Bill Brubaker

William Brubaker is deceased. He was an internationally acclaimed school architect. His long time association with Perkins and Will Architects in Chicago, Illinois, afforded him to design and build many schools across the globe. One of Mr. Brubaker's last major school project contributions was to Prairie Ridge High in Crystal Lake, Illinois.

Art Costa

Arthur L. Costa is an Emeritus Professor of Education at California State University, Sacramento, and Co-Director of the Institute for Intelligent Behavior in Berkeley, California. He has served as a classroom teacher, a curriculum consultant, an assistant superintendent for instruction and as the Director of Educational Programs for the National Aeronautics and Space Administration. He has made presentations and conducted workshops in all 50 states as well as Mexico, Central and South America, Canada, Australia, New Zealand, Africa, Europe, Asia, and the Islands of the South Pacific. Author of numerous journal articles, he edited the book *Developing Minds: A Resource Book for Teaching Thinking;* is the author of *The Enabling Behaviors, Teaching for Intelligent Behaviors,* and *The School as a Home for the Mind.* He is co-author of *Cognitive Coaching*[SM]: *A Foundation for Renaissance Schools,* and co-editor of *The Role of Assessment in the Learning Organization: Shifting the Paradigm* and *If Minds Matter.* Active in many professional organizations, Dr. Costa served as President of the California Association for Supervision and Curriculum Development and was the National President of A.S.C.D. from 1988 to 1989.

John Dyer

John Dyer, B. Ed., M.A., has had 27 years experience with the Calgary Board of Education, Calgary, Alberta, Canada, as a teacher, a Junior High School Principal, an Assistant Superintendent and as the Co-ordinator of Staff Development. He was formerly a senior associate with the Institute for Intelligent Behavior, Sacramento, CA, and worked collaboratively with Art Costa and Bob Garmston. For the past 10 years John has managed his own consulting and training company and is currently a training associate with the Center for Cognitive Coaching. John can be reached through email at jadyer@attglobal.net.

Bob Garmston

Bob Garmston is Professor Emeritus, School of Education, at California State University, Sacramento, and director of Facilitation Associates, an educational consulting firm specializing in leadership, learning and organizational development. He is co-developer of Cognitive Coaching^{SM} and co-founder of the Institute for Intelligent Behavior with Dr. Art Costa. He is co-developer of Adaptive Schools with Bruce Wellman, an initiative developing collaborative groups within schools intent on strengthening student achievement. He is an award winning author of books and articles, authoring over one hundred publications on educational leadership, learning, coaching and staff development. Formerly a principal in Saudi Arabia, he has been a teacher, principal, superintendent, and curriculum director. He has held leadership posts in professional organizations, including the California and International Association for Supervision and Curriculum Development (ASCD). He is a reviewer for the *International Journal of Leadership in Education* and lives in Sacramento, California, near his five children and four (bright and cute) grandchildren. Fabob@aol.com.

Jenny Edwards

Jenny Edwards, Ph.D., has been involved with Cognitive Coaching^{SM} since 1989. She has done research on Cognitive Coaching^{SM} and has written *Cognitive Coaching^{SM}: A Synthesis of the Research.* She has taught Cognitive Coaching^{SM} in Mexico, Italy, and the Philippines, as well as in the United States. She is on the faculty of the Educational Leadership and Change doctoral program at Fielding Graduate Institute in Santa Barbara, California.

Pat Forte

Pat Forte teaches in San Francisco Unified School District. She has worked in education overseas and in the United States in a variety of areas: staff development, beginning teacher support, specially funded projects, and administration. Currently Pat is teaching fourth- and fifth-grade students, using maps and tools that promote reflection. A curious, life-long learner, she is committed to facilitating quality learning experiences that support students in becoming more intentional and self-directed.

Peg Luidens

Peg Luidens is a national presenter who has been at the forefront of shaping coaching practices that support and accelerate individual, group, and organizational growth and development. Her initial coaching work was embedded in the teaching of writing to K-12 students and teachers. Her publications in this area focus upon coaching conversations that draw out a writer's inherent ideas and engage writers in self-assessment. Peg has extensive experience with school site and district wide planning, developing collaborative teams, facilitating crisis management, and creating school cultures that inspire the pursuit of excellence and the achievement of peak performance. Her work is dedicated to building skills for pro-active leadership and immediate application in an ever-changing educational world.

Laura Mitchell

Laura Mitchell is an assistant principal at Buffalo Creek Elementary in Spring Branch Independent School District, Houston, Texas. She completed her B.S. degree in Bilingual Education from Southwest Texas State University in San Marcos and her Masters degree in Educational Leadership from the University of Houston. Laura has been a classroom teacher and a bilingual coordinator for 17 years and an assistant principal for 3 years. Cognitive Coaching[SM] has given her the strategies and tools to work in an educational setting with teachers, students, and parents. These strategies and tools have increased her capacity to be an administrator who supports teachers in a challenging but innovative teaching environment.

William Powell

William (Bill) Powell has severed as an international school educator for the past 25 years. He has taught in the United States, Saudi Arabia, Indonesia, and Tanzania. He is currently the Headmaster of the International School of Kuala Lumpur in Malaysia. Bill is the author of numerous journal articles on inclusion and empowering children and has recently finished co-authoring the book with his wife, Ochan Kusuma-Powell, *Count Me In! Developing Inclusive International Schools.* He is also the author of *School Board Governance Training: A Sourcebook of Case Studies.* When he is not working with children or writing, Bill can be found roaming the French countryside near his home in the foothills of the Pyrenees.

Sandy Ripplinger

Sandy Ripplinger is the principal of Eldorado K–8 School in Superior, Colorado. A lifetime educator, she has been a teacher, assistant principal, and principal and is also the mother of six children. In 1999, Ms. Ripplinger was given the professional growth opportunity of opening a new K–8 school, one of three in the Boulder Valley School District. She believes that collaboration, shared mission, vision, and values and a commitment towards continuous improvement among staff are vital to the creation of a learning environment that supports all children in achieving their highest potential.

Joe Saban

A retired school superintendent, Joe Saban is currently a full time Assistant Professor in the College of Education at Northern Illinois University in DeKalb. His responsibilities at NIU include teaching Master and Doctoral candidates in the Graduate School and overseeing the leadership intern programs. Joe consults widely on organizational development, change, and cognitive neuroscience. After spending 34 rewarding years (15 as a teacher) in the public schools, he cites Cognitive Coaching^{SM} as one of the most effective and productive programs he has had the opportunity to weave into a school district's culture. Joe is dedicated to the education of all children in our nation and is a firm believer in positive change through thoughtful and respectful dialogue.

Lynn Sawyer

Lynn Sawyer is Coordinator of Professional Development for Washoe County School District, Reno, Nevada, a Cognitive Coaching^{SM} Training Associate, and a member of the ASCD faculty. She does consulting projects with teachers and administrators on Cognitive Coaching^{SM}, teacher performance and evaluation, and effective pedagogical strategies. Believing that classroom teachers have the greatest influence on students' love of learning and ability to achieve their personal goals, Lynn's life mission is to support teachers' professional growth.

Yaso Thiru

Yaso Thiru is an assistant professor of accounting and management at Alaska Pacific University. Her specialties include teaching and research in curriculum development and organizational change. As an instructor in the long-distance education program at the university, she uses coaching to facilitate on line courses. She continues to experiment and use coaching in classrooms, collaborative research projects, and in guiding her elementary school aged children.

Julia Versaw

Julie Versaw currently teaches third grade at Shelton Elementary School in Golden, Colorado. She has taught at the third-grade level for most of her teaching career. It is her desire to use every strategy available to increase student learning. She became interested in Cognitive Coaching[SM] as a tool for students when she was training to mentor other teachers. She asked the question, "Since it is so effective for adult learning, why not let young students use it as well?" Her contribution is the result of her experiences as she sought to answer that question.

Index